Thomas DeWitt Talmage

Evils of the cities

A series of practical and popular discourses delivered in the Brooklyn Tabernacle

Thomas DeWitt Talmage

Evils of the cities
A series of practical and popular discourses delivered in the Brooklyn Tabernacle

ISBN/EAN: 9783744726757

Printed in Europe, USA, Canada, Australia, Japan

Cover: Foto ©Thomas Meinert / pixelio.de

More available books at **www.hansebooks.com**

EVILS OF THE CITIES

A

SERIES OF

PRACTICAL AND POPULAR DISCOURSES

DELIVERED

IN THE BROOKLYN TABERNACLE

BY

T. DE WITT TALMAGE, D. D.

———

ILLUSTRATED

"That church was built as the result of that book you gave me thirty years ago."—See story, page 56.

———

CHICAGO

RHODES, & MCCLURE PUBLISHING

Preface

The reader will find in this volume a series of practical and popular discourses, delivered in the Brooklyn Tabernacle, treating upon the evils of the day, giving a clear and full exposition of said evils, and suggesting the remedies by which they may be overcome.

The usual clearness, fullness and earnestness of Dr. Talmage, and the great desire that all may be saved through the redemption of Christ, characterize all these sermons, and render them decidedly salutary and entertaining.

The Saviour's great willingness to receive back all, as shown by story and facts, is fully commensurate with the great evils which are so fully, earnestly, and inoffensively handled. Young and old, and all alike, may read this book with interest and profit, for the pathway of safety and happiness is made to shine most conspicuously through all, and the model home, with its happy family is in the front ground of every picture.

J. B. McCLURE.

Chicago.

CONTENTS.

———

WHAT KEEPS HIM AWAY?"

EVILS OF THE CITIES.

PLAGUE OF GAMBLING.

"Let my people go that they may serve me, for I will at this time send all my plagues." Ex. ix, 13, 14.

Last winter, in the museum at Cairo, Egypt, I saw the mummy, or embalmed body of Pharaoh, the oppressor of the ancient Israelites. Visible are the very teeth that he gnashed against the Israelitish brick-makers, the sockets of the merciless eyes with which he looked upon the overburdened people of God, the hair that floated in the breeze of the Red Sea, the very lips with which he commanded them to make bricks without straw. Thousands of years after, when the wrappings of the mummy were unrolled, old Pharaoh lifted up his arm as if in imploration, but his skinny bones cannot again clutch his shattered scepter. It was to compel that tyrant to let the oppressed go free that the memorable ten plagues were sent.

Sailing the Nile and walking amid the ruins of the Egyptian cities I saw no remains of those plagues that smote the water or the air. None of the frogs croaked in the one, none of the locusts sounded their

rattle in the other, and the cattle bore no sign of
the murrain; and through the starry nights hovering about
the pyramids no destroying angel swept his wing, But
there are ten plagues still stinging and befouling and
cursing our cities, and like angels of wrath smiting not
only the firs born but the last born.

PRIDE OF CITY.

Brooklyn, New York and Jersey City, though called
three, are practically one. The bridge already fastening
two of them together will be followed by other bridges
and by tunnels from both New Jersey and Long Island
shores, until what is true now will, as the years go by,
become more emphatically true. The average condition
of public morals in this cluster of cities is as good if not
better than in any other part of the world. Pride of city
is natural to men in all times, if they live or have lived
in a metropolis noted for dignity or prowess. Caesar
boasted of his native Rome, Lycurgus of Sparta, Virgil
of Andes, Demosthenes of Athens, Archimedes of Syra-
cuse, and Paul of Tarsus. I should suspect a man of
base heartedness who carried about with him no feelings
of complacency in regard to the place of his residence;
who gloried not in its arts or arms or behavior; who
looked with no exultation upon its evidences of prosperity, its artistic embellishments and its scientific attain-
ments.

I have noticed that men never like a place where they
have not behaved well. Men who have free rides in
prison vans never like the city that furnishes the vehicle.
When I see in history, Argo, Rhodes, Smyrna, Chios,
Colophon and several other cities claiming Homer, I

conclude that Homer behaved well. Let us not war against this pride of city, nor expect to build up ourselves by pulling others down.

BOSTON, AND PHILADELPHIA.

Let Boston have its commons. its Faneuil hall and its magnificent scientific and educational institutions. Let Philadelphia talk about its Mint, and Independence hall, and Girard college, and its old families, as virtuous as venerable. When I find a man living in one of those places who has nothing to say in favor of them I feel like asking him, "What mean thing did you do that you do not like your native city?" New York is a goodly city, and when I say that, I mean the region between Spuyten Duyvil creek and Jamaica in one direction and Newark flats in the other direction. That which tends to elevate a part elevates all. That which blasts part blasts all. Sin is a giant, and he comes to the Hudson or Connecticut river and passes it as easily as we step across a figure in the carpet. The blessing of God is an angel, and when it stretches out its two wings one of them hovers over that and the other over this.

THE GREAT CITY OF NEW YORK.

In infancy the great metropolis was laid down by the banks of the Hudson. Its infancy was as feeble as that of Moses sleeping in the bulrushes by the Nile; and, like Miriam, there our fathers stood and watched it. The royal spirit of American commerce came down to the water to bathe, and there she found it. She took it in her arms, and the child grew and waked strong, and the ships of foreign lands brought gold and spices to its feet, and stretching itself up into the porportions of a metropolis, it has looked up to the mountains and off upon the sea—the mightiest of the energies of American civilization.

The character of a founder of a city will be seen for many years in it inhabitants. Romulus impressed his life upon Rome. The Pilgrims relaxed not their hold upon the cities of New England. William Penn has left Philadelphia an inheritance of integrity and fair dealing, and on any day in that city you may see in the manners, customs and principles of its people his tastes, his coat, his hat, his wife's bonnet and his plain meeting house The Hollanders still wield an influence over New York.

Grand old New York! What southern thoroughfare was ever smitten by pestilence, when our physicians did not throw themselves upon the sacrifice! What distant land has cried out in the agony of famine, and our ships have not put out with breadstuffs! What street of Damascus or Beyrout or Madras that has not heard the step of our missionaries! What struggle for national life in which our citizens have not poured their blood into the trenches? What gallery of exquisite art in which our painters have not hung their pictures! What department of literature or science to which our scholars have not contributed! I need not speak of our public schools, where the cordwainer and milkman and glassblowers stand by the side of the flattered sons of merchant princes; or of the insane asylums on all these islands where they who went cutting themselves, among the tombs, now sit, clothed and in their right minds; or of the Magdalen asylums, where the lost one of the street comes to bathe the Saviour's feet with her tears, and wipe them with the

hair of her head—confiding in the pardon of him who
said: ''Let him who is without sin cast the first stone at
her.'' I need not speak of the institutions for the blind,
the lame, the deaf, and the dumb, for the incurables, the
widow, the orphan, and the outcast; or of the thousand
armed machinery that sends streaming down from the
reservoirs the clear, bright, sparkling, God given water
that rushes through our aqueducts, and dashes out of
the hydrants, and tosses up in our fountains, and hisses
in our steam engines, and showers out the conflagration,
and sprinkles from the baptismal font of our churches; and
with silver note, and golden sparkle, and crystalline
chime, says to hundreds of thousands of our population,
in the authentic words of him who said: ''I will; be
thou clean!''

THE CURSE OF GAMBLING.

All this I promise in opening this course of sermons on
the ten plagues of these three cities, lest some stupid
man might say I am deprecating the place of my residence. I speak to you to-day concerning the plague of
gambling. Every man and woman in this house ought
to be interested in this theme.

Some years ago, when an association for the suppression of gambling was organized, an agent of the association came to a prominent citizen and asked him to patronize the society. He said, ''No, I can have no interest
in such an organization. I am in no wise affected by
that evil.'' At that very time his son, who was his
partner in business, was one of the heaviest players in
Hearne's famous gambling establishment. Another refused his patronage on the same ground, not knowing

that his first book-keeper, though receiving a salary of only a thousand dollars, was losing from fifty to one hundred dollars per night. The president of a railroad company refused to patronize the institution, saying, "That society is good for the defense of merchants, but we railroad people are not injured by this evil;" not knowing that, at the very time, two of his conductors were spending three nights of each week at faro tables in New York. Directly or indirectly, this evil strikes at the whole world.

GAMBLING DEFINED.

Gambling is the risking of something more or less valuable in the hope of winning more than you hazard. The instruments of gaming may differ but the principle is the same. The shuffling and dealing cards, however full of temptation, is not gambling, unless stakes are put up; while, on the other hand, gambling may be carried on without cards or dice, or billiards, or ten-pin alley. The man who bets on horses, on elections, on battles—the man who deals in "fancy" stocks, or conducts a business which hazards extra capital, or goes into transactions without foundation, but dependent upon what men call "luck," is a gambler. Whatever you expect to get from your neighbor without offering an equivalent in money or time or skill is either the product of theft or gambling. Lottery tickets and lottery policies come into the same category. Fairs for the founding of hospitals, schools and churches, conducted on the raffling system, come under the same denomination. Do not, therefore, associate gambling necessarily with any instrument, or game, or time or place, or think the principle depends upon whether you play for a glass of wine or one hundred shares of railroad stock. Whether you patronize "auction pools," "French mutuals," or "book-making," whether you employ faro or billiards, rondo and keno, cards or bagatelle, the very idea of the thing is dishonest, for it professes to bestow upon you a good for which you give no equivalent.

$80,000,000,00 DAILY FOR GAMBLING.

It is estimated that every day in Christendom eighty million dollars pass from hand to hand through gambling practices, and every year in Christendom one hundred and twenty-three billion one hundred million dollars change hands in that way. There are in this cluster of cities about eight hundred confessed gambling establishments; how many of them do you suppose profess to be honest? Ten. These ten profess to be honest because they are merely the ante-chamber to the seven hundred and ninety that are acknowledged fraudulent. There are first class gambling establishments. ⁄ You go up the marble stairs. You ring the bell. The liveried servant introduces you. The walls are lavender tinted. The mantels are of Vermont marble. The pictures are "Jephthah's Daughter" and Dore's "Dante's and Virgil's Frozen Region of Hell"—a most appropriate selection, this last, for the place. There is the roulette table, the finest, the costliest, most exquisite piece of furniture in the United States. There is the banqueting room, where free of charge to the guests, you may find the plate and viands and wines and cigars sumptuous beyond parallel.

Then you come to the second class gambling establishment. To it you are introduced by a card through some "r⸺er-in." Having entered, you must either gamble or fight. Sanded cards, dice loaded with quicksilver, poor drinks, will soon help you to get rid of all your money to a tune in short meter with staccato passages. You wanted to see. You saw. The low villians of that place watch you as you come in. Does not the panther, squat in the grass, know a calf when he sees it? Wrangle not for your rights in that place, or your body will be thrown bloody into the street, or dead into the East river. You go along a little further and find the policy establsh-ment. In that place you bet on numbers. Betting on two numbers is called a "saddle," betting on three num-bers is called a "gig," betting on four numbers is called a "horse," and there are thousands of our young men leaping into that "saddle" and mounting that "gig" and behind that "horse" riding to perdition. There is always one kind of sign on the door—"Exchange." a most ap-propriate title for the door, for there, in that room, a man exchanges health, peace and heaven for loss of health, loss of home, loss of family, loss of immortal soul. Exchange sure enough and infinite enough.

Men wishing to gamble will find places just suited to their capacity, not only in underground oyster cellar, or at the table back of the curtain, covered with greasy cards, or in the steamboat smoking cabin, where the bloated wretch with rings in his ears instead of his nose, deals the pack, and winks in the unsuspecting traveler —providing free drinks all around—but in gilded parlors and amid gorgeous surroundings.

HAZARDING AN ESTATE FOR HELL.

A young man having suddenly heired a large property,

sits at the hazard table and takes up in a dice box the estate won by a father's lifetime sweat, and shakes it, and tosses it away. Intemperance soon stigmatizes its victim, kicking him out, a slavering fool, into the ditch, or sending him, with the drunkard's hiccough, staggering up the street where his family lives. But gambling does not in that way expose it victims. The gambler may be eaten up by the gambler's passion, yet you have only dis covered it by the greed in his eyes, the hardness of his features, the nervous restlessness, the threadbare coat and his embarrassed business. Yet he is on the road to hell, and no preacher's voice, or startling warning, or wife's entreaty, can make him stay for a moment his head-long career. The infernal spell is on him; a giant is aroused within; and though you bind him with cables, they would part like thread; and though you fasten him seven times around with chains, they would snap like rusted wire; and though you piled up in his path heaven high Bibles, tracts and sermons, and on the top should set the cross of the son of God, over them all the gamb-ler would leap, like a roe over the rocks, on his way to perdition.

GAMBLING KILLS INDUSTRY.

Again, this sin works ruin by killing industry. A man used to reaping scores or hundreds or thousands of dollars from the gaming table will not be content with slow work. He will say, ''What is the use of trying to make these fifty dollars in my store when I can get five times that in half an hour down at 'Billy's?' You never knew a confirmed gambler who was industrious. The men given to this vice spend their time, not actively engaged in the game, in idleness, intoxication or sleep, or in corrupting new victims.   This sin has dulled the car-penter's saw and cut the band of the factory wheel, sunk the cargo, broken the teeth of the farmer's harrow and sent a strange lightning to shatter the .battery of the philosopher.   The very first idea in gaming is at war with all the industries of society.

THE WHOLE WORLD IS ROBBED.

The crime is getting its lever under many a mercantile house in our great cities, and before long down will come the great establishment, crushing reputation, home, comfort, and immortal souls.   How it diverts and sinks capital may be inferred from some authentic statement before us.   The ten gaming houses that once were au-thorized in Paris passed through the bank, yearly, three hundred and twenty-five millions of francs.   Where does all the money come from?   The whole world is robbed! What is most sad, there are no consolations for the loss and suffering entailed by gaming.   If men fail in lawful business, God pities and society commiserates; hut where in the Bible or in society is there any consolation for the gambler?   From what tree of the forest oozes there a balm that can soothe the gamester's heart?   In that bottle where God keeps the tears of his children are there any tears of the gambler?   Do the winds that come to kiss the faded cheek of sickness, and to cool the heated brow of the laborer, whisper hope and cheer to the emaciated victim of the game of hazard?   When an honest man is in trouble he has sympathy.   "Poor fellow!" they say. But do gamblers come to weep at the agony of the gambler? Ay, there is no sympathy for him in sorrows!

MR. PORTER'S SAD HISTORY.

In Northumberland was one of the finest estates in England. Mr. Porter owned it, and in a year gambled it all away. Having lost the last acre of the estate, he came down from the saloon, and got his carriage, went back, staked his horses and carriage and town house, and played. He threw and lost, He started home, and in a side alley met a friend from whom he borrowed ten guineas; went back to the saloon and before a great while had won twenty thousand pounds. He died at last a beggar in St. Giles. How many gamblers felt sorry for Mr. Porter? Who consoled him on the loss of his estate? What gambler subscribed to put a stone over the poor man's grave? Not one!

GAMBLING THE CAUSE OF OTHER CRIMES.

Furthermore, this sin is the source of uncounted dishonesties. The game of hazard itself is often a game of cheat. How many tricks and deceptions in the dealing of the cards! The opponents hand is ofttimes found out by fraud. Cards are marked so that they may be designated from the back. Expert gamesters have their accomplices, and one wink may decide the game. The dice have been found loaded with platina, so that "doublets" come up every time. These dice are introduced by gamblers, unobserved by honest men who have come into the play; and this accounts for the fact that ninety-nine out of a hundred who gamble, however wealthy they began, at the end are found to be poor, miserable, ragged wretches, that would not now be allowed to sit on the doorstep of the house that they once owned. In a gambling house in San Francisco a young man having just come from the mines deposited a large sum upon the ace, and won twenty-two thousand dollars. But the tide turns. Intense excitement comes upon the countenances of all. Slowly the cards went forth. Every eye is fixed. Not a sound is heard until the ace is revealed favorable to the bank. There are shouts of ''Foul!' ''Foul!" but the keepers of the table produce their pistols, and the uproar is silenced and the bank has won ninety-five thousand dollars. Do you call this a game of chance? There is no chance about it.

IT UTTERLY RUINS.

But these dishonesties in the carrying on of the game are nothing when compared with the frauds which are committed in order to get money to go on with the nefarious work. Gambling with its greedy hand has snatched away the widow's mite and the portion of the orphans? has sold the daughter's virtue to get the means to continue the game; has written the counterfeit signature, emptied the banker's money vault and wielded the assassin's dagger. There is no depths of meanness to which it will not stoop. There is no cruelty at which it is appalled. There is no warning of God that it will not dare. Merciless, unappeasable, fiercer and wilder, it blinds, it hardens, it rends, it blasts, it crushes, it damns. It has peopled our prisons and lunatic asylums. How many railroad agents and cashiers and trustees of funds it has driven to disgrace, incarceration and suicide! Witness years ago a cashier of a railroad who stole one hundred and three thousand dollars to carry on his gaming practices. Witness forty thousand dollars stolen from a Brooklyn bank within the memory of many of you, and the one hundred and eighty thousand dollars taken from a Wall street insurance company for the same purpose! These are only illustrations on a large scale of the robberies every day committed for the purpose of carrying out the designs of gamblers. Hundreds of thousands of dollars every year leak out without observation from the merchant's till into the gambling hell.

A man in London keeping one of these gambling houses boasted that he had ruined a nobleman a day; but if all the saloons of this land were to speak out they might utter a more infamous boast, for they have destroyed a thousand noble men a year.

IT DESTROYS DOMESTIC HAPPINESS.

Notice also the effect of this crime upon domestic happiness. It has. sent its ruthless plowshare through hundreds of families, until the wife sat in rags, and the daughters were disgraced, and the sons grew up to the same infamous practices or took a short cut to destruction across the murderer's scaffold. Home has lost all charms for the gambler. How tame are the children's caresses and a wife's devotion to the gambler! How drearily the fire burns on the domestic hearth! There must be louder laughter, and something to win and something to lose; an excitement to drive the heart faster and fillip the blood and fire the imagination. No home, however bright, can keep back the gamester. The sweet call of love bounds back from his iron soul, and all endearments are consumed in the flame of his passion. The family Bible will go after all other treasures are lost, and if his crown in heaven were put into his hand he would cry: "Here goes one more game, my boys! On this one throw I stake my crown of heaven."

A SAD, SAD STORY AND LETTER.

A young man in London, on coming of age, received a fortune of one hundred and twenty thousand dollars, and, through gambling, in three years was thrown on his mother for support. An only son went to a southern city; he was rich, intellectual and elegant in manners. His parents gave him on his departure from home their last blessing. The sharpers got hold of him. They flattered him. They lured him to the gaming table, and let him win almost every time for a good while, and patted him on the back and said, "First rate player.' But fully in their grasp they fleeced him, and his thirty thousand dollars were lost. Last of all he put up his watch and lost that. Then he began to think of his home and his old father and mother, and wrote thus:

"My Beloved Parents—You will doubtless feel a momentary joy at the reception of this letter from the child of your bosom, on whom you have lavished all the favors of your declining years. But should a feeling of joy for a moment spring up in your hearts when you should have received this from me cherish it not. I have fallen deep —never to rise. Those gray hairs that I should have honored and protected I shall bring down with sorrow to the grave. I will not curse my destroyer, but oh? may God avenge the wrongs and impositions practiced upon the unwary in a way that shall best please Him. This, my dear parents, is the last letter you will ever receive from me. I humbly pray your forgiveness. It is my dying prayer. Long before you have received this letter from me the cold grave will have closed upon me forever. Life to me is insupportable. I cannot, nay, I will not, suffer the shame of having ruined you. Forget and forgive is the dying prayer of your unfortunate son."

The old father came to the postoffice, got the letter and fell to the floor. They thought he was dead at first; but they brushed back the white hair from his brow and fanned him. He had only fainted. I wish he had been dead, for what is life worth to a father after his son is destroyed? When things go wrong at the gambling table they shout "Foul! foul!" Over all the gaming tables of the world I cry out: "Foul! foul! Infinitely foul."

A VIVID PICTURE OF THE GAMBLER'S LIFE.

Shall I sketch the history of the gambler? Lured by bad company he finds his way into a place where honest men ought never to go. He sits down to his first game, but only for pastime and the desire of being thought sociable. The players deal out the cards. They unconsciously play into Satan's hands, who takes all the tricks and both the players' souls for trumps—he being a sharper at any game. A slight stake is put up just to add interest to the play. Game after game is played. Larger stakes and still larger. They begin to move nervously on their chairs. Their brows lower and eyes flash, until now they who win, and they who lose, fired alike with passion, sit with set jaws, and compressed lips, and clinched fists and eyes like fire balls that seem starting from their sockets, to see the final turn before it comes; if losing, pale with envy and tremulous with unuttered oaths cast back red hot upon the heart—or, winning, with hysteric laugh—"Ha! ha! I have it! I have it!

A few years have passed and he is only the wreck of a man. Seating himself at the game ere he throws the first card, he stakes the last relic of his wife, and the marriage ring which sealed the solemn vows between them. The game is lost, and staggering back in exhaustion he dreams. The bright hours of the past mock his agony, and in his dreams fiends with eyes of fire and tongue of flames circle about him with joined hands to dance and sing their orgies with hellish chorus, chanting ''Hail! brother!'' kissing his clammy forehead until their loathsome locks, flowing with serpents, crawl into his bosom and sink their sharp fangs and suck up his life's blood, and coiling around his heart pinch it with chills and shudders unutterable.

BE WARNED IN TIME.

Take warning! You are no stronger than tens of thousands who have by this practice been overthrown. No young man in our cities can escape being tempted. Beware of the first beginnings! This road is a down grade, and every instant increases the momentum. Launch not upon this treacherous sea. Split hulks strew the beach. Everlasting storms howl up and down tossing unwary crafts into the Hellgate. I speak of what I have seen with my own eyes. I have looked off into the abyss, and I have seen the foaming, and the hissing, and the whirling of the horrid deep in which the mangled victims writhed, one upon another, and struggled, strangled, blasphemed and died—the death stare of eternal despair upon their countenances as the waters gurgled over them.

To a gambler's deathbed there comes no hope. He will probably die alone. His former associates come not nigh his dwelling. When the hour comes his miserable soul will go out of that miserable life into a miserable eternity. As his poor remains pass the house where he was ruined, old companions may look out a moment and say, "There goes the old carcass—dead at last," but they will not get up from the table. Let him down now into his grave. Plant no tree to cast its shade there, for the long, deep, eternal gloom that settles there is shadow enough. Plant no "forget-me-nots" or eglantines around the spot, for flowers were not made to grow on such a blasted heath. Visit it not in the sunshine, for that would be mockery, but in the dismal night, when no stars are out and the spirits of darkness come down horsed on the wind, then visit the grave of the gambler!

DRUNKENNESS.

"Noah planted a vineyard; and he drank of the wine and was drunken." Genesis ix, 20, 21.

This Noah did the best and the worst thing for the world. He built an ark against the deluge of water, but introduced a deluge against which the human race has ever since been trying to build an ark—the deluge of drunkenness. In my text we hear his staggering steps. Shem and Japheth tried to cover up the disgrace, but there he is, drunk on wine at a time in the history of the world, when, to say the least, there was no lack of water. Inebriation, having entered the world, has not retreated. Abigail, the fair and heroic wife, who saved the flocks of Nabal, her husband, from confiscation by invaders, goes home at night and finds him so intoxicated she cannot tell him the story of his narrow escape. Uriah came to see David, and David got him drunk and paved the way for the despoliation of a house hold. Even the church bishops needed to be charged to be sober and not given to too much wine, and so familiar were people of Bible times with the staggering and falling motion of the inebriate that, Isaiah, when he comes to describe the final dislocation of worlds, says, "The earth shall reel to and fro like a drunkard."

A WORLD WIDE TEMPTATION.

Ever since apples and grapes and wheat grew the world has been tempted to unhealthful stimulants. But the

[34]

INTEMPERANCE.

intoxicants of the olden time were an innocent beverage, a harmless orangeade, a quiet syrup, a peaceful soda water as compared with the liquids of modern inebriation, into which a madness and a fury, and a gloom, and a fire, and a suicide, and a retribution have mixed and mingled. · Fermentation was always known, but it was not until a thousand years after Christ that distillation was invented.   While we must confess that some of the ancient arts have been lost, the Christian era is superior to all others in the bad eminence of whisky and rum and gin. The modern drunk is a hundred fold worse than the ancient drunk.   Noah in his intoxication became imbecile, but the victims of modern alcoholism have to struggle with whole menageries of wild beasts, and jungles of hissing serpents, and perditions of blaspheming demons.

An arch fiend arrived in our world and he built an invisible caldron of temptation.   He built that caldron strong and stout for all ages and all nations.   First he squeezed into the caldron the juices of the forbidden fruit of Paradise.   Then he gathered for it a distillation from the harvest fields and the orchards of the hemispheres. Then he poured into this caldron capsicum, and copperas and logwood and deadly nightshade and assault and battery and vitriol and opium and rum and murder and sulphuric acid and theft and potash and cochineal and red carrots and poverty and death and hops.   But it was a dry compound, and it must be moistened, and it must be liquefied, and so the arch fiend pours into that caldron the tears of centuries of orphanage and widowhood, and he poured in the blood of twenty thousand assassinations.

And then the arch fiend took a shovel that he had brought up from the furnaces beneath, and he put that shovel into this great caldron and began to stir, and the caldron began to heave and rock and boil and sputter and hiss and smoke, and the nations gathered around it with cups and tankards and demijohns and kegs, and there was enough for all, and the arch fiend cried: "Aha! champion fiend am I! Who has done more than I have for coffins and graveyards and prisons and insane asylums and the populating of the lost world? And when this caldron is emptied I'll fill it again and I'll stir it again, and it will smoke again, and that smoke will join another smoke, the smoke of torment that ascendeth for ever and ever. I drove fifty ships on the rocks of Newfoundland, and the Skeeries, and the Goodwins. I have ruined more senators than gathered this winter in the national councils. I have ruined more lords than are now gathered in the house of peers. The cup out of which I ordinarly drink is a bleached human skull, and the upholstery of my palace is so rich a crimson, because it is dyed in human gore, and the mosaic of my floors is made up of the bones of children dashed to death by drunken parents, and my favorite music—sweeter than Te Deum or triumphal march—my favorite music is the cry of daughters turned out at midnight on the street because father has come home from the carousal, and the seven hundred voice shriek of the sinking steamer, because the captain was not himself when he put the ship on the wrong course. Champion fiend am I! I have kindled more fires, I have wrung out more agonies, I have stretched out more midnight shadows, I have opened more Golςothas, I have rolled more Juggernauts, I have damned more souls than any other emissary of diabolism. Champion fiend am I!"

THE NATION'S GREATEST EVIL.

Drunkenness is the greatest evil of this nation, and it takes no logical process to prove to this audience that a drunken nation cannot long be a free nation. I call your attention to the fact that drunkenness is not subsiding; certainly that it is not at a standstill, but that it is on an onward march, and it is a double quick. There is more rum swallowed in this country, and of a worse kind, than was ever swallowed since the first distillery began its work of death. Where there was one drunken home there are ten drunken homes. Where there was one drunkard's grave there are twenty drunkard's graves. It is on the increase. Talk about crooked whisky—by which men mean the whisky that does not pay the tax to government—I tell you all strong drink is crooked. Crooked Otard, crooked Cognac, crooked schnapps, crooked beers, crooked wine, crooked whisky—because it makes a man's path crooked, and his life crooked, and his death crooked, and his eternity crooked.

If I could gather all the armies of the dead drunkards and have them come to resurrection, and then add to that host all the armies of living drunkards, five and ten abreast, and then if I could have you mount a horse and ride along that line for review, you would ride that horse until he dropped from exhaustion, and you would mount another horse and ride until he fell from exhaustion, and you would take another and another, and you would ride along hour after hour and day after day.

Great host, in regiments, in brigades.   Great armies of
them.   And then if you had voice stentorian enough to
make them all hear, and you could give the command,
"Forward,   march!" their first tramp would make the
earth tremble.   I do not care which way you look in the
community to-day, the evil is increasing.

Is drunkenness a state or national evil?   Does it belong to the north, or does it belong to the south?   Does
it belong to the east, or does it belong to the west?
Ah! there is not an American river into which its tears
have not fallen and into which its suicides have not
plunged.   What ruined that southern plantation?—
every field a fortune, the proprietor and his family once
the most affluent supporters of summer watering places.
What threw that New England farm into decay and turned the roseate cheeks that bloomed at the foot of the
Green Mountains into the.pallor of despair?   What has
smitten every street of every village, town and city of
this continent with a moral pestilence?   Strong drink.

MAINE AND GEORGIA.

To prove that this is a national evil I call up two
states in opposite directions—Maine and Georgia.   Let
them testify in regard to this.   State of Maine says, "It
is so great an evil up here we have anathematized it as a
state."   State of Georgia says, "It is so great an evil
down here that ninety counties of this state have made
the sale of intoxicating drink a criminality."   So the
word comes up from all parts of the land.   Either drunk.
enness will be destroyed in this country or the American.
government will be destroyed.   Drunkenness and free

institutions are coming into a terrible death grapple.

HEREDITARY APPETITE.

I call attention to the facts that there are thousands of people born with a thirst for strong drinks—a fact too often ignored. Along some ancestral lines there runs the river of temptation. There are children whose swaddling clothes are torn off the shrould of death. Many a father has made a will of this sort: "In the name of God, amen. I bequeath to my children my houses and lands and estates; share and share shall they alike. Hereto I affix my hand and seal in the presence of witnesses." And yet perhaps that very man has made another will that the people have never read, and that has not been proved in the courts. That will put in writing, would read something like this: "In the name of disease and appetite and death, amen. I bequeath to my children my evil habits, my tankards shall be theirs, my wine cup shall be theirs, my destroyed reputation shall be theirs. Share and share alike shall they in the infamy. Hereto I affix my hand and seal in the presence of all the applauding harpies of hell."

From the multitude of those who have the evil habit born with them this army is being augumented. And I am sorry to say that a great many of the drug stores are abetting this evil, and alcohol is sold under the name of bitters. It is bitters for this and bitters for that and bitters for some other thing, and good men deceived, not knowing there is any thraldom of alcoholism coming from that source, are going down, and some day a man sits with the bottle of black bitters on his table, and the cork flies out, and after it flies a fiend and clutches the man by his throat and says: ''Aha! I have been after you for ten years. I have got you now. Down with you! down with you!'' Bitters! Ah! yes. They make a man's family bitter, and his home bitter, and his disposition bitter, and his death bitter, and his hell bitter. Bitters! A vast army, all the time increasing.

It seems to me it is about time for the 17,000,000 professors of religion in America to take sides. It is going to be an out and out battle with drunkenness and sobriety, between heaven and hell, between God and the devil Take sides before there is any further national decadence take sides before your sons are sacrificed and the new home of your daughter goes down under the alcoholism of an imbruted husband. Take sides while your voice, your pen, your prayer, your vote may have an influence in arresting the despoliation of this nation. If the 17,-000,000 professors of religion should take sides on this subject it woutd not be very long before the destiny of this nation would be decided in the right direction.

THE GREAT ENEMY OF LABOR.

Gather up the money that the working classes have spent for rum during the last thirty years, and I will build for every workingman a house, and lay out for him a garden, and clothe his sons in broadcloth and his daughters in silks, and stand at his front door a prancing span of sorrels or bays, and secure him a policy of life insurance so that the present home may be well maintained after he is dead. The most persistent, most overpowering enemy of the working classes is intoxicating liquor. It is the anarchist of the centuries, and has boycotted and is now boycotting the body and mind and soul of American labor. It annually swindles industry out of a large percentage of its earnings. It holds out its blasting solicitations to the mechanic or operative on his way to work, and at the noon spell, and on his way home at eventide. On Saturday when the wages are paid, it snatches a large part of the money that might come to the family and sacrifices it among the saloon keepers. Stand the saloons of this country side by side, and it is carefully estimated that they would reach from New York to Chicago.

This evil is pouring its vitriolic and damnable liquors down the throats of hundreds of thousands of laborers, and while the ordinary strikes are ruinous both to employers and employes, I proclaim a universal strike against strong drink, which strike, if kept up, will be the relief of the working classes and the salvation of the nation. I will undertake to say that there is not a healthy laborer in the United States who, within the next twenty years, if he will refuse all intoxicating beverages and be saving, may not become a capitalist on a small scale.

CANNOT SOMETHING BE DONE?

Oh, how many are waiting to see if something cannot be done for the stopping of intemperance! Thousands of drunkards waiting who cannot go ten minutes in any direction without having the temptation glaring before their eyes or appealing to their nostrils, they fighting against it with enfeebled will and diseased appetite, conquering, then surrendering, conquering again and surrendering again, and crying: "How long, O Lord! how long before these infamous solicitations shall be gone?" And how many mothers are waiting to see if this national curse cannot lift? Oh, is that the boy who has the honest breath who comes home with breath vitiated or disguised? What a change! How quickly those habits of early coming home have been exchanged for the rattling of the night key in the door long after the last watchman has gone by and tried to see that every thing was closed up for the night!

THE WAYWARD BOY.

Oh! what a change for that young man, who we had hoped would do something in merchandise or in artisanship or in a profession that would do honor to the family name, long after mother's wrinkled hands are folded from the last toil! All that exchanged for startled look when the door bell rings, lest something has happened; and the wish that the scarlet fever twenty years ago had been fatal, for then he would have gone directly to the bosom of his Saviour. But alas! poor old soul, she has lived to experience what Solomon said, "A foolish son is a heaviness to his mother."

Oh! what a funeral it will be when that boy is brought home dead! And how mother will sit there and say: "Is this my boy that I used to fondle, and that I walked the floor with in the nights when he was sick? Is this the boy that I held to the baptismal font for baptism? Is this the boy for whom I toiled until the blood burst from the tips of my fingers, that he might have a good start and a good home? Lord, why hast thou let me live to see this? Can it be that these swollen hands are the ones that used to wander over my face when rocking him to sleep? Can it be that this swollen brow is that I once so rapturously kissed? Poor boy! how tired he does look. I wonder who struck him that blow across the temples? I wonder if he uttered a dying prayer? Wake up, my son; don't you hear me? Wake up! Oh! he can't hear me! Dead! dead! dead! 'Oh, Absalom, my son. my son, would God that I had died for thee, oh, Absalom, my son, my son!"

WAITING WIVES.

I am not much of a mathematician and I cannot estimate it, but is there anyone here quick enough at figures to estimate how many mothers there are waiting for something to be done? Ay, there are many wives waiting for domestic rescue. He promised something different from that when after the long acquaintance and the careful scrutiny of character, the hand and the heart were offered and accepted. What a hell on earth a woman lives in who has a drunken husband! O death, how lovely thou art to her, and how soft and warm thy skeleton hand! The sepulcher at midnight in winter is a king's drawing room compared with that woman's home. It is not so much the blow on the head that hurts as the blow on the heart:

The rum fiend came to the door of that beautiful home, and opened the door and stood there and said: "I curse this dwelling with an unrelenting curse. I curse that father into a manaic, I curse that mother into a pauper. I curse those sons into vagabonds. I curse those daughters into profligacy. Cursed be bread tray and cradle. Cursed be couch and chair, and family Bible with record of marriages and births and deaths. Curse upon curse." Oh, how many wives are there waiting to see if something cannot be done to shake these frosts of the second death **off the orange blossoms! Yea, God is waiting, the God** who works through human instrumentalities, waiting to see whether this nation is going to overthrow this evil, and if it refuse to do so God will wipe out the nation as he did Phœnicia; as he did Rome, as he did Thebes, as he did Babylon.

Ay, he is waiting to see what the church of God will do. If the church does not do its work, then he will wipe it out as he did the church of Ephesus, church of Thyatira, church of Sardis. The Protestant and Roman Catholic churches to-day stand side by side, with an impotent look, gazing on this evil, which costs this country more than a billion dollars a year to take care of the 800,000 paupers, and the 315,000 criminals, and the 30,000 idiots, and to bury the 75,000 drunkards. Protagoras boasted that out of the sixty years of his life forty years he had spent in ruining youths; but this evil may make the more infamous boast that all its life it has been ruining the bodies, minds and souls of the human race.

THE POLITICIANS ARE DOING NOTHING.

Put on your spectacles and take a candle and examine the platforms of the two leading political parties of this country, and see what they are doing for the arrest of this evil, and for the overthrow of this abomination. Resolutions— oh! yes, resolutions about Mormonism! It is safe to attack that organized nastiness two thousand miles away. But not one resolution against drunkenness, which would turn this entire nation into one bestial Salt Lake City. Resolutions against political corruption, but not one word about drunkenness, which would rot this nation from scalp to heel. Resolutions about protection against competition with foreign industries, but not one word about protection of family and church and nation against the scalding, blastings, all consuming. damning tariff of strong drink put upon every financial, individual, spiritual, moral, national interest.

THE POWER OF THE CHURCH.

I look in another direction. The Church of God is the grandest and most glorious institution on earth. What has it in solid phalanx accomplished for the overthrow of drunkenness? Have its forces ever been marshaled? No, not in this direction. Not long ago a great ecclesiastical court assembled in New York, and resolutions arrainging strong drink were offered, and clergymen with strong drink on their tables and strong drink in their cellars defeated the resolutions by threatening speeches. They could not bear to give up their own lusts.

I tell this audience what many of you may never have thought of, that to-day—not in the millennium, but to-day—the church holds the balance of power in America; and if Christian people—the men and the women who profess to love the Lord Jesus Christ and to love purity and to be the sworn enemies of all uncleanness and debauchery and sin—if all such would march side by side and shoulder to shoulder, this evil would soon be overthrown. Think of three hundred thousand churches and Sunday schools in Christendom marching shoulder to shoulder! How very short a time it would take them to put down this evil, if all the churches of God, transatlantic and cisatlantic, were armed on this subject!

Young men of America, pass over into the army of teetotalism. Whisky, good to preserve corpses, ought never to turn you into a corpse. Tens of thousands of young men have been dragged out of respectability, and out of purity, and out of good character, and into darkness by this infernal stuff called strong drink. Do not touch it! Do not touch it!

A SAD STORY ABOUT "JOE."

In the front door of our church in Brooklyn, a few summers ago, this scene occurred: Sabbath morning a young man was entering for divine worship. A friend passing along the street said, "Joe, come along with me; I am going down to Coney Island and we'll have a gay Sunday.,' "No," replied Joe; "I have started to go here to church, and I am going to attend service here." "Oh, Joe," his friend said, "you can go to church any time! The day is bright, and we'll go to Coney Island, and we'll have a splendid time." The temptation was too strong, and the twain went to the beach, spent the day in drunkenness and riot. The evening train started up from Brighton. The young men were on it. Joe, in his intoxication, when the train was in full speed, tried to pass around from one seat to another and fell and was crushed.

Under the lantern as Joe lay bleeding his life away on the grass, he said to his comrade: "John, that was a bad business, you taking me away from church; it was a very bad business. You ought not to have done that, John. I want you to tell the boys to-morrow when you see them that rum and Sabbath breaking did this for me. And John, while you are telling them, I will be in hell, and it will be your fault." Is it not time for me to pull out from the great organ of God's word, with many banks of keys, the tremolo stop? "Look not upon the wine when it is red, when it moveth itself aright in the cup, for at last it biteth like a serpent and stingeth like an adder.

THIS EVIL WILL BE ARRESTED.

But this evil will be arrested. Blucher came up just before night and saved the day at Waterloo. At 4 o'clock, in the afternoon it looked very badly for the English. Generals Ponsonby and Pickton fallen. Sabers broken, flags surrendered, Scots Grays annihilated. Only forty-two men left out of the German brigade. The English army falling back and falling back. Napoleon rubbed his hands together and said; "Aha! aha! we"ll teach that little Englishman a lesson. Ninety chances out of a hundred are in our favor. Magnificent! magnificent!" even sent messages to Paris to say he had won the day.

But before sundown Blucher came up, and he who had been the conqueror of Austerlitz became the victim of Waterloo. The name which had shaken all Europe and filled even America with apprehension, that name went down, and Napoleon, muddy and hatless, and crazed with his disasters, was found feeling for the stirrup of a horse, that he might mount and resume the conflict.

Well, my friends, alcoholism is imperial, and it is a conqueror, and there are good people who say the night of national overthrow is coming, and that it is almost night. But before sundown the Conqueror of earth and heaven will ride in on a white horse, and alcoholism, which has had its Austerlitz of triumph, shall have its Waterloo of defeat. Alcoholism having lost its crown, the grizzly and cruel breaker of human hearts, crazed with the disaster, will be found feeling in vain for the stirrup on which to remount its foaming charger. "So, O Lord, Let thine enemies perish."

PLAGUE OF BAD BOOKS.

"And the frogs came up and covered the land of Egypt.   And the magicians did so with their enchantments, and brought frogs upon the land of Egypt." Ex. viii, 6, 7.

There is almost a universal aversion to frogs, and yet with the Egyptians they were honored, they were sacred, and they were objects of worship while alive, and after death they were embalmed, and to-day their remains may be found among the sepulchres of Thebes.

THE ANCIENT PLAGUE OF FROGS.

These creatures, so attractive once to the Egyptians, at divine behest became obnoxious and loathsome, and they went croaking and hopping and leaping into the palace of the king, and into the bread trays and the couches of the people, and even the ovens, which are now uplifted above the earth and on the side of chimneys, but then were small holes in the earth with sunken pottery, were filled with frogs when the housekeepers came to look at then.   If a man sat down to eat, a frog alighted on his plate.   If he attempted to put on a shoe, it was preoccupied by a frog.   If he attempted to put his head upon a pillow, it had been taken possession of by a frog.

Frogs high and low and everywhere, loathsome frogs, slimy frogs, besieging frogs, innumerable frogs, great plague of frogs.   What made the matter worse the magicians said there was no miracle in this, and that they could by sleight-of-hand produce the same thing, and they seemed to succeed, for by sleight-of-hand wonders may be wrought. After Moses had thrown down his staff and by miracle it became a serpent, and then he took hold of it and by miracle it again became a staff, the serpent charmers imitated the same thing, and knowing that there were serpents in Egypt which by a peculiar pressure on the neck would become as rigid as a stick of wood, they seemed to change the serpent into the staff, and then, throwing it down, the staff became the serpent.

So likewise these magicians tried to imitate the plague of frogs, and perhaps by smell of food attracting a great number of them to a certain point, or by shaking them out from a hidden place, the magicians sometimes seemed to accomplish the same miracle. While these magicians made the plague worse, none of them tried to make it better. "Frogs came up and covered the land of Egypt, and the magicians did so with their enchantment, and brought up frogs upon the land of Egypt."

THE MODERN PLAGUE OF FROGS.

Now that plague of frogs has come back upon the earth. It is abroad to-day. It is smiting this nation. It comes in the shape of corrupt literarture. The frogs hop into the store, the shop, the office, the banking house, the factory—into the home, into the cellar, into the garret, on the drawing room table, on the shelf of the library. While the lad is reading the bad book the teacher's face is turned the other way, one of these frogs hops upon the page. While the young woman reads the forbidden novelette after retiring at night, reading by gaslight, one of these frogs leaps upon the page. Indeed they have hopped upon the news stands of the country, and the mails at the postoffice shake out in the letter trough hundreds of them.   The plague has taken at different times possession of this country.   It is one of the most loathsome, one of the most frightful, one of the most ghastly of the ten plagues of our modern cities.

There is a vast number of books and newspapers printed and published which ought never to see the light. They are filled with a pestilence that makes the land· swelter with a moral epidmic. The greatest blessing that ever came to this nation is that of an elevated literature, and· the greatest scourge has been that of unclean literature.   This last has its victims in all occupations and departments.   It has helped to fill insane asylums and penitentiaries and almhouses and dens of shame.   The bodies of this infection lie in the hospitals and in the graves, while their souls are being tossed over into a lost eternity, an avalanche of horror and despair.

The London plague was nothing to it.   That counted its victims by thousands, but this modern pest has already shoveled its millions into the charnel house of the morally dead.   The longest rail train that ever ran over the Erie or Hudson tracks was not long enough nor large enough to carry the beastliness and putrefaction which have been gathered up in bad books and newspapers of this land in the last twenty years.   The literature of a nation decides the fate of a nation.   Good books, good morals.   Bad books, bad morals.

I begin with the lowest of all the literature, that which does not even pretend to be respectable—from **cover to** cover a blotch of leprosy. There are many whose entire business it is to dispose of that kind of literature. They display it before the schoolboy on his way home. They get the catalogues of schools and colleges, take the names and postoffice addresses, and send their advertisements, and their circulars, and their pamphlets, and their books to every one of them.

THE AMOUNT OF BAD LITERATURE.

In the possession of these dealers in bad literature were found nine hundred thousand names and postoffice addresses, to whom it was thought it might be profitable to send these corrupt things. In the year 1870 there were one hundred and sixty-five establishments engaged in publishing cheap, corrupt literature. From one publishing house there went out twenty different styles of corrupt books. Although over thirty tons of vile literature have been destroyed by the Society for the Suppression of Vice, still there is enough of it left in this country to bring down upon us the thunderbolts of an incensed God.

THE LAWS AGAINST BAD BOOKS.

In the year 1868 the evil had become so great in this country that the congress of the United States passed a law forbidding the transmission of bad literature through the United States mails, but there were large loops in that law through which criminals might crawl out, and the law was a dead failure—that law of 1868. But in 1873 another law was passed by the congress of the United Stares against the transmission of corrupt literature through the mails—a grand law, a potent law, a Christian law,—and under that law multitudes of these scoundrels have been arrested, their property confiscated

and they themselves thrown into the penitentiaries where
they belonged.

HOW ARE WE TO WAR AGAINST IT?

Now, my friends, how are we to war against this corrupt literature, and how are the frogs of this Egyptian
plague to be slain?　First of all by the prompt and inexorable execution of the law.　Let all good postmasters
and United States district attorneys, and detectives and
reformers concert in their action to stop this plague.
When Sir Rowland Hill spent his life in trying to secure
cheap postage not only for England, but for all the world,
and to open the blessing of the postoffice to all honest
business, and to all messages of charity and kindness
and affection, for all healthful intercommunication, he
did not mean to make vice easy or to fill the mail bags
of the United States with the scabs of such a leprosy.

It ought not to be in the power of every bad·man who
can raise a one cent stamp for a circular or a two cent
stamp for a letter to blast a man or destroy a home.　The
postal service of this country must be clean, and we
must all understand that the swift retributions of the
United States government hover over every violation of
the letter box. ·

ENFORCE THE LAW.

There are thousands of men and women in this country,
some for personal gain, some through innate depravity,
some through a spirit of revenge, who wish to use this
great avenue of convenience and intelligence for purposes
revengeful, salacious and diabolic.　Wake up the law.
Wake up all its penalties.　Let every court room on this
subject be a Sinai thunderous and aflame.　Let the con-

victed offenders be sent for the full term to Sing Sing or Harrisburg.

I am not talking about what cannot be done. I am talking now about what is being done. A great many of the printing presses that gave themselves entirely to the publication of vile literature have been stopped or have gone into business less obnoxious. What has thrown off, what has kept off the rail trains of this country for some time back nearly all the leprous periodicals? Those of us who have been on the rail trains have noticed a great change in the last few months and the last year or two. Why have nearly all those vile periodicals been kept off the rail trains for some time back? Who effected it? These societies for the purificaticn of railroad literature gave warning to the publishers, and warning to railroad companies, and warning to conductors, and warning to newsboys, to keep the infernal stuff off the trains.

Many of the cities have successfully prohibited the most of that literature even from going on the news stands. Terror has seized upon the publishers and the dealers in impure literature, from the fact that over a thousand arrests have been made, and the aggregate time for which the convicted have been sentenced to the prison is over one hundred and ninety years, and from the fact that about two million of their circulars have been destroyed, and the business is not as profitable as it used to be.

THE LAW! THE LAW! WHAT IT IS DOING.

How have so many of the news stands of our great cities been purified? How has so much of this iniquity been balked? By moral suasion? Oh, no. You might as well go into a jungle of the East Indies and pat a cobra on the neck, and with profound argument try to persuade it that it is morally wrong to bite and sting and to poison anything. The only answer to your argument would be an uplifted head and a hiss and a sharp, reeking tooth struck into your arteries. The only argument for a cobra is a shotgun, and the only argument for these dealers in impure literature is the clutch of the police and bean soup in a penitentiary. The law! the law! I invoke to consummate the work so grandly begun!

ANOTHER WAY.

Another way in which we are to drive back this plague of Egyptian frogs is by filling the minds of our young people with a healthful literature. I do not mean to say that all the books and newspapers in our families ought to be religious books and newspapers, or that every song ought to be sung to the tune of ''Old Hundred.'' I have no sympathy with the attempt to make the young, old. I would rather join in a crusade to keep the young, young. Boyhood and girlhood must not be abbreviated. But there are good books, good histories, good biographies, good works of fiction, good books of all styles with which we are to fill the minds of the young, so that there will be no more room for the useless and the vicious than there is room for chaff in a bushel measure which is already filled with Michigan wheat.

Why are 50 per cent of the criminals in the jails and penitentiaries of the United States to-day under twenty-one yea;s of age! Many of them under seventeen, under sixteen, under fifteen, under fourteen, under thirteen. Walk along one of the corridors of the Tombs prison in

New York and look for yourselves. Bad books, bad newspapers, bewitched them as soon as they got out of the cradle. Beware of all those stories which end wrong. Beware of all those books which make the road that ends in perdition seem to end in Paradise. Do not glorify the dirk and the pistol. Do not call the desperado brave or the libertine gallant. Teach our young people that if they go down into the swamps and marshes to watch the jack-o'-lanterns dance on the decay and rottenness they will catch the malaria and death.

"Oh," says some one, "I am a business man, and I have no time to examine what my children read. I have no time to inspect that come into my household." If your children were threatened with typhoid fever, would you have time to go for the doctor? Would you have time to watch the progress of the disease? Would you have time for the funeral? In the presence of my God I warn you of the fact that your children are threatened with moral and spiritual typhoid, and that unless the thing be stopped it will be to them funeral of body, funeral of mind, funeral of soul. Three funerals in one day.

My word is to this vast multitude of young people: Do not touch, do not borrow, do not buy a corrupt book, or a corrupt picture. A book will decide a man's destiny for good or for evil. The book you read yesterday may have decided you for time and for eternity, or it may be a book that may come into your possession to-morrow.

THE POWER OF A BAD BOOK.

A good book—who can exaggerate its power?
Benjamin Franklin said that his reading of Cotton

Mather's "Essays to Do Good" in childhood gave him holy aspirations for all the rest of his life.

George Law declared that a biography he read in childhood gave him all his subsequent prosperities.

A clergyman many years ago, passing to the far west, stopped at a hotel. He saw a woman copying something from Doddrige's "Rise and Progress." It seemed that she had borrowed the book, and there were some things she wanted especially to remember.

The clergyman had in his satchel a copy of Doddrige's "Rise and Progress," and so he made her a present of it. Thirty years passed on. The clergyman came that way, and he asked where the woman was whom he had seen so long ago.

"She lives yonder in that beautiful house."

He went there and said to her. "Do you remember me?"

She said, "No I do not."

He said, "Do you remember a man gave you Doddrige's 'Rise and Progress' thirty years ago?"

"Oh, yes; I remember. That book saved my soul. I loaned the book to all my neighbors, and they read it and they were converted to God, and we had a revival of religion which swept through the whole community. We built a church and called a pastor. You see that spire yonder, don't you? That church was built as the result of that book you gave me thirty years ago."

Oh, the power of a good book! But, alas! for the influence of a bad book.

John Angel James, than whom England never had a holier minister, stood in his pulpit at Birmingham and said: "Twenty-five years ago a lad loaned to me an infamous book. He would loan it only fifteen minutes, and then I had to give it back, but that book has haunted me like a specter ever since. I have in agony of soul, on my knees before God, prayed that he would obliterate from my soul the memory of it, but I shall carry the damage of it until the day of my death."

The assassin of Sir William Russell declared that he got the inspiration for his crime by reading what was then a new and popular novel, "Jack Sheppard."

Homer's "Iliad" made Alexander the warrior. Alexander said so. The story of Alexander made Julius Cæsar and Charles XII both men of blood.

Have you in your pocket, or in your trunk, or in your desk at business a bad book, a bad picture; a bad pamphlet? In God's name I warn you to destroy it.

THE CHRISTIAN PRESS.

Another way in which we shall fight back this corrupt literature and kill the frogs of Egypt is by rolling over them the Christian printing press, which shall give plenty of healthful reading to all adults. All these men and women are reading men and women. What are you reading? Abstain from all those books which, while they have some good things about them, have also an admixture of evil. You have read books that had two elements in them—the good and the bad. Which stuck to you? The bad! The heart of most people is like a sieve, which lets the small particles of gold fall through, but keeps the great cinders. Once in a while there is a mind like a loadstone, which, plunged amid steel and brass fillings, gathers up the steel and repels the brass. But it is generally the opposite. If you attempt to plunge through a fence of burrs to get one blackberry, you will get more burrs than blackberries.

You cannot afford to read a bad book, however good you are. You say, "The influence is insignificant." I tell you that the scratch of a pin has sometimes produced lockjaw. Alas, if through curiosity, as many do, you pry into an evil book, your curiosity is as dangerous as that of the man who would take a torch into a gunpowder mill merely to see whether it would really blow up or not.

In a menagerie a man put his arm through the bars of a black leopard's cage. The animal's hide looked so sleek and bright and beautiful. He just stroked it once. The monster seized him, and he drew forth a hand torn and mangled and bleeding.

Oh, touch not evil even with the faintest stroke! Though it may be glossy and beautiful, touch it not lest you pull forth your soul torn and bleeding under the clutch of the black leopard.

"But," you say, "how can I find out whether a book is good or bad without reading it?" There is always something suspicious about a bad book. I never knew an exception—something suspicious in the index or style of illustration. This venemous reptile almost always carries a warning rattle.

The clock strikes midnight. A fair form bends over a romance. The eyes flash fire. The breath is quick and irregular. Occasionally the color dashes to the cheek, and then dies out. The hands tremble as though a guardian spirit were trying to shake the deadly book out of the grasp. Hot tears fall. She laughs with a shrill voice that drops dead at its own sound. The sweat on her brow is the spray dashed up from the river of death. The clock strikes four, and the rosy dawn soon after begins to look through the lattice upon the pale form that looks like a detained specter of the night. Soon in a mad house she will mistake her ringlets for curling serpents, and thrust her white hand through the bars of the prison, and smite her head, rubbing it back as though to push the scalp from the skull, shrieking: ''My brain! my brain!" Oh, stand off from that! Why will you go sounding your way amid the reefs and warning buoys, when there is such a vast ocean in which you may voyage, all sail set?

We see so many books we do not understand what a book is. Stand it on end. Measure it—the height of it, the depth of it, the length of it, the breadth of it. You cannot do it. Examine the paper and estimate the progress made from the time of the impressions on clay, and then on to the bark of trees, and from the bark of trees to papyrus, and from papyrus to the hide of wild beasts, and from the hide of wild beasts on down until the miracles of our modern paper manufactories, and then see the paper, white and pure as an infant's soul, waiting for God's inscription.

A book! Examine the type of it. Examine the printing of it, and see the progress from the time when Solon's laws were written on oak planks, and Hesiod's poems were written on tables of lead, and the Sinaitic commands were written on tables of stone, on down to Hoe's perfecting printing press.

A book! It took all the universities of the past, all the

martyr fires, all the civilizations, all the battles, all the victories, all the defeats, all the glooms, all the brightnesses, all the centuries to make it possible.

A book! It is the chorus of ages; it is the drawing room in which kings and queens and orators and poets and historians come out to greet you.   If I worshipped anything on earth I would worship that.   If I burned incense to any idol I would build an altar to that.

Thank God for good books, healthful books, inspiring books, Christian books, books of men, books of women, Book of God.   It is with these good books that we are to overcome corrupt literature.   Upon the frogs swoop with these eagles.   I depend much for the overthrow of iniquitous literature upon the mortality of books.   Even good books have a hard struggle to live.

Polybius wrote forty books; only five of them left. Thirty books of Tacitus have perished.   Twenty books of Pliny have perished.   Livy wrote one hundred and forty books; only thirty-five of them remain.   Æschylus wrote one hundred dramas; only seven remain. Euripides wrote over a hundred; only nineteen remain. Varro wrote the biographies of over seven hundred great Romans. All that wealth of biography has perished.   If good and valuable books have such a struggle to live, what must be the state of those that are deceased and corrupt and blasted at the very start.   They will die as the frogs when the Lord turned back the plague.   The work of Christianization will go on until there will be nothing left but good books, and they will take the supremacy of the world.   May you and I live to see the illustrious day! **Against** every bad pamphlet send a good pamphlet;

against every unclean picture send an innocent picture; against every scurrilous song send a Christian song; against every bad book send a good book; and then it will be as it was in ancient Toledo, where the Toletum missals were kept by the saints in six churches, and the sacrilegious Romans demanded that those missals be distroyed, and that the Roman missals be substituted; and the war came on, and I am glad to say that the whole matter having been referred to champions, the champion of the Toletum missals with one blow brought down the champion of the Roman missals.

So it will be in our day. The good literature, the Christian literature, in its championship for God and the truth, will bring down the evil literature in its championship for the devil. I feel tingling to the tips of my fingers and through all the nerves of my body, and all the depths of my soul, the certainty of our triumph. Cheer up, oh, men and women who are toiling for the purification of society! Toil with your faces in the sunlight. "If God be for us, who, who can be against us?"

LADY STANHOPE.

Lady Hester Stanhope was the daughter of the third Earl of Stanhope, and after her nearest friends had died she went to the far east, took possession of a deserted convent, threw up fortresses amid the mountains of Lebanon, opened the castle to the poor, and the wretched, and the sick who would come in. She made her castle a home for the unfortunate. She was a devout Christian woman. She was waiting for the coming of the Lord. She expected that the Lord would descend in person, and she thought upon it until it was too much for her reason.   In the magnificent stables of her palace she had two horses groomed and bridled and saddled and caparisoned and all ready for the day in which her Lord should descend, and He on one of them and she on the other should start for Jerusalem, the city of the Great King. It was a fanaticism and a delusion; but there was romance, and there was splendor, and there was thrilling expectation in the dream!

Ah, my friends, we need no earthly palfreys groomed and saddled and bridled and caparisoned for our Lord when He shall come.   The horse is ready in the equerry of heaven, and the imperial rider is ready to mount. "And I saw, and behold a white horse, and He that sat on him had a bow; and a crown was given unto him; and he went forth conquering and to conquer. And the armies which were in heaven followed him on white horses, and on his vesture and on his thigh were written, King of kings, and Lord of lords."

Horse-men of heaven, mount!   Cavalry of God, ride on! Charge! charge! until they shall be hurled back on their haunches—the black horse of famine, and the red horse of carnage, and the pale horse of death.   Jesus forever!

AMUSEMENTS.

AMUSEMENTS.

"Let the young men now arise and play before us." II Samuel, 2, 14

There are two armies encamped by the pool of Gibeon. The time hangs heavily on their hands. One army proposes a game of sword-fencing. Nothing could be more healthful and innocent. The other army accepts the challenge. Twelve men against twelve men, the sport opens. . But something went adversely. Perhaps one of the swordsmen got an unlucky clip, or in some way had his ire aroused, and that which opened in sportfulness ended in violence, each one taking his contestant by the hair, and then with the sword thrusting him in the side; so that that which opened in innocent fun ended in the massacre of all the twenty four sportsmen. Was there ever a better illustration of what was true then, and is true now, that that which is innocent may be made destructive? What of a wordly nature is more important and strengthening and innocent than amusement, and yet what has counted more victims? I have no sympathy with a straight-jacket religion. This is a very bright world to me, and I propose to do all I can to make it bright for others.

A BEAUTIFUL WORLD.

I never could keep step to a dead march. A book years ago issued says that a Christian man has a right to some amusements; for instance, if he comes home at night weary from his work, and, feeling the need of recreation, puts on his slippers and goes into his garret, and walks lively around the floor several times, there can be no harm in it. I belleve the Church of God has made a tremendous mistake in trying to suppress the sportfulness of youth, and drive out from men their love of amusement. If God ever implanted anything in us he implanted this desire. But instead of providing for this demand of our nature the Church of God has, for the main part, ignored it. As in a riot the Mayor plants a battery at the end of the street, and has it fired off, so that everything is cut down that happens to stand in the range, the good as well as the bad, so there are men in the church who plant their batteries of condemnation and fire away indiscriminately. Everything is condemned. But my Bible commends those who use the world without abusing it, and in the natural world God has done everything to please and amuse us. In poetic figure we sometimes speak of natural objects as being in pain, but it is a mere fancy. Poets say the clouds weep, but they never yet shed a tear; and that the winds sigh, but they never did have any trouble; and that the storm howls, but it never lost its temper. The world is a rose, and the universe a garland.

And I am glad to know that in all our cities there are plenty of places where we may find elevated moral entertainment. But all honest men and good women will agree with me in the statement that one of the worst plagues of these cities is corrupt amusement. Multitudes have gone down under the blasting influence, never to rise. If we may judge of what is going on in many of the places of amusement by the Sodomic pictures on board-fences, and in many of the show-windows, there is not a much lower depth of profligacy to reach.   At Naples, Italy, they keep such pictures locked up from indiscriminate inspection.   Those pictures were exhumed from Pompeii and are not fit for public gaze.   If the effrontery of bad places of amusement in hanging out improper advertisement of what they are doing night by night grows worse in the same proportion, in fifty years New York and Brooklyn will beat not only Pompeii but Sodom.

RIGHT AND WRONG RECREATION.

To help stay the plague now raging, I project certain principles by which you may judge in regard to any amusement or recreation, finding out for yourselves whether it is right, or whether it is wrong.

I remark, in the ffrst place, that you can judge of the moral character of any amusement by its healthful result, or by its baleful reaction.   There are people who seem made up of hard facts.   They are a combination of multiplication tables and statistics.   If you show them an exquisite picture, they will begin to discuss the pigments involved in the coloring.   If you show them a beautiful rose, they will submit it to a botanical analysis, which is only the post mortem examination of a flower. They have no rebound in their nature.   They never do anything more than smile.   There are no great tides of feeling surging up from the depths of their soul, in billows of reverberating laughter.   They seem as if nature had built them by contract, and made a bungling job out of it But, blessed be God, there are people in the worla who have bright faces, and whose life is a song, an anthem, a pæan of victory.   Even their troubles are like the vines that crawl up the side of a great tower, on the top of which the sunlight sits, and the soft airs of summer holds perpetual carnival. They are people you like to have come 'to your house: they are the people I like to have come to my house. If you but touch the hem of their garments you are healed.

Now it is these exhilarent, sympathetic, and warm-hearted people that are most tempted to pernicious amusements. In proportion as a ship is swift it wants a strong helmsman; in proportion as a horse is gay, it wants a stout driver; and these people of exuberant nature will do well to look at the reaction of all their amusements. If an amusement sends you home at night nervous, so that you cannot sleep, and you rise up in the morning, not because you have slept out, but because your duty drags you from your slumbers, you have been where you ought not to have been. There are amusements that send a man next day to his work bloodshot, yawing, stupid, nauseated; and there are wrong kinds of amusements. They are entertainments that give a man disgust with the drudgery of life, with tools because they are not swords, with working aprons because they are not robes, with cattle because they are not infuriated bulls of the arena. If any amusement sends you home longing for a life of romance and thrilling adventure, love that takes poison and shoots itself, moonlight adventures and hair-breadth escapes, you may depend upon it that you are the sacrificed victims of unsanctified pleasure. Our re-creations are intended to build us up, and if they pull us down as to our moral or as to our physical strength, you may come to the conclusion that they are obnoxious.

There is nothing more depraving than an attendance upon amusements that are full of innuendo and low suggestions. The young man enters. At first he sits far back, with his hat on and his coat-collar up, fearful that somebody there may know him. Several nights pass on. He takes off his hat earlier, and puts his coat-collar down. The blush that first came into his cheek when anything indecent was enacted comes no more to his cheek. Farewell, young man! You have probably started on the long road which ends in consummate destruction. The stars of hope will go out one by one, until you will be left in utter darkness. Hear you not the rush of the maelstrom, in whose outer circle your boat now dances, making merry with the whirling waters? But you are being drawn in, and the gentle motion will become terrific agitation. You cry for help. In vain! You pull at the oar to put back, but the struggle will not avail! You will be tossed, and dashed, and shipwrecked, and swallowed in the whirlpool that has already crushed in its wrath 10,000 hulks. Young men who have just come from country residence to city residence will do well to be on guard, and let no one induce you to places of improper amusement. It is mightily alluring when a young man, long a citizen, offers to show a new-comer all around.

Still further; those amusements are wrong which lead you into expenditure beyond your means. Money spent in recreation is not thrown away. It is all folly for us to come to a place of amusement feeling that we have wasted our money and time. You may by it have made an investment worth more than the transaction that yielded you hundreds of thousands of dollars. But how many properties have been riddled by costly amusements.

MY FIRST EXPERIENCE IN A LARGE CITY.

The first time I ever saw the city—it was the city of Philadelpia—I was a mere lad. I stopped at a hotel, and I remember in the even-tide one of these men plied me with his infernal art. He saw I was green. He wanted to show me the sights of the town. He painted the path of sin until it looked like emerald; but I was afraid of him. I shoved back from the basilisk—I made up my mind he was a basilisk. I remember how he wheeled his chair around in front of me, and with a con-centered and diabolical effort, attempted to destroy my soul; but there were good angels in the air that night. It was no good resolution on my part, but it was the all-en-compassing grace of a good God that delivered me. Be-ware! beware! oh, young man. "There is a way that seemeth right unto a man, but the end thereof is death." The table has been robbed to pay the club. The cham-pagne has cheated the children's wardrobe. The carousing party has burned up the boy's primer. The table cloth of the corner saloon is in debt to the wife's faded dress. Excursions that in a day make a tour around a whole month's wages; ladies whose life time business is to "go shopping;" large bets on horses, have their counterparts in uneducated children, bankruptcies that shock the money market and appall the church; and that send drunkenness staggering accross the richly-figured carpet of the mansion, and dashing into the mirror, and drown-ing out the carol of music with the whooping of bloated sons come home to break their old mother's heart.

I saw a beautiful home, where the bell rang violently

late at night. The son had been off in sinful indulgences. His comrades were bringing him home. They carried him to the door. They rang the bell at 1 o'clock in the morning. Father and mother came down. They were waiting for the wandering son, and then the comrades, as soon as the door was opened threw the prodigal headlong into the doorway, crying, ''There he is, drunk as a fool. Ha, ha!'' When men go into amusements that they cannot afford, they first borrow what they cannot earn, and then they steal what they cannot borrow. First they go into embarrassment, and then into lying, and then into theft; and when a man gets as far on as that, he does not stop short of the penitentiary. There is not a prison in the land where there are not victims of unsanctified amusements.

ON THE DOWN GRADE.

Merchants of Brooklyn, or New York, is there a dis. arangement in your accounts? Is there a leakage in your money drawer? Did not the cash account come out right last night? I will tell you. There is a young man in your store wandering off into bad amusements! The salary you give him may meet lawful expenditures, but not the sinful indulgences in which he has entered, and he takes by theft that which you do not give him in lawful salary.

How brightly the path of unrestrained amusement opens! The young man says, ''Now I am off for a good time. Never mind economy. I'll get money somehow! What a fine road! What a beautiful day for a ride! Crack the whip, and over the turnpike! Come, boys, fill high you glasses. Drink! Long life, health, plenty of rides just like this!" Hard-working men hear the clatter of the hoofs, and look up and say: "Why, I wonder where those fellows get their money from! We have to toil and drudge; they do nothing!" To these gay men life is a thrill and an excitement. They stare at other people, and in turn are stared at. The watch-chain jingles. The cup foams. The cheeks flush. The eyes flash. The midnight hears their guffaw. They swagger. They jostle decent men off the side-walk. They take the name of God in vain. They parody the hymn they learned at their mother's knee; and to all pictures of disaster they cry out, "Who cares!" and to the counsel of some Christian friend, "Who are you?"

THE CRASH!

Passing along the street some night, you hear a shriek in grogshop, the rattle of the watchman's club, the rush of the police. What is the matter now? Oh, the reckless young man has been killed in a grogshop fight. Carry him home to his father's house. Parents will come down and wash his wounds, and close his eyes in death. They forgive him all he ever did, although he cannot in his silence ask it. The prodigal has got home at last. Mother will go to her little garden and gather the sweetest flowers and twist them into a chaplet for the silent heart of the wayward boy, and push back from the bloated brow the long locks that were once her pride. And the air will be rent with agony. The great dramatist says; "How sharper than a serpent's tooth it is to have a thankless child."

I go further, and say those are unchristian amusements which become the chief business of a man's life. Life

is an earnest thing. Whether we were born in a palace
or hovel; whether we are affluent or pinched, we have to
work. If you do not sweat with toil, you will sweat with
disease. You have a soul that will be transfigured amidst
the pomp of a judgement day; and after the sea has sung
its last chant, and the mountain shall have come down
in an avalanche of rock, you will live and think and act,
high on a throne where seraphs sing, or deep in a dungeon where demons howl. In a world where there is so
much to do for yourselves, and so much to do for others,
God pity that man who has nothing to do.

AMUSEMENTS ARE MEANS TO AN END.

Your sports are merely means to an end. They are
alleviations and helps. The arm of toil is the only arm
strong enough to bring up the bucket out of the deep well
of pleasure. Amusement is only the bower where business and philanthropy rest while on their way to stirring
achievements. Amusements are only the vines that grow
about the anvil of toil, and the blossoming of the hammers. Alas for the man who spends his time in labor-
iously doing nothing, his days in looking up lounging
places and loungers, his nights in seeking out some gas-
lighted foolery! The man who always has on his sporting
jacket, ready to hunt for the game in the mountain or
fish in the brook, with no time to pray, or work, or read,
is not so well off as the greyhound that runs by his side,
or the fly bait with which he whips the streams.

A man who does not work does not know how to play.
If God had intended us to do nothing but laugh he would
not have given us shoulders with which to lift, and hands
with which to work, and brains with which to think.

The amusements of life are merely the orchestra playing while the great tragedy of life plunges through its five acts—infancy, childhood, manhood, old age and death. Then exit the last earthly opportunity. Enter the overwhelming realities of an eternal world!

I go further, and say that all those amusements are wrong which lead into bad company. If you go to any place where you have to associate with the intemperate, with the unclean, with the abandoned, however well they may be dressed, in the name of God quit it. They will despoil your nature. They will undermine your moral character. They will drop you when you are destroyed. They will give not one cent to support your children when you are dead. They will weep not one tear at your burial. They will chuckle over your damnation.

DOWNFALL OF A FRIEND.

I had a friend at the West—a rare friend. He was one of the first to welcome me to my new home. To fine personal appearance he added a generosity, frankness, and ardor of nature that made me love him like a brother. But I saw evil people gathering around him. They came up from the saloons, from the gambling hells. They plied him with a thousand arts. They seized upon his social nature, and he could not stand the charm. They drove him on the rocks, like a ship full winged, shivering on the breakers. I used to admonish him. I would say:

"Now, I wish you would quit these bad habits, and become a Christian."

"**Oh,**" he would reply, "I would like to; I would like

to; but I have gone so far I don't think there is any way back."

In his moments of repentance he would go home and take his little girl of eight years, and embrace her convulsively, and cover her with adornments, and strew around her pictures and toys, and everything that could make her happy: and then, as though hounded by an evil spirit, he would go out to the enflaming cup and the house of shame, like a fool to the correction of the stocks.

AT HIS DEATH BED.

I was summoned to his death-bed. I hastened. I entered the room. I found him, to my surprise, lying in full everyday dress on the top of the couch. I put out my hand. He grasped it excitedly, and said:

"Sit down, Mr. Talmage, right there." I sat down.

He said: "Last night I saw my mother, who has been dead twenty years, and she sat just where you sit now. It was no dream. I was wide-awake. There was no delusion in the matter. I saw her just as plainly as I see you.. Wife, I wish you would take these strings off of me. There are strings spun all around my body. I wish you would take them off of me."

I saw it was delirium.

"Oh," replied the wife. "my dear there is nothing there, there is nothing there."

He went on, and said: Just where you sit, Mr. Talmage, my mother sat. She said to me:

"Henry I do wish you would do better." I got out of bed, put my arms around her and said, 'Mother, I want to do better. I have been trying to do better. Won't you help me to do better? You used to help me.' No mistake about it, no delusion.   I saw her—the cap and the apron and the spectacles, just as she used to look twenty years ago—but I do wish you would take these strings away.   They annoy me so.   I can hardly talk. Won't you take them away?"

I knelt down and prayed, conscious of the fact that he did not realize what I was saying.   I got up.   I said "Good-bye; I hope you will be better soon."

He said, "Good-bye, good-bye."

That night his soul went to the God who gave it. Arrangements were made for the obsequies.   Some said, "Don't bring him in the church; he was too dissolute."

"Oh," I said, "bring him.   He was a good friend of mine while he was alive, and I shall stand by him now that he is dead.   Bring him to the church."

AT HIS FUNERAL.

As I sat in the pulpit and saw his body coming up through the aisle, I felt as if I could weep tears of blood. I told the people that day, "This man had his virtues and a good many of them.   He had his faults and a good many of them.   But if there is any man in this audience who is without sin, let him cast the first stone at this coffin lid."   On one side the pulpit sat the little child, rosy, sweet-faced, as beautiful as any little child that sat at your table this morning, I warrant you.   She looked up wistfully, not knowing the full sorrows of an orphan child.   Oh, her countenance haunts me to-day, like some sweet face looking upon us through a horrid dream

HIS DESTROYERS.

On the other side of the pulpit were the men who had

destroyed him.   There they sat, hard-visaged, some of
them pale from exhausting disease, some of them flushed
until it seemed as if the fires of iniquity flamed through
the cheek and crackled the lips.   They were the men
who had done the work.   They were the men who had
bound him hand and foot.   They had kindled the fires.
They had poured the wormwood and gall into that
orphan's cup.   " Did they weep?   No.   Did they sigh
repentingly?   No.   Did they say: "What a pity that
such a brave man should be slain?"   No, no; not one
bloated hand was lifted to wipe a tear from a bloated
cheek: They sat and looked at the coffin like vultures
gazing at the carcass of a lamb whose heart they had
ripped out! I cried in their ears as plainly as I cou'd:
"There is a God and a judgement day!"   Did they
tremble.   Oh, no, no.   They went back from the house
of God, and that night, though their victim lay in Oak-
wood Cemetery, I was told that they blasphemed, and
they drank, and they gambled, and there was not one less
customer in all the houses of iniquity.   This destroyed
man was a Samson in physical strenglh. but Delilah
sheared him, and the Philistines of evil companionship
dug his eyes out and threw them into the prison of evil
habits.   But in the hour of his death he rose up and took
hold of the two pillared curses of God against drunkenness and uncleanness, and threw himself forward, until
down upon him and his companions there came the
thunders of an eternal catastrophe.

Again: Any amusement that gives you a distaste for
domestic life is bad.   How many bright domestic circles
have been broken up by sinful amusements! The father

went off, the mother went off, the child went off. There
are to-day the fragments before me of blasted households. Oh, if you have wandered away, I would like to
charm you back by the sound of that one word "home."
Do you not know that you have but little more time to
give to domestic welfare? Do you not see, father, that
your children are soon to go out into the world, and all
the influence for good you are to have over them you
must have now? Death will break in on your conjugal
relations, and alas, if you have to stand over the grave of
one who perished from your neglect!

GIVE TO HOME YOUR BEST AFFECTIONS.

I saw a waywaad husband standing at the death-bed of
his Christian wife, and I saw her point to a ring on her
finger, and heard her say to her husband, "Do you see
that ring?" He replied, "Yes, I see it." "Well," said
she, "Do you remember who put it there?" "Yes," said
he, "I put it there;" and all the past seemed to rush
upon him. By the memory of that day when, in the
presence of men and angels, you promised to be faithful
in joy or sorrow, and in sickness and health; by the
memory of those pleasant hours when you sat together in
your new home talking of a bright future; by the cradle
and the joyful hour when one life was spared and another
given; by that sick-bed, when the little one lifted up the
hands and called for help, and you knew he must die,
and he put one arm around each of your necks and brought
you very near together in that dying kiss; by the little
grave in Greenwood that you never think of without a
rush of tears; by the family Bible, where amidst stories
of heavenly love, is the brief but expressive record of

births and deaths; by the neglects of the past, and by the agonies ot the future; by a judgement day, when husbands and wives, parents and children, in immortal groups, will stand to be caught up in shining array, or to shrink down into darkness; by all that, I beg you to give to home your best affections.

· FINAL FALL OF THE CURTAIN.

Ah, my friends, there is an hour coming when our past life will probably pass before us in review. It will be our last hour. If from our death pillow we have to look back and see a life spent in sinful amusement, there will be a dart that will strike through our soul sharper than the dagger with which Virginius slew his child. The memory of the past will make us quake like Macbeth. The iniquities and rioting through which we have passed will come upon us, weird and skeleton as Meg Merrillies. Death, the old Shylock, will demand, and take the remaining pound of flesh, and the remaining drop of blood; and upon our last opportunity for repentance, and our last chance for heaven, the curtain will forever drop.

THE PLAGUE OF LIES.

"Ye shall not surely die" Genesis iii, 4.

hat was a point blank lie. Satan told it to Eve to induce her to put her semicircle of white, beau-. tiful teeth into a forbidden apricot or plum or peach or apple. He practically said to her: . "Oh, Eve, just take a bite of this and you will be omnipotent and omniscient. You shall be as gods." Just opposite was the result. It was the first lie that was ever told in our world. It opened the gate for all the falsehoods that. have ever alighted on this planet. It introduced a plague that covers all nations—the plague of lies. Far worse than the plagues of Egypt, for they were on the banks of the Nile, but this on the banks of the Hudson, on the banks of the East River, on the banks of the Ohio, and the Mississisppi, and the Thames, and the Rhine, and the Tiber, and on both sides of all rivers. The Egyptian plagues lasted only a few weeks, but for six thousand years has raged this plague of lies.

WHITE AND BLACK LIES.

There are a hundred ways of telling a lie. A man's entire life may be a falsehood, while with his lips he may not once directly falsify. There are those who state what is positively untrue, but afterward say "may be" softly. These departures from the truth are called "white lies;" but there is really no such thing as a white lie.

The whitest lie that was ever told was as black as per--

JOSEPH SOLD INTO EGYPT.

dition. No inventory of public crimes will be sufficient that omits this gigantic abomination. There are men high in church and state actually useful, self denying and honest in many things, who, upon certain subjects and in certain spheres, are not at all to be depended upon for veracity. Indeed, there are many men and women who have their notions of truthfulness so thoroughly perverted that they do not know when they are lying. With many it is a cultivated sin; with some it seems a natural infirmity. I have known people who seem to have been born liars. The falsehoods of their lives extended from cradle to grave. Prevarications, misrepresentation and dishonesty of speech appeared in their first utterances, and were as natural to them as any of their infantile diseases, and were a sort of moral croup or spiritual scarlatina. But many have been placed in circumstances where this tendency has day by day and hour by hour been called to larger developments. They have gone from attainment to attainment and from class to class until they have become regularly graduated liars.

THE CITIES ARE FULL OF LIES.

The air of the city is filled with falsehoods. They hang pendent from the chandeliers of our finest residences; they crowd the shelves of some of our merchant princess; they fill the sidewalk from curb stone to brown stone facing; they cluster around the mechanic's hammer, and blossom from the end of the merchant yard-stick, and sit in the doors of churches. Some call them ''fiction.'' Some style them ''fabrication.'' You might say that they were subterfuge, disguised, delusion, romance, evasion, pretense, fable, deception, misrepresentation; but, as I am ignorant of anything to be gained by the hiding of a God defying outrage under a lexicographer's blanket, 1 shall call them what my father taught me to call them — lies.

I shall divide them into agricultural, mercantile, mechanical, ecclesiastical and social lies.

AGRICULTURAL LIES.

First, then, I will speak of those that are more particularly agricultural. There is something in the perpetual presence of natural objects to make a man pure. The trees never issue "false stock." Wheat fields are always honest. Rye and oats never move out in the night, not paying for the place they have occupied. Corn shocks never make false assignments. Mountain brooks are always "current." The gold on the grain is never counterfeit. The sunrise never flaunts in false colors. The dew sports only genuine diamonds. Taking farmers as a class, I believe they are truthful and fair in dealing and kind hearted. But the regions surrounding our cities do not always send this sort of men to our markets. Day by day there creak through our streets and about the market houses farm wagons that have not an honest spoke in their wheels or a truthful rivet from tongue to tailboard.

During the last few years there have been times when domestic economy has foundered on the farmer's firkin. Neither high taxes, nor the high price of dry goods, nor the exorbitancy of labor, could excuse much that the city has witnessed in the behavior of the yeomanry. By the quiet firesides in Westchester and Orange counties I hope there may be seasons of deep reflection and hearty repentance. Rural districts are accustomed to rail at great cities as given up to fraud and every form of unrighteousness, but our cities do not absorb all the abominations. Our citizens have learned the importance of not always trusting to the size and style of apples in the top of a farmer's barrel as an indication of what may be found farther down. Many of our people are accustomed to watch and see how correctly a bushel or beets is measured, and there are not many honest milk cans.

Deceptions do not all cluster around city halls. When our cities sit down and weep over their sins, all the surrounding countries ought to come in and weep with them. There is often hostility on the part of producers against traders, as though the man who raises the corn was necessarily more honorable than the grain dealer who pours it into his mammoth bin. There ought to be no such hostility. Yet producers often think it no wrong to snatch away from the trader; and they say to the bargain maker, "You get your money easy." Do they get it easy? Let those who in the quiet field and barn get their living exchange places with those who stand to-day amid the excitements of commercial life and see if they find it so very easy.

While the farmer goes to sleep with the assurance that his corn and barley will be growing all the night, moment by moment adding to his revenue, the merchant tries to go to sleep conscious that that moment his cargo may be broken on the rocks or damaged by the wave that sweeps clear across the hurricane deck, or that reckless speculators may that very hour be plotting some momentary revolution, or the burgulars be prying open his safe, or his debtors fleeing the town, or his landlord raising the rent, or the fires kindling on the block that contains all his estate. Easy! Is it? God help the merchants! It is hard to have the palms of the hand blistered with outdoor work, but a more dreadful process when through mercantile anxieties the brain is consumed.

MERCANTILE LIES.

In the next place we notice mercantile lies, those before the counter and behind the counter. I will not attempt to specify the different forms of commercial falsehood. There are merchants who excuse themselves for what they call commercial custom. In other words, the multiplication and university of a sin turns it into a virtue. There have been large fortunes gathered where there was not one drop of unrequited toil in the wine; nor one spark of bad temper flashing from the bronze bracket; nor one drop of needle woman's heart blood in the crimson plush, while there are other great estsblishments in which there is not one door knob, not one brick, not one trinket, not one thread of lace but has upon it the mark of dishonor. What wonder if, some day, a hand of toil that had been wrung and worn out and blistered until the skin came off should be placed against the elegant wall paper, leaving its mark of blood—four fingers and a thumb—or that some day, walking the halls, there should be a voice accosting the occupant, saying, ''Six cents for making a shirt," and, flying the room another voice should say, ''Twelve cents for an army blanket," and the man should try to sleep at night, but ever and anon be aroused, until, getting up on one elbow, he shrieks out, ''Who's there?" One Sabbath night, in the vestibule of my church after service, a woman fell in convulsions. The doctor said she needed medicine not so much as something to eat. As she began to revive in her delirium, she said graspingly: "Eight cents! Eight cents! Eight cents! I wish I could get it done; I am so tired! I wish I could get some sleep, but I must get it done! Eight cents! Eight cents!" We found afterward she was making garments for eight cents apiece, and that she could make but three of them in a day! Three times eight are twenty-four! Hear it, men and women who have comfortable homes!

THE WORST VILLIANS OF THE CITY.

Some of the worst villians of the city are the employers of these women. They beat them down to the last penny, and try to cheat them out of that. The woman must deposit a dollar or two before she gets the garment to work on. When the work is done it is sharply inspected, the most insignificant flaws picked out, and the wages refused, and sometimes the dollar deposited not given back. The Women's Protective Union reports a case where one of these poor souls, finding a place where she could get more wages, resolved to change employers, and went to get her pay for work done. The employer says, "I hear you are going to leave me." "Yes," she said, "I am come to get what you owe me." He made no answer. She said, "Are you not going to pay me?" "Yes," he said, "I will pay you;" and he kicked her down the stairs.

There are thousands of fortunes made in commercial spheres that are throughout righteous. God will let His favor rest upon ever scroll, every pictured wall, every traceried window, and the joy that flashes from the lights, and showers from the music and dances in the children's quick feet, pattering through the hall, will utter the congratulations from men and the approval of God.

THERE IS NO NEED OF FALSEHOOD.

A merchant can, to the last item, be thoroughly honest. There is never any need of falsehood. Yet how many will, day by day, hour by hour, utter what they know to be wrong. You say that you are selling at less than cost. If so, then it is right to say it. But did that cost you lest than what you ask for it? If not, then you have falsffied. You say that that article cost you twenty-five dollars. Did it? If so, then all right. If it did not, then you have falsified.

Suppose you are a purchaser. You are "beating down" the goods. You say that that article for which five dollars is charged is not worth more than four. Is it worth no more than four dollars? Then all right. If it be worth more, and for the sake of getting it less than its value, you wilfully depreciate it, you have falsified. You may call it a sharp trade. The recording angel writes it down on the ponderous tomes of eternity. "Mr. So-and-so, merchant on Wall street or in Eight street or in State street, or Mrs. So-and-so, keeping house on Beacon street or on Madison avenve or Rittenhouse square or Brooklyn Heights or Brooklyn Hill, told one falsehood." You may consider it insignificant because relating to an insignificant purchase. You would despise the man who would falsify in regard to some great matter in which the city or the whole country was concerned; but this is only a box of buttons, or a row of pins, or a case of needles. Be not deceived. The article purchased may be so small you can put it in your vest pocket, but the sin was bigger than the Pyramids, and the echo of the dishonor will reverberate through all the mountains of eternity.

LYING DOES NOT PAY.

You throw on your counter some specimens of handkerchiefs. Your customer asks: "Is that all silk? No cotton in it?" You answer, "It is all silk." Was it all silk? If so, all right. But was it partly cotton? Then you have falsified. Moreover, you lost by the falsehood. The customer, though he may live at Lynn or Doylestown or Poughkeepsie, will find out that you have defrauded him, and next spring when he again comes shopping he will look at your sign and say: "I will not try there! That is the place where I got that handkerchief." So that by that one dishonest bargain you picked your own pocket and insulted the Almighty.

Would you dare to make an estimate of how many falsehoods in trade were yesterday told by hardware men and clothiers and fruit dealers, and dry goods establishments and importers and jewelers and lumbermen and coal merchants and stationers and tobacconists? Lies about saddles, about buckles, about ribbons, about carpets, about gloves, about coats, about shoes, about hats, about watches, about carriages, about books—about everything. In the name of the Lord Almighty, I arraign commercial falsehoods as one of the greatest plagues in city and town.

MECHANICAL LIES.

In the next place I notice mechanical lies. There is no class of men who administer more to the welfare of the city than artisans. To their hand we must look for the buildings that shelter us, for the garments that clothe us, for the car that carries us. They wield a widespread influence. There is much derision of what is called "Muscular Christianity," but in the latter day of the world's prosperity I think that the Christian will be muscular. We have a right to expect of those stalwart men of toil the highest possible integrity. Many of them answer all our expectations, and stand at the front of religious and philanthropic enterprises. But this class, like the others that I have named, has in it those who lack in the element of veracity. They cannot all be trusted: In times when the demand for labor is great it is impossible to meet the demands of the public, or do work with that promptness and perfection that would at other times be possible.

But there are mechanics whose word cannot be trusted at any time. No man has a right to promise more work than he can do. There are mechanics who say that they will come on Monday, but they do not come until Wednesday. You put work in their hands that they tell you shall be completed in ten days, but it is thirty. There have been houses built of which it might be said that every nail driven, every foot of plastering put on, every yard of pipe laid, every shingle hammered, every brick mortared, could tell of falsehoods connected therewith. There are men attempting to do ten or fifteen pieces of work who have not the time or strength to do more than five or six pieces, but by promises never fulfilled keep all the undertakings within their own grasp. This is what they call "nursing" the job.

How much wrong to his soul and insult to God a

mechanic would save if he promised only so much as he expected to be able to do. Society has no right to ask of you impossibilities. You cannot always calculate correctly, and you may fail because you cannot get the help that you anticipate. But now I am speaking of the wilful making of promises that you know you cannot keep. Did you say that that shoe should be mended, that coat repaired, those bricks laid, that harness sewed, that door grained, that spout fixed or that window glazed by Saturday, knowing that you would neither be able to do it yourself nor get anyone else to do it? Then, before God and man you are a liar. You may say that it makes no particular difference, and that if you had told the truth you would have lost the job, and that people expect to be disappointed, but that excuse will not answer. Their is a voice of thunder rolling among the drills and planes and shoe lasts and shears which says, "All liars shall have their part in the lake that burneth with fire and brimstone."

ECCLESIASTICAL LIES.

I next notice ecclesiastical lies—that is, falsehoods told for the purpose of advancing churches and sects, or for the purpose of depleting them. There is no use in asking many a Calvinist what an Arminian believes, for he will be apt to tell you that the Arminian believes that a man can convert himself; or to ask the Arminian what the Calvinist believes, for he will tell you that the Calvanist believes that God made some men just to damn them. There is no need in asking a pædo-Baptist what a Baptist believes, for he will be apt to say that the Baptist believes immersion to be positively necessary to

salvatlon.   It is almost impossible for one denomination
of Christians, without prejudice or misrepresentation, to
state the sentiment of an opposing sect.   If a man hates
Presbyterians, and you ask him what Presbyterians believe, he will tell you that they believe that there are in-
fants in hell a span long!

It is strange, also, how individual churches will sometimes make misstatements about other individual churches.
It is especially so in regard to falsehoods told with reference to prosperous enterprises.   As long as a church
is feeble, and the singing is discordant, and the minister,
through the poverty of the church, must go with a threadbare coat, and here and there a worshipper sits in the
end of a pew, having all the seat to himself, religious
sympathizers of other churches will say, "What a pity!"
But let a great day of prosperity come, and even ministers of the Gospel, who ought to be rejoiced at the large-
ness and extent of the work, denounce and misrepresent
and falsify, starting the suspicion in regard to themselves
that the reason they do not like the corn is because it is
not ground in their own mill.   How long before we shall
learn to be fair in our religious criticisms!   The keenest
jealousies on earth are church jealousies.   The field of
Christian work is so large that there is no need that our
hoe handles hit.

SOCIAL LIES.

Next I speak of social lies.   This evil makes much of
society insincere.   You know not what to believe.   When
people ask you to come, you do not know whether or not
they want you to come.   When they send their regards,
you do not know whether it is an expression of their

heart, or an external civility. We have learned to take almost everything at a discount. Word is sent "Not at home," when they are only too lazy to dress themselves. They say, "The furnace has just gone out," when in truth they have had no fire in it all winter. They apologize for the unusual barrenness of their table, when they never live any better. They decry their most luxurious entertainments to win a shower of approval. They apologize for their appearance, as though it were unusual, when always at home they look just so. They would make you believe that some nice sketch on the wall was the work of a master painter. "It was an heirloom, and once hung on the wall of a castle, and a duke gave it to their grandfather." When the fact is, that painting was made by a man "down east," and baked so as to make it look old, and sold with others for ten dollars a dozen. People who will lie about nothing else, will lie about a picture. On a small income we must make the world believe that we are affluent, and our life becomes a cheat, a counterfeit and a sham.

Few persons are really natural. When I say this I do not mean to slur cultured manners. It is right that we should have more admiration for the sculptured marble than for the unknown block of the quarry. From many circles in life insincerity has driven out vivacity and enthusiasm. A frozen dignity instead floats about the room, and iceberg grinds against iceberg. You must not laugh outright; it is vulgar. You must smile. You must not dash rapidly across the room; you must glide. There is a round of bows and grins and flatteries and ohs! and ahs! and simpering, and nambypambyism—a

world of which, is not worth one good, round, honest
peal of laughter. From such a hollow round, the tor-
tured guest retires at the close of the evening and assures
his host that he has enjoyed himself!

What a round of insincerities many people run in order
to win the favor of the world! Their life is a sham and
their death an unspeakable sadness. Alas for the poor
butterflies when the frost strikes them!

Compare the life and death of such a one with that of
some Christian aunt who was once a blessing to your
household. I do not know that she was ever offered the
hand in marriage. She lived single, that untrammeled
she might be everybody's blessing. Whenever the sick
were to be visited, or the poor to be provided with bread,
she went with a blessing. She could pray, or sing
"Rock of Ages" for any sick pauper who asked her. As
she got older there were days when she was a little sharp,
but auntie was a sunbeam—just the one for Christmas
eve. She knew better than any one else how to fix things.
Her every prayer, as God heard it, was full of everybody
who had trouble. The brightest things in all the house
dropped from her fingers. She had peculiar notions,
but the grandest notion she ever had was to make you
happy. She dressed well—auntie always dressed well;
but her highest adornment was that of a meek and quiet
spirit, which, in the sight of God, is of great price.
When she died you all gathered lovingly about her, and
as you carried her out to rest the Sunday school class almost covered the coffin with japonicas, and the poor
people stood at the end of the alley, with their aprons to
their eyes, sobbing bitterly; and the man of the world

said, with Solomon, "Her price was above rubies," and Jesus, as unto the maiden in Judea commanded, "I say unto thee, arise!"

But to many, through insincerity, this life is a masquerade ball. As at such entertainments gentlemen and ladies appear in the dress of kings or queens, mountain bandits or clowns, and at the close of the dance throw off their disguises, so in this dissipated life all unclean passions move in mask. Across the floor they trip merrily. The lights sparkle along the wall or drop from the ceiling —a cohort of fire? The music charms. The diamonds glitter. The feet bound. Gemmed hands stretched out clasp gemmed hands. Dancing feet respond to dancing feet. Gleaming brow bends to gleaming brow. On with the dance! Flash and rustle and laughter and immeasurable merry making! But the languor of death comes over the limbs and blurs the sight!

Lights lower! Floor hollow with sepulchral echo. Music saddens into a wail. Lights lower! The maskers can hardly now be seen. Flowers exchange their fragrance for a sickening odor, such as comes from garlands that have lain in vaults of cemeteries. Lights lower! Mists fill the room. Glasses rattle as though shaken by sullen thunder. Sighs seem caught among the curtains. Scarfs fall from the shoulder of beauty—a shroud! Lights lower! Over the slippery boards, in dance of death, glide jealousies, disappointments, lust, despair. Torn leaves and withered garlands only half hide the ulcered feet. The stench of smoking lamp wicks almost quenched. Choking damps. Chilliness. Feet still. Hands folded. Eyes shut. Voices hushed. Lights out.

THE PLAGUE OF INFIDELITY.

"Let God be true, but every man a liar.". Romans iii, 4.

That is if God says one thing and the whole human race says the opposite, Paul would accept the Divine veracity. But there are many in our time who have dared arraign the Almighty for falsehood. Infidelity is not only a plague, but it is the mother of plagues.

A LONG SENTENCE OF STRANGE INFIDEL ASSERTIONS.

It seems from what we hear on all sides that the Christian religion is a huge blunder; that the Mosaic account of the creation is an absurdity large enough to throw all nations into rollicking guffaw; that Adam and Eve never existed; that the ancient flood and Noah's ark were impossibilities; that there never was a miracle; that the Bible is the friend of cruelty, of murder, of polygamy, of all forms of base crime; that the Christian religion is woman's tyrant and man's stultification; that the Bible from lid to lid is a fable, a cruelty, a humbug, a sham, a lie; that the martyrs who died for its truth were miserable dupes; that the church of Jesus Christ is properly gazetted as a fool; that when Thomas Carlyle, the skeptic, said, "The Bible is a noble book," he was dropping into imbecility; that when Theodore Parker declared in Music Hall, Boston, "Never a boy or girl in all Christendom but was profited by that great book," he was becoming very weak minded; that it is something to bring

R.G. Ingersoll

a blush to the cheek of every patriot, that John Adams, the father of American Independence, declared, "The Bible is the best book in all the world;" and that lion hearted Andrew Jackson turned into a sniveling coward when he said, "That book, sir, is the rock on which our republic rests;" and that Daniel Webster abdicated the throne of his intellectual power and resigned his logic, and from being the great expounder of the constitution, and the great lawyer of his age, turned into an idiot when he said, "My heart assures and reassures me that the gospel of Jesus Christ must be a divine reality. From the time that at my mother's feet or on my father's knee I first learned to lisp verses from the sacred writings they have been my daily study and vigilant contemplation, and if there is anything in my style or thought to be commended, the credit is due to my kind parents in instilling into my mind an early love of the Scriptures;" and that William H. Seward, the diplomatist of the century, only showed his puerility when he declared, "The whole hope of human progress is suspended on that ever growing influence of the Bible;" and that it is wisest for us to take that book from the throne in the affections of uncounted multitudes and put it under our feet, to be trampled upon by hatred and hissing contempt; and that your old father was hoodwinked, and cajoled, and cheated and befooled, when he leaned on this as a staff after his hair grew gray, and his hands were tremulous, and his steps shortened as he came up to the verge of the grave; and that your mother sat with a pack of lies on her lap while reading of the better country, and of the ending of all her aches and pains, and reunion, not only with those of you who stood around her, but with the children she must buried with infinite heartache, so shat she could read no more until she took off her spectacles and wiped from them the heavy mist of many tears. Alas! that for forty and fifty years they should have walked under this delusion and had it under their pillow when they lay a-dying in the back room, and asked that some words from the vile page might be cut upon the tombstone under the shadow of the old country meeting house where they sleep to-day, waiting for a resurrection that will never come.

INFIDELITY'S PROPOSITION.

This book, having deceived them, and having deceived the mighty intellects of the past, must not be allowed to deceive our larger, mightier, vaster, more stupendous intellects. And so out with the book from the court room, where it is used in the solemnization of testimony. Out with it from under the foundation of church and asylum. Out with it trom the domestic circle. Gather together all the Bibles— the children's Bibles, the family Bibles, those newly bound, and those with lid nearly worn out and pages almost obliterated by the fingers long ago turned to dust—bring them all together, and let us make a bonfire of them, and by it warm our cold criticism, and after that turn under with the plowshare of public indignation the polluted ashes of that loathsome, adulterous, obscene, cruel and deathful book which is so antagonistic to man's liberty, and woman's honor, and the world's happiness.

ITS DEATHFUL LAUGHTER.

Now that is the substance of what infidelity proposes

and declares, and the attack on the Bible is accompanied
by great jocosity, and there is hardly any subject about
which more mirth is kindled than about the Bible. I
like fun; no man was ever built with a keener apprecia-
tion of it. There is health in laughter instead of harm
—physical health, mental health, moral health, spiritual
health—providing you laugh at the right thing. The
morning is jocund. The Indian, with its own mist bap-
tizes the cataract Minnehaha, or Laughing Water. You
have not kept your eyes open or your ears alert if you
have not seen the sea smile, or heard the forests clap
their hands, or the orchards in blossom week aglee with
redolence. But there is a laughter which is deathful,
there is a laughter which has the rebound of despair. It
is not healthy to giggle about God, or chuckle about
eternity, or smirk about the things of the immortal soul.

STOPPING THE TRAIN.

You know what caused the accident years ago on the
Hudson River railroad. It was an intoxicated man who
for a joke pulled the string of the air brake and stopped
the train at the most dangerous point of the journey.
But the lightning train, not knowing there was any im-
pediment in the way, came down, crushing out of the
mangled victims the immortal souls that went speeding
instantly to God and judgment. It was only a joke.
He thought it would be fun to stop the train. He stopped
it. And so infidelity is chiefly anxious to stop the long
train of the Bible, and the long train of the churches,
and the long train of the Christian influences, while
coming down upon us are death, judgment and eternity,
coming a thousand miles a minute, coming with more

force than all the avalanches that ever slipped from the Alps, coming with more strength than all the lightning express trains that ever whistled or shrieked or thundered across the continent.

Now in this jocularity of infidel thinkers I cannot join, and I propose to give you some reasons why I cannot be an infidel, and so I will try to help out of this present condition any who may have been struck with the awful plague of skepticism.

WHY I CANNOT BE AN INFIDEL.

First, I cannot be an infidel because infidelity has no good substitute for the consolation it proposes to take away. You know there are millions of people who get their chief consolation from this book. What would you think of a crusade of this sort? Suppose a man should resolve that he would organize a conspiracy to destroy all the medicines from all the apothecaries and from all the hospitals of the earth The work is done. The medicines are taken, and they are thrown into the river, or the lake, or the sea.

A patient wakes up at midnight in a paroxysm of distress, and wants an anodyne. "Oh." says the nurse, "the anodynes are all destroyed; we have no drops to give you, but instead of that I'll read you a book on the absurdities of morphine and on the absurdities of all remedies." But the man continues to writhe in pain, and the nurse says: "I'll continue to read some discourses on anodynes, the cruelities of anodynes, the indecencies of anodynes, the absurdities of anodynes. For your groan I'll give you a laugh."

Here in the hospital is a patient having a gangrened

limb amputated. He says: "Oh, for ether! Oh, for chloroform!" The doctor says: "Why, they are all destroyed; we don't have any more chloroform or ether, but I have got something a great deal better. I'll read you a pamphlet against James Y. Simpson, the discoverer of chloroform as an anæsthetic, and against Drs. Agnew and Hamilton and Hosack and Mott and Harvey and Abernethy." "But," says the man, "I must have some anæsthetics." "No," says the doctor, "they are all destroyed, but we have got something a great deal better." "What is that?" "Fun" Fun. about medicines. Lie down, all ye patients in Bellevue hospital, and stop your groaning; all ye broken hearted of all the cities, and quit your crying; we have the catholicon at last!

Here is a dose of wit, here is a strengthening plaster of sarcasm, here is a bottle ef ribaldry that you are to keep well shaken up and take a spoonful of it after each meal, and if that does not cure you here is a solution of blasphemy in which you may bathe, and here is a tincture of derision. Tickle the skeleton of death with a repartee! Make the Kings of Terror cackle! For all the agonies of all the ages a joke! Millions of people willing with uplifted hand toward heaven to affirm that the gospel of Jesus Christ is full of consolation for them, and yet infidelity proposes to take it away, giving nothing absolutely nothing, except fun. Is there any greater height or depth or length or breadth or immensity of meanness in all God's universe?

"DON'T KNOWS" OF INFIDELITY!

Infidelity is a religion of "Don't knows." Is there a God? Don't know! Is the soul immortal? Don't know!

If we should meet each other in the future world will we recognize each other? Don't know! A religion of "don't knows" for the religion of "I know," "I know in whom I have believed," "I know that my Redeemer liveth." Infidelity proposes to substitute a religion of awful negatives for our religion of glorious positives, showing right before us a world of reunion and ecstacy and high companionship and glorious worship and stupendous victory, the mightiest joy of earth not high enough to reach to the base of the Himalaya of uplifted splendor awaiting all those who on wing of Christian faith willl soar toward it.

PUTTING OUT ALL THE LIGHT HOUSES!

Have you heard of the conspiracy to put out all the lighthouses on the coast? Do you know that on a certain night of next month, Eddystone lighthouse, Bell Rock lighthouse, Sherryvore lighthouse, Montauk lighthouse, Hatteras lighthouse, New London lighthouse, Barnegat llghthouse, and the 640 lighthouses on the Atlantic and Pacific coasts are to be extinguished? "Oh," you say, "what will become of the ships on that night? What will be the fate of the one million sailors following the sea? What will be the doom of the millions of passengers? Who will arise to put down such a conspiracy?" Every man, woman and child in America and the world. But that is only a fable. That is what infiedlity is trying to do—put out all the lighthouses on the coast of eternity, letting the soul go up the "Narrows" of death with no light, no comfort, no peace—all that coast covered with the blackness of darkness. Iustead of the great lighthouse, a glowworm of wit, a firefly of jocosity. Which do you like the better, O voyager for eternity, the firefly or the lighthouse?

THE AWFUL MISSION OF INFIDELITY.

What a mission infidelity has started on! The extinguishment of lighthouses, the breaking up of lifeboats, the dismissal of all the pilots, the turning of the inscription on your child's grave into a farce and a lie. Walter Scott's "Old Mortality," chisel in hand, went through the land to cut out into plainer letters the half obliterated inscriptions on the tombstones, and it was a beautiful mission; but infidelity spends its time with hammer and chisel trying to cut out from the tombstones of your dead all the story of resurrection and heaven. It is the iconoclast of every village graveyard and of every city cemetery and of Westminster Abbey. Instead of Christian consolation for the dying, a freezing sneer. Instead of prayer a grimace. Instead of Paul's triumphant defiance of death, a going out you know not where, to stop you know not when, to do you know not what. That is infidelity.

FALSE CHARGES OF INFIDELITY.

Furthermore: I cannot be an infidel, because of the false charges infidelity is all the time making against the Bible. Perhaps the slander that has made the most impression and that some Christians have not been intelligent enough to deny is that the Bible favors polygamy. Does the God of the Bible uphold polygamy, or did He? How many wives did God make for Adam? He made one wife. Does not your common sense tell you when God started the marriage institution He started it as He wanted it to continue. If God had favored polygamy he could have created for Adam five wives or ten wives or twenty wives just as easily as he made one.

At the very first of the Bible, God shows himself in favor of monogamy and antagonistic to polygamy. Genesis ii, 24, ''Therefore shall a man leave his father and mother, and shall cleave unto his wife.'' Not his wives, but his wife. How many wives did God spare for Noah in the ark? Two and two the birds; two and two the cattle; two and two the lions; two and two the human race. If the God of the Bible had favored a multiplicity of wives he would have spared the plurality of wives. When God first launched the human race he gave Adam one wife. At the second launching of the human race he spares for Noah one wife, for Ham one wife, for Shem one wife, for Japheth one wife! Does that look as though God favored polygamy? In Leviticus xviii, 18, God thunders his prohibition of more than one wife.

God permitted Polygamy. Yes; just as he permits to-day's murder and theft and arson and all kinds of crime. He permits these things as you well know, but he does not sanction them. Who would dare to say he sanctions them? Because the Presidents of the United States have permitted polygamy in Utah, you are not, therefore, to conclude that they patronized it, they denounced it. All of God's ancient Israel knew that the God of the Bible was against polygamy, for in the four hundred and thirty years of their stay in Egypt their is only one case of polygamy recorded—only one. All the mighty men of the Bible stood aloof from polygamy except those who, falling into the crime, were chastised within an inch of their lives. Adam, Aaron, Noah, Joseph, Joshua, Samuel, monogamists.　But you say, ''Didn't David and Solomon favor polygamy?"　Yes; and did they not get well punished for it?

DAVID AND SOLOMON PUNISHED FOR SINS.

Read the lives of these two men and you will come to the conclusion that all the attributes of God's nature were against their behavior.　David suffered for his crimes in the caverns of Adullam and Makkedah, in the wilderness of Mahanaim, in the bereavement of Ziklag.　The Bedouins after him, sickness after him, Absalom after him, Ahithopel after him, Adonijah after him, the Edomites after him, the Syrians after him, the Moabites after him, death after him, the Lord God Almighty after him.　The poorest peasant in all the empire married to the plainest jewess was happier than the king in his marital misbehavior.　How did Solomon get along with his polygamy? Read his warnings in Proverbs; read his self disgust in Ecclesiastes.　He throws up his hands in loathing and cries out, ''Vanity of vanities, all is vanity."　His seven hundred wives nearly pestered the life out of him.　Solomon got well paid for his crimes—well paid.

I repeat that all the mighty men of the Scriptures were aloof from polygamy, save as they were pounded and flailed and cut to pieces for their insult to holy marriage.　If the Bible is the friend of polygamy why is it that in all the lands where the Bible predominates polygamy is forbidden, and in the lands where there is no Bible, it is favored?　Polygamy all over China, all over India, all over Africa, all over Persia, all over heathendom, save as the missionaries have done their work, while polygamy does not exist in England and the United

States except in defiance of law. The Bible abroad, God honored monogamy. The Bible not abroad, God abhorred polygamy.

THE GLORY OF CHRISTIAN WOMANHOOD.

Another false charge which infidelity has made against the Bible is that it is antagonistic to woman, that it enjoins her degradation and belittles her mission. Under this impression many women have been overcome of this plague of infidelity. Is the Bible the enemy of woman?

A BIBLE PICTURE GALLERY.

Come into the picture gallery, the Louvre, the Luxembourg of the Bible, and see which pictures are the more honored.

Here is Eve, a perfect woman; as perfect a woman as could be made by a perfect God.

Here is Deborah, with her womanly arm hurling a host into battle.

Here is Miriam, leading the Israelitish orchestra on the banks of the Red sea.

Here is motherly Hannah, with her own loving hand replenishing the wardrobe of her son Samuel the prophet.

Here is Abigail, kneeling at the foot of the mountain until the four hundred wrathful men, at the sight of her beauty and prowess halt, halt—a hurricane stopped at the sight of a water lily, a dew drop dashing back Niagara.

Here is Ruth putting to shame all the modern slang about mothers-in-law as she turns her back on her home and her country, and faces wild beasts and exile and death that she may be with Naomi, her husband's mother. Ruth, the queen of the harvest fields. Ruth, the grandmother of David. Ruth, the ancestress of Jesus Christ. The story of her virtues and her life sacrificed is the most beautiful pastoral ever written.

Here is Vashti defying the bacchanal of a thousand drunken lords, and Esther willing to throw her life away that she may deliver her people.

And here is Dorcas, the sunlight of eternal fame gilding her philanthropic needle, and the woman with perfume in a box made from the hills of Alabastron, pouring the holy chrism on the head of Christ, the aroma lingering all down the corridor of the centuries.

Here is Lydia, the merchantess of Tyrian purple immortalized for her Christian behavior.

Here is the widow with two mites, more famous than the Peabodys and the Lenoxes of all the ages, while here comes in slow of gait and with careful attendants and with especial honor and high favor, leaning on the arm of inspiration, one who is the joy and pride of any home so rarely fortunate as to have one, an old Christian grandmother, Grandmother Lois. Who has more worshipers to-day than any being that ever lived on earth except Jesus Christ? Mary.

For what purpose did Christ perform His first miracle upon earth? To relieve the embarrassment of a womanly housekeeper at the falling short of a beverage. Why did Christ break up the silence of the tomb, and tear off the shroud, and rip up the rocks? It was to stop the bereavement of the two Bethany sisters. For whose comfort was Christ most anxious in the hour of dying excruciation? For a woman, an old woman, a wrinkle faced woman, a woman who in other days had held him in her arms, his first friend, his last friend, as it is very apt to be, his mother.　　All the pathos of the ages compressed into one utterance, ''Behold thy mother.''　Does the Bible antagonize woman?

If the Bible is so antagonistic to woman, how do you account for the difference in woman's condition in China and Central Africa, and her condition in England and America?　There is no difference except that which the Bible makes.　In lands where there is no Bible she is hitched like a beast of burden to the plows, she carries the hod, she submits to indescribable indignities.　She must be kept in a private apartment, and if she come forth she must be carefully hooded and religiously veiled as though it were a shame to be a woman.　Do you not know that the very first thing that the Bible does when it comes into a new country is to strike off the shackles of woman's serfdom?　O woman, where are your chains to-day?　Hold up both your arms and let us see your handcuffs.　Oh, we see the handcuffs.　They are bracelets of gold bestowed by husbandly or fatherly or brotherly or sisterly or loverly affection.　Unloosen the warm robe from your neck, O woman, and let us see the yoke of your bondage.　Oh, I find the yoke a carcanet of silver, or a string of carnelians, or a cluster of pearls, that must gall you very much.　How bad you must all have it.

Since you put the Bible on your stand in the sitting room, has the Bible been to you, O woman, a curse or a blessing?　Why is it that a woman when she is troubled will go to her worst enemy, the Bible?　Why do you not go for comfort to some of the great infidel books, Spin-

oza's "Ethics," or Hume's "Natural History of Religion,"
or Paine's "Age of Reason," or Dedro's Dramas, or any
one of the 260 volumes of Voltaire?   No, the silly, de-
luded woman persists in hanging about the Bible verses,
"Let not your heart be troubled,"   "All things work together for good," "Weeping may endure for a night," "I
am the resurrection," "Peace, be still."

INFIDELITY DOES NO GOOD FOR THE WORLD.

Furthermore, rather than invite I resist this plague of
infidelity because it has wrought no positive good for the
world and is always a hindrance.   I ask you to mention
the names of the merciful and the educational institution which infidelity founded and is supporting, and has
supported all the way through—institutions pronounced
against God and the Christian religion, and yet pronounced in behalf of suffering humanity.   What are the
names of them?   Certainly not the United States Christian commission or the sanitary commission, for Christian
George H. Stuart was the president of the one, and
Christian Henry W. Bellows was the president of the
other.

Where are the asylums and merciful institutions founded by infidelity and supported by infidelity, pronounced
against God and the Bible, and yet doing work for the
alleviation of suffering?   Infidelity is so very loud in its
braggadocio it must have some to mention.   Certainly,
if you come to speak of educational institutions it is not
Yale, it is not Harvard, it is not Princeton, it is not
Middletown, it is not Cambridge or Oxford, it is not any
institution from which a diploma would not be a disgrace.
Do you point to the German universities as exceptions?

I have to tell you that all the German universities to-day are under positive Christian influences, except the University of Heidelberg, where the ruffianly students cut and maul and mangle and murder each other as a matter of pride instead of infamy.. Do you mention Girard college, Philadelphia, as an exception, that college established by the will of Mr. Girard which forbade religious instruction and the entrance of clergymen within its gates? My reply is that I lived for seven years near that college and knew many of its professors to be Christian instructors, and no better Christian influences are to be found in any college than in Girard college.

CHRISTIANITY AND INFIDELITY COMPARED.

There stands Christianity. There stands infidelity. Compare what they have done. Compare their resources. There is Christianity, a prayer on her lip; a benediction on her brow; both hands full of help for all who want help; the mother of thousands of colleges; the mother of thousands of asylums for the oppressed, the blind, the sick, the lame, the imbecile; the mother of missions for the bringing back of the outcast; the mother of thousands of reformatory institutions for the saving of the lost; the mother of innumerable Sabbath schools bringing millions of children under a drill to prepare them for respectability and usefulness, to say nothing of the great future. That is Christianity.

Here is infidelity; no prayer on her lips, no benediction on her brow, both hands clenched—what for? To fight Christianity. That is the entire business. The complete mission of infidelity to fight Christianity. Where are her schools, her colleges, her asylums of mercy?

Let me throw you down a whole ream of foolscap paper that yon may fill all of it with the names of her beneficent institutions, the colleges, and the asylums, the institutions of mercy and of learning, founded by infidelity and supported alone by infidelity, pronounced against God and the Christian religion, and yet in favor of making the world better.

"Oh," you say, "a ream of paper is to much for the names of those institutions."

Well, then, I throw you a quire of paper. Fill it all up now. I will wait until you get all the names down.

"Oh," you say, "that is too much."

Well, then, I will just hand you a sheet of letter paper. Just fill up the four sides while we are talking of this matter with the names of the merciful institutions and the educational institutions founded by infidelity and supported all along by infidelity, pronounced against God and the Christian religion, yet in favor of humanity.

"Oh," you say, "that is too much room. We don't want a whole sheet of paper to write down the names."

Perhaps I had better tear out one leaf from my memorandum book and ask you to fill up both sides of it with the names of such institutions.

"Oh," you say, "That would be too much room. I wouldn't want so much room as that."

Well, then, suppose you count them on your ten fingers.

"Oh," you say, "not quite so much as that."

Well, then, count them on the fingers of one hand.

"Oh," you say, "we don't want quite so much room as that."

Suppose, then, you halt and count on one finger the name of any institution founded by infidelity, supported entirely by infidelity, pronounced against God and the Christian religion, yet toiling to make the world better. Not one! Not one!

ALAS, FOR THE MEANNESS OF INFIDELITY!

Is infidelity so poor, so starveling, so mean, so useless? Get out, you miserable pauper of the universe! Crawl into some rathole of everlasting nothingness. Infidelity standing to-day amid the suffering, groaning, dying nations, and yet doing absolutely nothing save, trying to impede those who are toiling until they fall exhausted into their graves in trying to make the world better.

Gather up all the work, all the merciful work, that infidelity has ever done, add it all together, and there is not so much nobility in it as in the smallest bead of that sister of charity who last night went up the dark alley of the town, put a jar of jelly for an invalid appetite on a broken stand, and then knelt on the bare floor praying the mercy of Christ upon the dying soul.

Infidelity scrapes no lint for the wounded, bakes no bread for the hungry, shakes up no pillow for the sick, rouses no comfort for the bereft, gilds no grave for the dead.

THANKS FOR THE GOODNESS OF CHRISTIANITY.

While Christ, our Christ, our wounded Christ, our risen Christ, the Christ of this old fashioned Bible— blessed be his glorious name forever! our Christ stands this hour pointing to the hospital, or to the asylum, saying: "I was sick and ye gave me a couch, I was lame and ye gave me a crutch, I was blind and ye physicianed my

eyesight, I was orphaned and ye mothered my soul, I
was lost on the mountains and ye brought me home; in-
asmuch as ye did it to one of the least of these, ye did it
to me."

But I thank God that this plague of infidelity will be
stayed. Many of those who hear me now by the Holy
Ghost upon their hearts will cease to be scoffers and will
become disciples, and the day will arrive when all nations will accept the Scriptures. The book is going to
keep right on until the fires of the last day are kindled.
Some of them will begin on one side and some on the
other side of the old book. They will not find a bundle
of loose manuscripts easily consumed like tinder thrown
into the fire. When the fires of the last day are kindled,
some will burn on this side, from Genesis toward Revelation, and others will burn on this side, from Revelation
toward Genesis, and in all their way, they will not find a
single chapter or a single verse out of place. That will
be the first time we can afford to do without the Bible.

What will be the use of the book of Genesis, descrip-
tive of how the world was made, when the world is de-
troyed? What will be the use of the prophecies when
they are fulfilled? What will be the use of the evangelistic or Pauline description of Jesus Christ when we see
him face to face? What will be the use of his photograph
when we have met him in glory? What will be the use
of the book of Revelation, standing as you will with your
foot on the glassy sea, and your hand on the ringing
harp, and your forhead chapleted with eternal coronation,
amid the amethystine and twelve gated glories of heaven?
The emerald dashing its green against the beryl, and the

beryl dashing its blue against the sapphire, and the sapphire throwing its light on the jacinth, and the jacinth dashing its fire against the chrysoprasus, and you and I standing in the glories of ten thousand sunsets.

"I AM GUILTY".

THE PLAGUE OF CRIME.

"All the waters that were in the river were turned to blood.'
Exodus vii, 20.

Among all the Egyptian plagues none could have been worse than this. The Nile is the wealth of Egypt. Its fish the food, its waters the irrigation of garden and fields. Its condition decides the prosperity or the doom of the empire. What happens to the Nile happens to all Egypt. And now in the text that great river is incarnadined. It is a red gash across an empire. In poetic license we speak of wars which turn the rivers into blood. But my text is not a poetic license. It was a fact, a great crimson, appalling condition described. The Nile rolling deep of blood. Can you imagine a more awful plague?

CRIME IN OUR CITIES.

The modern plague which nearest corresponds with that is the plague of crime in all our cities. It halts not for bloodshed. It shrinks from no carnage. It bruises and cuts and strikes down and destroys. It revels in the blood of body and soul, this plague of crime rampant for ages, and never bolder or more rampant than now.

The annual police reports of these cities as I examine them are to me more suggestive than Dente's Inferno, and all Christian people as well as reformers need to awaken to a present and tremendous duty. If you want this "Plague of Crime" to stop there are several kinds of

(111)

persons you need to consider. First, the public criminals. You ought not to be surprised that these people
make up a large portion in many communities. The
vast majority of the criminals who take ship from Europe come into our own port. In 1869, of the forty-
nine thousand people who were incarcerated in the
prison of the country, thirty-two thousand were of foreign
birth. Many of them were the very desperadoes of
society, oozing into the slums of our city, waiting for
an opportunity to riot and steal and debauch, joining the
large gang of American thugs and cut-throats.

There are in this cluster of cities (New York, Jersey
City and Brooklyn) four thousand people whose entire
business in life is to commit suicide. That is as much
their business as jurisprudence or medicine or merchandise is your business. To it they bring all their energies
of body, mind and soul, and they look upon the inter-
vals which they spend in prison as so much unfortunate
loss of time, just as you look upon an attack of influenza
and rheumatism which fastens you in the house for a few
days. It is their lifetime business to pick pockets, and
blow up safes, and shop lift, and play the panel game,
and they have as much pride of skill in their business as
you have in yours when you upset the argument of an
opposing counsel, or cure a gunshot fracture which other
surgeons have given up, or fore-see a turn in the market
as you buy goods just before they go up 20 per cent.
It is their business to commit crime, and I do not suppose that once in a year the thought of the immorality
strikes them.

Added to these professional criminals, American and

foreign, there is a large class of men who are more or less industrious in crime. In one year the police in this cluster of cities arrested ten thousand people for theft, and ten thousand for assault and battery, and fifty thousand for intoxication. Drunkenness is responsible for much of the theft, since it confuses a man's ideas of propriety, and he gets his hands on things that do not belong to him. Rum is responsible for much of the assault and battery, inspiring men to sudden bravery, which they must demonstrate though it be on the face of the next gentlemen.

SOCIETY THREATENED ON ALL SIDES.

Ten million dollars' worth of property stolen in this cluster of cities in one year! You cannot, as good citizens, be independent of that fact. It will touch your pockets, since I have to give you the fact that these three cities pay about eight million dollars' worth of taxes a year to arraign, try and support the criminal population. You help to pay the board of every criminal, from the sneak thief that snatches a spool of cotton up to some man who swamps a bank. More than that, it touches your heart in the moral depression of the community. You might as well think to stand in a closely confined room where there are fifty people, and yet not breathe the vitiated air, as to stand in a community where there is such a great multitude of the depraved, without somewhat being contaminated. What is the fire that burns your store down compared with the conflagration which consumes your morals? What is the theft of the gold and silver from your money safe, compared with the theft of your children's virtue? We are all ready to arraign criminals.   We shout at the top of our voice, "Stop thief!" and when the police get on the track we come out haltless and in our slippers, and assist in the arrest.   We come around the bawling ruffian and hustle him off to justice, and when he gets in prison what do we do for him?   With great gusto we put on the handcuffs, and the hopples; but what preparation are we making for the day when the handcuffs and the hopples come off?   Society seems to say to these criminals, "Villain, go in there and rot," when it ought to say, "You are an offender against the law, but we mean to give you an opportunity to repent; we mean to help you. Here are Bibles, and tracts, and Christian influences. Christ died for you.   Look and live."

Vast improvements have been made by introducing industries into the prison; but we want something more than hammers and shoe lasts to reclaim these people. Aye, we want more than sermons on the sabbath day. Society must impress these men with the fact that it does not enjoy their suffering, and that it is attempting to reform and elevate them.   The majority of criminals suppose that society has a grudge against them, and they in turn have a grudge against society.   They are harder in heart and more infuriate when they come out of jail than when they went in.   Many of the people who go to prison, go again and again and again.

STARTLING FIGURES!

Some years ago, of fifteen hundred prisoners, who during the year had been in Sing Sing, four hundred had been there before,   In a house of correction in the country, where during a certain reach of time, there had been five thousand people, more than three thousand had been there before. So in one case the prison, and in the other, the house of correction, left them just as bad as they were before The secretary of one of the benevolent societies of New York saw a lad of fifteen years of age who had spent three years of his life in prison, and he said to the lad:

"What have they done for you to make you better?"

"Well," replied the lad, "the first time I was brought up before the judge he said:

'You ought to be ashamed of yourself.'

And then I committed a crime again, and I was brought up before the same judge, and he said:

'You rascal!'

And after a while I committed some other crime, and I was brought before the same judge, and he said:

'You ought to be hanged.'"

That was all they had done for him in the way of reformation and salvation. "Oh" you, say "these people are incorrigible." I suppose there are hundreds of persons this day lying in the prison bunks who would leap up at the prospect of reformation if society would only allow them a way into decency and respectability.

THE CONTAMINATION OF CORRUPT SURROUNDINGS!

"Oh" you say, "I have no patience with these rogues." I ask you in reply, how much better would you have been under the same circumstances? Suppose your mother had been a blasphemer and your father a sot, and you had started life with a body stuffed with evil proclivities, and you had spent much of your time in a cellar amid obscenities and cursing, and if at ten years of age you had been compelled to go out and steal, battered and banged at night if you came in without any spoil, and suppose your early manhood and womanhood had been covered with rags and filth, and decent society had turned its back upon you, and left you to consort with vagabonds and wharf rats—how much better would you have been? I have no sympathy with that executive clemency which would let crime run loose, 'or which would sit in the gallery of the court room weeping, because some hard hearted wretch is brought to justice; but I do say that the safety and life of the community demand more potential influences in behalf of public offenders.

SOME OE THE SAD SIGHTS I HAVE SEEN.

In some of the city prisons the air is like that of the Black Hole of Calcutta. I have visited prisons where, as the air swept through the wicket, it almost knocked me down. No sunlight. Young men who had committed their first crime crowded in among old offenders. I saw in one prison a woman, with a child almost blind, who had been arrested for the crime of poverty, who was waiting until the slow law could take her to the almshouse, where she rightfuly belonged; but she was thrust n there with her child, amid the most abandoned wretches of the town. Many of the offenders in that prison slept on the floor, with nothing but a vermin covered blanket over them. Those people crowded and wan and wasted and half suffocated and infuriated. I said to the men, "How do you stand it here?" "God knows," said one man, "we have to to stand it." Oh, they will pay you when they get out. Where they burned down one house they will burn three They will strike deeper the assassin's knife. They are this minute plotting worse burglaries.

JAILS ARE OFTEN CRIMINAL MANUFACTORIES.

Some of the city jails are the best places I know of to manufacture footpads, vagabonds and cut-throats. Yale college is not so well calculated to make scholars, nor Harvard so well calculated to make scientists, nor Princeton so well calculated to make theologians, as many of our jails are calculated to make criminals. All that those men do not know of crime, after they have been in the dungeon for some time, . Satanic machination cannot teach them, In the insufferable stench and sickening surroundings of such places, there is nothing but disease for the body, idiocy for the mind, and death for the soul. Stifled air, and darkness, and vermin, never turned a thief into an honest man.

We want men like John Howard, and Sir William Blackstone, and women like Elizabeth Fry, to do for the prisons of the United States, what those people did in other days for the prisons of England. I thank God for what Isaac T. Hopper, and Dr. Wines, and Mr. Harris, and scores of others, have done in the way of prison reform, but be want something more radical before will come the blessings of Him who said: "I was in prison and ye came unto me."

UNTRUSTWORTHY OFFICALS.

Again, in your effort to arrest this plague of crime you need to consider untrustworthy officials. "Woe nnto thee, O land, when thy king is a child, and thy princes drink in the morning." It is a great calamity to a city when bad men get into public authority. Why was it that in New York there was such unparalleled crime betweeu 1866 and 1871? It was because the judges of police in that city at that time for the most part were as corrupt as the vagabonds that came before them for trial. Those were the days of high carnival for election frauds, assassination, and forgery. We had all kinds of rings. There was one man during those years that got one hundred and twenty-eight thousand dollars in one year for serving the public.

$50,000,000,00 SQUANDERED.

In a few years it was estimated that there were fifty millions of public treasure squandered. In those times the criminal had only to wink to the judge, or his lawyer would wink for him, and the question was decided for the defendent. Of the eight thousand people arrested in that city in one year, only three thousand were punished. These little matters were "fixed up," while the interests of society were "fixed down." You know as well as I do that one villain who escapes, only opens the door for other criminalities. When the two pickpockets snatched the diamond pin from the Brooklyn gentlemen in a Broadway stage, and the villains were arrested, and the trial was set down for the general sessions, and then the trial never came, and never anything more was heard of the case, the public officials were only bidding higher for more crime.

It is no compliment to public authority when we have in all the cities of the country, walking abroad, men and women notorious for criminality unwhipped of justice. They are pointed out to you in the street, day by day.

There you find what are called the "fences," the men who stand between the thief and the honest man, sheltering the thief, and at a great price handing over the goods to the owner to whom they belong. There you will find those who are called the "skinners," the men who hover around Wall street, with great sleight of hand in bonds and stocks. There you find the funeral thieves, the people who go and sit down and mourn with families and pick their pockets. And there you find the "confidence men," who borrow money of you because they have a dead child in the house and want to bury it, when they never had a house or a family; or they want to go to England and get a large property there, and they want you to pay their way and they will send the money black by the very next mail.

"SHOPLIFTERS," "PICKPOCKETS," ETC.

There are the "harbor thieves," the "shoplifters," the "pickpockets," famous all over the cities. Hundreds of them with their faces in the Rogues' Gallery, yet doing nothing for the last five or ten years but defraud society and escape justice. When these people go unarrested and unpunished it is putting a high premium upon vice and saying to the young criminals of this country, "What a safe thing it is to be a great criminal!" Let the law swoop upon them. Let it be known to this country that crime will have no quarter; that the detectives are after it; that the police club is being brandished; that the iron door of the prison is being opened; that the judge is ready to call on the case. Too great leniency to criminals is too great severity to society.

Again in your effort to arrest the plague of crime you

need to consider the idle population. Of course I do not refer to people who are getting old, or to the sick, or to those who cannot get work, but I tell you to look out for those athletic men and women, who will not work. When the French nobleman was asked why he kept busy when he had so large a property he said, "I keep on engraving so I may not hang myself." I do not care who the man is, you cannot afford to be idle. It is from the idle classes that the criminal classes are made up. Character, like water, gets putrid if it stands still too long. Who can wonder that in this world, where there is so much to do, and all the hosts of the earth and heaven and hell are plunging into the conflict, and angels are flying, and God is at work, and the universe is a-quake with the marching and counter marching, that God lets his indignation fall upon a man who chooses idleness?

THE DO-NOTHINGS.

I have watched these do-nothings who spend their time stroking their beard and retouching their toilet and criticising industrious people, and pass their days and nights in bar rooms and club houses, lounging, and smoking, and chewing, and card playing. They are not only useless, but they are dangerous. How hard it is for them to while away the hours! Alas, for them! If they do not know how to while away an hour, what will they do when they have all eternity on their hands? These men for a while smoke the best cigars, and wear the best clothes, and move in the highest spheres, but I have noticed that very soon they come down to the prison, the almshouse or stop at the gallows.

The police stations of this cluster of cities furnish annually between two and three hundred thousand lodgings. For the most part these two and three hundred thousand lodgings are furnished to able bodied men and women—people as able to work as you and I are. When they are received no longer at one police station because they are "repeaters," they go to some other station, and so they keep moving around. They get their food at house doors, stealing what they can lay their hands on in the front basement while the servant is spreading the bread in the back basement. They will not work. Time and again in the country districts, they have wanted hundreds and thousands of laborers. These men will not go. They do not want to work.

I have tried them. I have set them to sawing wood in my cellar to see whether they wanted to work. I offered to pay them well for it. I have heard the saw going for about three minutes, and then I went down, and lo! the wood, but no saw! They are the pest of society, and they stand in the way of the Lord's poor who ought to be helped, and must be helped and will be helped.

While there are thousands of industrious men who cannot get any work, these men who do not want any work come in and make that plea. I am in favor of the restoration of the old fashioned whipping post for just this one class of men who will not work—sleeping at night at public expense in the station house, duriug the day get their food at our doorstep. Imprisonment does not scare them. They would like it. Blackwell's Island or Sing Sing would be a comfortable home for them.   They would have no objection to the almshouse, for they like thin soup, if they cannot get mock turtle.

WHAT I PROPOSE FOR THE DO NOTHINGS.

I propose this for them: On one side of them put some healthy work; on the other side put a rawhide, and let them take their choice.   I like for that class of people the scant bill of fare that Paul wrote out for the Thessalonian loafers,   "If any work not, neither should he eat."   By what law of God or man is it right that you and I should toil day in and out, until our hands are blistered, and our arms ache, and our brain gets numb, and then be called upon to support what in the United States are about two million loafers?   They are a very dangerous class.   Let the public authorities keep their eyes on them.

THE ILL TREATED BECOME DESPERATE.

Again, among the uprooting classes I place the oppressed poor.   Poverty to a certain extent is chastening, but after that, when it drives a man to the wall, and he hears his children cry in vain for bread, it some times makes him desperate.   I think there are thousands of honest men lacerated into vagabondism. . There are men crushed under burdens for which they are not half paid.   While there is no excuse for criminality, even in oppression, I state it as a simple fact that much of the scoundrelism of the commnnity is consequent upon ill treatment.   There are many men and women battered, and bruised, and stung, until the hour of despair has come, and they stand with the ferocity of a wild beast which, pursued until it can run no longer, turns round, foaming and bleeding, to fight the hounds.

UNDER GROUND NEW YORK AND BROOKLYN!

There is a vast underground New York and Brooklyn life that is appalling and shameful. It wallows and steams with putrefaction. You go down the stairs which are wet and decayed with filth, and at the bottom you find the poor victims on the floor, cold, sick, three fourths dead, slinking into a still darker corner under the gleam of the lantern of the police. There has not been a breath of fresh air in that room for five years, literally. The broken sewer empties its contents upon them, and they lie at night in the swimming filth. There they are, men, women, children; blacks, whites: Mary Magdelen without her repentance, and Lazarus without his God. These are ''the dives'' into which the pickpockets and the thieves go, as well as a great many who would like a different life, but cannot get it.

These places are the sores of the city, which bleed perpetual corruption. They are the underlying volcano that threatens us with a Caraccas earthquake. It rolls and roars, and surges, and heaves, and rocks, and blasphemes, and dies, and there are only two outlets for it—the police court and the Potter's field. In other words, they must either go to prison, or to hell. Oh, you never saw it, you say. You never will see it until on the day when those staggering wretches shall come up in the light of the judgment throne, and while all hearts are being revealed, God will ask you what you did to help them.

There is another layer of poverty and destination not so squalid, but almost as helpless. You hear the inces-

sant wailing for bread and clothes and fire.   Their eyes
are sunken.   Their cheek bones stand out.   Their
hands are damp with slow consumption.   Their flesh is
puffed up with dropsies.   Their breath is like that of the
charnel house.   They hear the roar of the wheels of fashion overhead and the gay laughter of men and maidens,
and wonder why God gave to others so much, and to
them so little.   Some of them thrust into an infidelity
like that of the poor German girl who, when told in the
midst of her wretchedness that God was good, said:
"No; no good God.   Just look at me.   No good God."

OUR 300,000 HONEST POOR.

In this cluster of cities whose cry of want I interpret
there are said to be, as far as I can figure it up from the
reports, aboat three hundred thousand honest poor who
are dependent upon iudividual, city and state charities.

·If all their voices could come up at once it would be
a groan that would shake the foundation of the city and
bring all earth and heaven to the rescue.   But for the
most part it suffers unexpressed.   It sits in silence gnash-
ing its teeth aiid sucking the blood of his own arteries
waiting for the judgment day.   Oh, I should not wonder if on that day it would be found that some of us had
somethings that belonged to them, some extra garment
which might have made tbem comfortable in cold days;·
some bread thrust into the ash barrel that might have
appeased their hunger for a little while; some wasted
candle, or gas jet, that might have kindled up their
darkness; some fresco on the ceiling that would have
given them a roof; some jewel which, brought to the
orphan girl in time, might have kept her from being

crowded off the precipices of an unclean life; some New
Testament that would have told them of Him who
"came to save that which was lost."

Oh, this wave of vagrancy and hunger and nakedness
that dashes against our front door step! If the roofs
of all the houses of destitution could be lifted so we
could look down into them just as God looks, whose nerves
would be strong enough to stand it? And yet there
they are! The fifty thousand sewing wonen in these
three cities, some of them in hunger and cold, working
night after night, until sometimes the blood spurts from
nostril and lips. How well their grief was voiced by
that despairing woman who stood by her invalid husband and invalid child, and said to the city missionary:
"I am down hearted, everything's against us; and then
there are other things."

"What other things?" said the city missionary.

"Oh," she repeated, "my sin."

"What do you mean by that?"

"Well," she said, I never hear or see any thing good.
It's work from Monday morning till Saturday night, and
and then when Sunday comes I can't go out, and 1 walk
the floor, and it makes me tremble to think that I have
got to meet God. Oh, sir, its so hard for us. We have
to work so, and then we have so much trouble, and then
we are getting along so poorly; and see this wee little
thing growing weaker and weaker; and then to think we
are not getting nearer to God but floating away from
Him. Oh, sir, I do wish I was ready to die."

I should not wonder if they had a good deal better
time than we in the future, to make up for the fact

that they had such a bad time here.   It would be just
like Jesus to say: ''Come up and take the highest seat.
you suffered with me on earth; now be glorified with me
in heaven. ''   O thou weeping One of Bethany! O thou
dying One of the cross!   Have mercy on the starving,
freezing, homeless poor of these great cities!

MY REASONS FOR PREACHING THIS SERMON.

I have preached this sermon for four or five practical
reasons: Because I want you to know who are the uprooting classes of society.   Because I want you to be
more discriminating in your charities.   Because I want
your hearts open with generosity, and your hands open
with charity.   Because I want you to be made the
sworn friends of all city evangelization, and all newsboys' lodging houses, and all children's aid societies, and
Dorcas societies, under the skillful manipulation of wives
and mothers and sisters and daughters; let the spare garments of your wardrobes be fitted to the limbs of the
wan and shivering.   I should not wonder if that hat
that you gave come back a jeweled coronet, or if that
garment you hand out from your wardrobe should mys-
teriously be whitened, and somehow be wrought into the
Saviour's own robe, so in the last day he would run his
hand over it and say, ''I was naked and ye clothed me.''
That would be putting your garments to glorious uses.

But more than that, I have preached the sermon because I thought in the contrast you would see how very
kindly God had dealt with you, and I thought that thousands of you would go to your comfortable homes and
sit at your well filed tables and at your warm registers,
and look at the round faces of your children, and that

then you would burst into tears at the review of God's goodness to you, and that you would go to your room and lock your door and kneel down and say:

"O Lord, I have been an ingrate; make me thy child. O Lord, there are so many hungry and unclad and unsheltered to day, I thank thee that all my life thou hast taken such good care of me. O Lord there are so many sick and crippeled children to-day, I thank the mine are well—some of them on earth, some of them in heaven. Thy goodness, O Lord breaks me down. Take me once and forever. Sprinkled as I was many years ago at the altar, while my mother held me, now I consecrate my soul to Thee in a holier baptism of repenting tears."

> "For sinners, Lord, thou cam'st to bleed,
> And I'm a sinner vile indeed;
> Lord, I believe thy grace is free,
> O magnify that grace to me."

THE WAR OF CAPITAL AND LABOR IN THE CITIES.

"Whatsoever ye would that men should do to you, do ye even so to them." Matt. vii, 12.

Two hundred and fifty thousand laborers in Hyde park, London, and the streets of American and European cities filled with processions of workmen carrying banners, brings the subject of Labor and Capital to the front. That all this was done in peace, and that as a result, in many places, arbitration has taken place, is a hopeful sign.

A WAR OF FIVE CONTINENTS.

The greatest war the world has ever seen is between capital and labor. The strife is not like that which in history is called the Thirty Years' War, for it is a war of centuries, it is a war of the five continents, it is a war hemispheric. The middle classes in this country, upon whom the nation has depended for holding the balance of power and for acting as mediators between the two extremes, are diminishing; and if things go on at the same ratio as they have for the last twenty years been going on, it will not be very long before there will be no middle class in this country, but all will be very rich or very poor, princes or paupers, and the country will be given up to palaces and hovels.

The antagonistic forces have again and again closed in upon each other. You may pooh pooh it; you may say that this trouble, like an angry child, will cry itself to sleep; you may belittle it by calling it Foulerism, or Socialism, or St. Simonism, or Nihilism, or Communism, but that will not hinder the fact that it is the mightiest, the darkest, the most terrific threat of this century. Most of the attempts at pacification have been dead failures, and monopoly is more arrogant and the trades unions more bitter.

"Give us more wages," cry the employes.

"You shall have less," says the capitalists.

"Compel us to do fewer hours of toil in a day."

"You shall toil more hours," say the others.

"Then, under certain conditions, we will not work at all," say these.

"Then you shall starve," say those, and the workmen gradually using up that which they accumulated in better times, unless there be some radical change, we shall have soon in this country three million hungry men and women. Now, three million hungry people cannot be kept quiet. All the enactments of legislatures and all the constabularies of the cities, and all the army and navy of the United States cannot keep three million hungry people quiet. What then? Will this war between capital and labor be settled by human wisdom? Never. The brow of the one becomes more rigid, the fist of the other more clinched.

But that which human wisdom cannot achieve will be accomplished by Christianity if it be given full sway. You have heard of medicines so powerful that one drop would stop a disease and restore a patient, and I have to tell you that one drop of my text properly administered will stop all these woes of society and give convalescence and complete health to all classes.   ''Whatsoever ye would that men should do to you, do ye even so them." I shall grst show you this morning how this controversy between monopoly and hard work cannot be stopped, and then I, will show you how this controversy will be settled.

FUTILE REMEDIES.

In the first place there will come no pacification to this trouble through an outcry against rich men, merely because they are rich.   There is no laboring man on earth that would not be rich if he could be.   Sometimes through a fortunate invention, or through some accident of prosperity, a man who had nothing, comes to large estate, and we see him arrogant and supercilious, and taking people by the throat, just as other people took him by the throat.

There is something very mean about human nature when it comes to the top.   But it is no more a sin to be rich, than it is a sin to be poor.   There are those who have gathered a great estate through fraud, and then there are millionaires who have gathered their fortunes through foresight in regard to changes in the markets, and through brilliant business faculty, and every dollar of their estate is as honest as the dollar which the plumber gets for mending a pipe, or the mason gets for building a wall.   There are those who keep in poverty because of their own fault.   They might have been well off, but they smoked or chewed up their earnings, or they lived beyond their means, while others on the same wages and on the same salaries went on to competency. I know a man who is all the time complaining of his poverty, and crying out against rich men, while he himself keeps two dogs, and chews and smokes, and is filled to the chin with whisky and beer!

Micawber said to David Copperfield: "Copperfield, my boy, one pound income, twenty shillings and sixpence expenses; result, misery. But Copperfield, my boy, one pound income, expenses ninteen shillings and sixpence; result, happiness." And there are vast multitudes of people who are kept poor because they are the victims of their own improvidence. It is no sin to be rich, and it is no sin to be poor. I protest against this outcry which I hear against those who, through economy and self denial and assiduity, have come to large fortune. This bombardment of commercial success will never stop this controversy between capital and labor.

Neither will the contest be settled by cynical and unsympathetic treatment of the laboring classes. There are those who speak of them as though they were only cattle or draught horses. Their nerves are nothing, their domestic comfort is nothing. They have no more sympathy for them than a hound has for a hare, or a hawk for a hen, or a tiger for a calf. When Jean Valjean, the greatest hero of Victor Hugo's writings, after a life of suffering and brave endurance, goes into incarceration and death, they clap the book shut and say, "Good for him!" They stamp their feet with indignation and say just the opposite of "Save the working classes." They have all their sympathies with Shylock, and not with Antonio and Portia. They are plutocrats, and their feelings are infernal. They are filled with irritation and irascibility on this subject. **To stop this aw-**

ful imbroglio between capital and labor, they will lift not so much as the tip end of the little finger. .

Neither will there be any pacification of this angry controversy through violence. God never blessed murder. Blow up to-morrow the country seats on the banks of the Hudson, and all the fine houses on Madison square, and Brooklyn heights, and Brooklyn hill, and Rittenhouse square, and Beacon street, and all the bricks and timber and stone will just fall back on the bare head of American labor. The worst enemies of the working classes in the United States, and Ireland, are their demented coadjutors. A few yeary ago assassination—the assassination of Lord Frederick Cavendish and Mr. Burke in Phænix park, Dublin, Ireland, in the attempt to avenge the wrongs of Ireland—only turned away from that afflicted people millions of sympathizers. The attempt to blow up the house of commons, in London, had only this effect: to throw out of employment tens of thousands of innocent Irish people in England.

In this country the torch put to the factories that have discharged hands for good or bad reason; obstructions on the rail track in front of midnight express trains because the offenders do not like the president of the company; strikes on shipboard the hour they were going to sail, or to printing offices the hour the paper was to go to press; or in mines the day the coal was to be delivered, or on house scaffoldings so the builder fails in keeping his contract—all these are only a hard blow on the head of American labor, and cripple its arms, and lame its feet, and pierce its heart. As a result of one of our great American strikes you find that the operatives lost four hundred thousand dollars' worth of wages, and have had poor wages ever since. Traps sprung suddenly upon employers, and violence, never took one knot out of the knuckle of toil, or put one farthing of wages into a callous palm. Barbarism will never cure the wrongs of civilization. Mark that!

STORY OF FREDERICK THE GREAT AND THE MILLER.

Frederick the Great admired some land near his palace at Potsdam and he resolved to get it. It was owned by a miller. He offered the miller three times the value of the property. The miller would not take it, because it was the old homestead and he felt about it as Naboth felt about his vineyard when Ahab wanted it. Frederick the great was a rough and terrible man, and he ordered the miller into his presence; and the king with a stick in his hand—a stick with which he sometimes struck his officers of state—said to the miller:

"Now, I have offered you three times the value of that property, and if you won't sell it I'll take it anyhow."

The miller said: "Your majesty, you won't."

"Yes," said the king, "I will take it."

"Then," said the miller, "if your majesty does take it I will sue you in the chancery court."

At that threat Frederick the Great yielded his infamous demand. And the most imperious outrage against the working classes will yet cower before the law. Violence, and contrary to the law, will never accomplish anything, but righteousness and according to law, will accomplish it.

GOLDEN RULE REMEDY.

Well, if this controversy between capital and labor cannot be settled by human wisdom, it is time for us to look somewhere else for relief, and it points from my text roseate and jubilant, and puts one hand on the broadcloth shoulder of capital, and put the other hand on the homespun covered shoulder of toil, and says, with a voice that will grandly and gloriously settle this and settle everything. "Whatsoever ye would that men should do to you, do ye even so to them." That is, the lady of the household will say: "I must treat the maid in the kitchen just as I would like to be treated if I were downstairs, and it were my work to wash, and cook, and sweep, and it were the duty of the maid in the kitchen to preside in this parlor." The maid in the kitchen must say: "If my employer seems to be more prosperous than I, that is no fault of hers; I shall not treat her as an enemy. I will have the same industry and fidelity down stairs as I would expect from any subordinates if I happened to be the wife of a silk importer."

The owner of an iron mill, having taken a dose of my text before leaving home in the morning, will go into his foundry, and, passing into what is called the puddiug room, he will see a man there stripped to the waist, and besweated and exhausted with the labor and the toil, he will say to him: "Why it seems very hot in here. You look very much exhausted. I hear your child is sick with scarlet fever. If you want your wages a little earlier this week, so as to pay the nurse and get the medicines, just come into my office at any time."

After awhile, crash goes the money market, and there is no more demand for the articles manufactured in that iron mill, and the owner does not know what to do. He says, "Shall I stop the mill, or shall I run it on half

time, or shall I cut down the men's wages?" He walks
the floor of his counting room all day, hardly knowing
what to do. Toward evening he calls all the laborers
together. They stand all around, some with arms akimbo,
some folded arms, wondering what the boss is going to
do now. The manufacturer says: "Men, business is
bad; I don't make twenty dollars where I used to make
one hundred. Somehow, there is no demand now for
what we manufacture, or but very little demand. You
see, I am at vast expense, and I have called you together
this afternoon to see what you would advise. I don't
want to shut up the mill, because that would force you
out of work, and you have always been very faithful, and
I like you, and you seem to like me, and the bairns must
be looked after, and your wife will after awhile want a
new dress. I don't know what to do."

GRATEFUL WORKMAN.

There is a dead halt for a minute or two, and then one
of the workmen steps out from the ranks of his fellows
and says: "Boss, you have been very good to us, and
when you prospered we prospered, and now you are in a
tight place, and I am sorry, and we have got to sympa-
thize with you. I don't know how the others feel. but I
propose that we take off twenty percent from our wages,
and that when the times get good you will remember us
and raise them again." The workman looks around to
his comrades, and says: "Boys, what do you say to this?
All in favor of my proposition will say ay." "Ay! ay!
ay!" shout two hundred voices.

But the mill owner, getting in some new machinery,
exposes himself very much, and takes cold and it settles

into pneumonia and he dies. In the procession to the tomb are all the workmen, tears rolling down their cheeks and off upon the ground; but an hour before the procession gets to the cemetery the wives and the children of those workmen are at the grave waiting for the arrival of the funeral pageant. The minister of religion may have delivered an eloquent eulogium before they started from the house, but the most impressive things are said that day by the working classes standing around the tomb. That night in all the cabins of the working people where they have family prayers, the widowhood and the orphanage in the mansion are remembered. No glaring populations look over the iron fence of the cemetery; but, hovering over the scene, the benediction of God and man is coming for the fulfillment of the Christ-like injunction, "Whatsoever ye would that men should do to you, do ye even so to them."

GOLDEN RULE CORPORATIONS.

"Oh," says some man here, "that is all Utopian, that is apocryphal, that is impossible." No, I cut out of a paper this: "One of the pleasantest incidents recorded in a long time is reported from Sheffield, England. The wages of the men in the iron works at Sheffield are regulated by a board of arbitration, by whose decision both masters and men are bound. For some time past the iron and steel trade has been extremely unprofitable, and the employer cannot, without much loss, pay the wages fixed by the board, which neither the employers nor employed have the power to change. To avoid this difficulty, the workmen in one of the largest steel works in Sheffield hit upon a device as rare as it was generous.

They offered to work for their employers one week without any pay whatever. How much better that plan is than a strike would be."

MODEL BUSINESS HOUSES.

But you go with me and I will show you—not so far off as Sheffield, England—factories, banking houses, store houses, and costly enterprises where this Christlike injunction of my text is fully kept, and you could no more get the employer to practice an injustice upon his men, or the men to conspire against the employer, than you could get your right hand and your left hand, your right eye and your left eye, your right ear and your left ear, into physiological antagonism. Now, where is this to begin? In our homes, in our stores, on our farms—not waiting for other people to do their duty. Is there a divergance now between the parlor and the kitchen? Then there is something wrong, either in the parlor or in the kitchen, perhaps in both. Are the clerks in your store irate against the firm? Then there is something wrong, either behind the counter, or in the private office, or perhaps in both.

A STORY OF GEN. WASHINGTON.

The great want of the world to-day is the fulfillment of this Christlike injunction, that which He promulgated in his sermon Olivetic. All the political economists under the archivolt of the heavens in convention for a thousand years cannot settle this oontroversy between monopoly and hard work, between capital and labor. During the Revolutionary war there was a heavy piece of timber to be lifted, perhaps for some fortress, and a

corporal was overseeing the work, and he was giving the
commands to some soldiers as they lifted.

"Heave away, there! yo heave!"

Well, the timber was too heavy; they could not get if up.
There was a gentleman riding by on a horse, and he stopped and said to this corporal:

"Why don't you help them lift? That timber is too
heavy for them to lift."

"No," he said, "I won't; I am a corporal."

The gentleman got off his horse and came up to the
place. "Now," he said to the soldiers, "all together—
yo heave!" and the timber went to its place. "Now,"
said the gentleman to the corporal, "when you have a
piece of timber too heavy for the men to lift, and you
want help, you send to your commander-in-chief.

It was Washington! Now, that is about all the gospel
I know—the gospel of giving somebody a lift out of
earth into heaven. That is the gospel of helping somebody else to lift.

SUPPLY AND DEMAND A FRAUD.

"Oh," says some wiseacre, "talk as you will, the law
of demand and supply will regulate these things until the
end of time." No, it will not, unless God dies and the
batteries of the judgement day are spiked, and Pluto and
Proserpine, king and queen of the infernal regions, take full
possession of this world. Do you know who Supply and
Demand are? They have gone into partnership, and they
propose to swindle this earth, and are swindling it. You
are drowning. Supply and Demand stand on the shore
—one on one side, the other on the other side of the life
boat, and they cry out to you: 'Now, you pay us what

we ask you for getting you to shore, or go to the bottom!"
If you can borrow $5,000 you can keep from failing in
business. Supply and Demand say: "Now, you pay us
exorbitant usury or you go into bankruptcy!" This robber firm of Supply and Demand say to you: "The crops
are short. We bought up all the wheat and it is in our
bin. Now, you pay our price or starve!" That is your
magnificent law of supply and demand.

Supply and Demand own the largest mill on earth, and
all the rivers roll over their wheel, and into their hopper,
they put all the men, women and children they can shovel
out of the centuries, and the blood and the bones redden
the valley while the mill grinds. That diabolic law of
supply and demand will yet have to stand aside, and instead thereof will come the law of love, the law of co-
operation, the law of kindness, the law of sympathy, the
law of Christ.

RECONCILIATION IS PROMISED.

Have you no idea of the coming of such a time? Then
you do not believe the Bible. All the Bible is full of
promises on this subject, and as the ages roll on, the
time will come when men of fortune will be giving larger
sums to humanitarian and evangelistic purposes, and
there will be more James Lenoxes, and Peter Coopers,
and William E. Dodges, and George Peabodys. As that
time comes there will be more parks, more picture galleries, more gardens thrown open for the holiday people
and the working classes.

I was reading some time ago, in regard to a charge
that had been made in England against Lambeth palace,
that it was exclusive; and that charge demonstrated the

sublime fact that to the grounds of that wealthy estate eight hundred poor families had free passes, and forty croquet companies, and on the the half day holidays four thousand poor people recline on the grass, walk through the paths, and sit under the trees. That is gospel—gospel on the wing, gospel out of doors, worth just as much as gospel in doors. That time is going to come.

That is only a hint of what is going to be. The time is going to come when, if you have anything in your house worth looking at—pictures, pieces of sculpture—you are going to invite me to come and see it; you are going to invite my friends to come and see it, and you will say, "See what I have been blessed with! God has given me this, and, so far as enjoying it, it is yours also." That is gospel.

A STORY OF HENRY CLAY.

In crossing the Alleghany mountains, many years ago, the stage halted, and Henry Clay dismounted from the stage and went out on a rock at the very verge of the cliff, and he stood there with his cloak wrapped abou. him, and he seemed to be listening for something Some one said to him, "What are you listening for?" Standing there on the top of the mountain, he said: "I am listening to the tramp of the footsteps of the coming millions of this continent." A sublime posture for an American statesman! You and I to-day stand on the mountain top of privilege, and on the rock of ages, and we look off, and we hear coming from the future, the happy industries, and smiling populations, and the consecrated fortunes, and the innumerable prosperities of the closing Nineteenth and the opening Twentieth century.

And now I have two words, one to capitalists and the **other** to laboring men.

TO CAPITALISTS.

To the capitalists: Be your own executors. Make investments for eternity. Do not be like some capitalists I know, who walk around among their employes with a supercilious air, or drive up to the factory in a manner which seems to indicate they are the autocrats of the universe, with the sun and the moon in their vest pockets, chiefly anxious when they go among laboring men, not to be touched by the greasy or smirched hand, and have their broadcloth injured. Be a christian employer. Remember those who are under their charge are bone of your bone and flesh of your flesh, that Jesus Christ died for them, and that they are immortal. Divide up your estates, or portions of them, for the relief of the world before you leave it. Do not go out of the world like a man who died eight or ten years ago, leaving in his will twenty million dollars, yet giving, how much for the church of God? How much for the alleviation of human sufferings? He gave some money a little while before he died. That was well; but in all this will of twenty million dollars, how much? One million? No. Five hundred thousand? No. One hundred dollars? No. Two cents? No. One cent? No. These great cities groaning in anguish, nations crying out for the bread of everlasting life. A man in a will giving twenty millions of dollars, and not one cent to God! It is a disgrace to our civilization.

TO LABORERS.

To laboring men: I congratulate you on your prospects.

I congratulate you on the fact that you are getting your representatives at Albany, at Harrisburg, and at Washington. This will go on until you have representatives at all the headquarters, and you will have full justice. Mark that I congratulate you also on the opportunities for your children. You children are going to have vast opportunities. I congratulate you that you have to work, and that when you are dead, your children will have to work. I congratulate you also on your opportunities of information. Plato paid one thousand three hundred dollars for two books. Jerome ruined himself, financially, by buying one volume of Origen. What vast opportunities for intelligence for you and your children! A workingman goes along by the show window of some great publishing house and he sees a book that costs five dollars. He says, "I wish I could have that information. I wish I could raise five dollars for that costly and beautiful book." A few months pass on and he gets the value of that book for fifty cents in a pamphlet. There never was such a day for the workingmen of America as the day that is coming.

THE MUTUAL FRIEND AND MEDIATOR.

But the greatest friend of capitalist and toiler, and the one who will yet bring them together in complete accord, was born one Christmas night while the curtains of heavens swung, stirred by the winds angelic. Owner of all things —all the continents, all worlds, and all the islands of light. Capitalist of immensity, crossing over to our condition. Coming into our world, not by gate of palace, but by door of barn. Spending his first night amid the shepherds. Gathering afterward around him the fishermen to be his chief attendants. With adze, and saw, and chisel, and ax, and in a carpenter shop showing himself brother with the tradesmen. Owner of all things, and yet on a hillock back of Jerusalem one day resigning everything for others, keeping not so much as a shekel to pay for his obsequies. By charity buried in the suburbs of a city that had cast him out. Before the cross of such a capitalist, and such a carpenter, all men can afford to shake hands and worship. Here is the every man's Christ. None so high but he was higher. None so poor but he was poorer. At his feet the hostile extremes will yet renounce their animosities, and countenances which have glowered with predjudices and revenge of centuries shall brighten with the smile of heaven as he commands: "Whatsoever ye would that men should do to you, do ye even so to them."

HUMDRUM OF THE CHURCHES.
OR
LUGUBRIOUS CHRISTIANITY.

"Of spices great abundance; neither was there any such spice as the Queen of Sheba gave King Solomon.   II chronicles ix, 9.

What is that building out yonder glittering in the sun? Have you not heard? It is the house of the forest of Lebanon. King Solomon has just taken to it his bride, the princess of Egypt. You see the pillars of the portico, and a great tower, adorned with one thousand shields of gold, hung on the outside of the tower—five hundred of the shields of gold manufactured at Solomon's order, five hundred were captured by David, his father, in battle. See how they blaze in the noonday sun.

Solomon goes up to the ivory stairs of his throne between twelve lions in statuary, and sits down on the back of the golden bull, the head of the bronze beast turned toward the people. The family and attendants of the king are so many that the caterers of the place have to provide every day one hundred sheep and thirteen oxen, besides the birds and the venison. I hear the stamping and pawing of four thousand fine horses in the royal stables. They were important officials who had charge of the work of gathering the straw and the barley for these horses. King Solomon was an early riser, tradition says, and used to take a ride out at daybreak,

SOLOMON.
From the Painting by Doré.

and when in his white apparel, behind the swiftest horses of all the realm, and followed by mounted archers in purple, as the cavalcade dashed through the streets of Jerusalem I suppose it was something worth getting up at five o'clock in the morning to look at.

Solomon was not like some of the kings of the present day—crowned imbecility. All the splendor of his place and retinue was eclipsed by his intellectual power. Why he seemed to know everything. He was the first great naturalist the world ever saw. Peacocks from India strutted the basaltic walk, and apes chattered in the trees and deer stalked the parks, and there were aquariums with foreign fish and aviaries with foreign birds, and tradition says these birds were so well tamed that Solomon might walk clear across the city under the shadow of their wings as they hovered and flitted about him.

SOLOMON AND HIS RIDDLES.

More than this, he had a great reputation for the conundrums and riddles that he made and guessed. He and King Hiram his neighbor, used to sit by the hour and ask riddles, each one paying in money if he could not answer or guess the riddle. The Solomonic navy visited all the world, and the sailors, of course, talked about the wealth of their king, and about the riddles and enigmas that he made and solved, and the news spread until Queen Balkis, away down south, heard of it, and sent messengers with a few riddles that she would like to have Solomon solve, and a few puzzles which she would like to have him find out. She sent among other things to King Solomon a diamond with a hole so small that a needle would not penetrate it, asking him to thread that diamond. Solomon took a worm and put it at the opening in the diamond, and the worm crawled through, leaving the thread in the diamond.

The queen also sent a goblet to Solomon, asking him to fill it with water that did not pour from the sky, and that did not rush out from the earth, and immediately Solomon put a slave on the back of a swift horse and galloped him around and around the park until the horse was nigh exhausted, and from the perspiration of the horse the goblet was filled. She also sent King Solomon five hundred boys in girls' dress, and five hundred girls in boys' dress, wondering if he would be acute enough to find out the deception. Immediately Solomon, when he saw them wash their faces, knew from the way they applied the water it was all a cheat.

THE VISIT OF THE QUEEN.

Queen Balkis was so pleased with the acuteness of Solomon that she said, "I'll just go and see him for myself." Yonder it comes—the cavalcade—horses and dromedaries, chariots and charioteers, jingling harness and clattering hoofs, and blazing shields, and flying ensigns, and clapping cymbals. The place is saturated with perfumes She brings cinnamon and saffron and calamus and frankincense and all manner of sweet spices. As the retinue sweeps through the gate the armed guard inhale the aroma. "Halt!" cry the charioteers, as the wheels grind the gravel in front of the pillard portico of the king. Queen Balkis alights in an atmosphere bewitching with perfume. As the dromedaries are driven up to the king's storehouses, and the bundles of camphor

are unloaded, and the sacks of cinnamon, and the boxes
of spices are opened, the purveyors of the place
discover what my text announces, "Of spices, great
abundance; neither was there any such spices as the
Queen of Sheba gave to King Solomon."

Well, my friends, you know that all theologians agree
in making Solomon a type of Christ, and making the
Queen of Sheba a type of every truth seeker, and I
shall take the responsibility of saying that all the
spikenard and cassia and frankincense which the Queen
of Sheba brought to King Solomon are mightily suggestive of the sweet spice of our holy religion. Christianity
is not a collections of sharp technicalities and angular
facts and chronological tables and dry statistics. Our
religion is compared to frankincense and to cassia, but
never to nightshade. It is a bundle of myrrh. It is a
dash of holy light. It is an opening of opaline gates.
It is a collection of spices. Would to God that we
were as wise in taking spices to our Divine King as
Queen Balkis was wise in taking the spices to the earthly
Solomon! What many of us most need is to have the
humdrum driven out of our life and the humdrum out of
our religion. The American and English and Scottish
church will die of humdrum unless there be a change.

PEOPLE DO NOT GO TO CHURCH BECAUSE THEY CANNOT
STAND THE HUMDRUM.

An editor from San Francisco a few weeks ago wrote
me saying he was getting up for his paper a symposium
from many clergymen, discussing among other things
"Why do not people go to church?" and he wanted my
opinion, and I gave it in one sentence, "People do not

go to church because they cannot stand the humdrum.' The fact is that most people have so much humdrum in their wordly calling that they do not want to have added the humdrum of religion. We need in all our sermons the exhortations and songs and prayers more of what Queen Balkis brought to Solomon—namely, more spice.

The fact is that the duties and cares of this life, coming to us from time to time, are stupid often and insane and intolerable. Here are men who have been bartering and negotiating, climbing, pounding, hammering for twenty years, forty years, fifty years. One great long drudgery has their life been. Their faces, anxious, their feelings benumbed, their days monotonous. What is necessary to brighten up that man's life, and to sweeten that acid disposition, and to put sparkle into the man's spirits? The spicery of our holy religion. Why, if between the loss of life there dashed a gleam of an eternal gain; if between the betrayals of life there came the the gleam of the undying friendship of Christ; if in dull times in business we found ministering spirits flying to and fro in our office and store and shop, everyday life, instead of being a stupid monotone, would be a glorious inspiration, penduluming between calm satisfaction and high rapture.

HOW TO KEEP HOUSE PROPERLY.

How any woman keeps house without the religion of Christ to help her is a mystery to me. To have to spend the greater part of one's life, as many women do, in planning for the meals, in stitching garments that will soon be rent again, and deploring breakages, and supervising tardy subordinates, and driving off dust that

soon again will settle, and doing the same thing day
in and day out, and year in and year out, until their
hair silvers‘ and the back stoops, and the spectacles
crawl to the eyes, and the grave breaks open nnder the
thin sole of the shoe—oh, it is a long monotony! But
when Christ comes to the drawing room, and comes to
the kitchen, and comes to the nursery, and comes to the
dwelling, then how cheery becomes all woman's duties.
She is never alone now; Martha gets through fretting,
and joins Mary at the feet of Jesus.

All day long Deborah is happy because she can help
Lapidoth; Hannah, because she can make a coat for
young Samuel; Miriam, because she can watch her infant brother; Rachel, because she can help her father
water the stock; the widow of Sarepta, because the cruse
of oil is being replenished. O woman! having in your
pantry a nest of boxes containing all kinds of condiment,
why have you not tried in your heart and life the spicery
of our holy religion? ''Martha! Martha!' thou are careful and troubled about many things; but one thing is
needful, and Mary hath chosen that good part which
shall not be taken away from her.

LUGUBRIOUS CHRISTIANITY, MORE HARMFUL THAN ALL THE BOOKS OF INFIDELITY.

I must confess that a great deal of religion of this day
is utterly insipid. There is nothing piquant or elevating
about it. Men and women go around humming psalms
in a minor key, and culturing melancholy, and their
worship has in it more sighs than rapture. We do not
doubt their piety. Oh, no. But they are sitting at a
feast where the cook has forgotten to season the food.

Everything is flat in their experience and in their conversation. Emancipated from sin and death and hell, and on their way to a magnificent heaven, they act as though they were' trudging on toward an everlasting Botany bay. Religion does not seem to agree with them. It seems to catch in the windpipe, and becomes a tight strangulation, instead of an exhilaration.

All the infidel books that have been written, from Voltaire down to Herbert Spencer, have not done so much damage to our Christianity as lugubrious Christians. Who wants a religion woven out of the shadows of the night? Why go growling on your way to celestial enthronement? Come out of that cave and sit down in the warm light of the Sun of Righteousness. Away with your odes to melancholy and Hervey's "Meditations Among the Tombs." ·

> Then let our songs abound,
> And every tear be dry;
> We're marching through Emmanuel's ground
> To fairer world's on high.

MORE SPICE YE CHRISTIAN TEACHERS!

I have to say, also, that we need to put more spice and enlivenment in our religious teaching, whether it be in the prayer meeting, or in the Sabbath school, or in the church. We ministers need more fresh air and sunshine in our lungs and our heart and our head. Do you wonder that the world is so far from being converted when you find so little vivacity in the pulpit and in the pew? We want, like the Lord, to plant in our sermons, and exhortations, more lilies of the field. We want fewer rhetorical elaborations, and fewer sesquipedalian words, and when we talk about shadows, we do not want to say adumbrations; and when we mean queerness, we do not want to talk about idiosyncracies; or if a stitch in the back, we do not want to talk of lumbago, but in the plain vernacular, preach that gospel which proposes to make all men happy, honest, victorious, and free.

In other words, we want more cinnamon and less gristle. Let this be so in all the different departments of work to which the Lord calls us. Let us be plain. Let us be earnest. Let us be common sensical. When we talk to people in a vernacular they can understand they will be very glad to come and receive the truth we represent. Would to God that Queen Balkis would drive her spice laden dromedaries into all our sermons, and prayer meeting exhortations.

MORE SPICE YE CHRISTIAN WORKERS!

More than that, we want more life and spice in our Christian work. The poor do not want so much to be groaned over as sung to. With the bread and medicines and the garments you give them, let there be an accompaniment of smiles and brisk encouragement. Do not stand and talk to them about the wretchedness of their abode, and the hunger of their looks, and the hardness of their lot. Ah! they know it better than you can tell them. Show them the bright side of the thing, if there be any bright side. Tell them good times will come. Tell them that for the children of God there is immortal rescue. Wake them up out of their stolidity by an inspiring laugh, and while you send in help, like the Queen of Sheba also send in the spices.

There are two ways of meeting the poor.　One way is to come into their house with a nose elevated in disgust, as much as to say:

'I don't see how you live here in this neighborhood. It actually makes me sick.　There is that bundle; take it, you poor, miserable wretch, and make the most of it." Another way is to go into the abode of the poor in a manner which seems to say:

"The blessed Lord sent me.　He was poor Himself. It is not more for the good I am going to try to do you than it is for the good you can do me."　Coming in that spirit the gift will be as aromatic as the spikenard on the feet of Christ, and all the hovels in that alley will be fragrant with spice.

MORE SPICE YE CHRISTIAN SINGERS.

We need more spice and enlivenment in our church music.　Churches sit discussing whether they shall have choirs, or precentors, or organs, or bass viols, or cornets. I say, take that which will bring out the most inspiring music.　If we had half as much zeal and spirit in our churches as we have in the songs of our Sabbath schools it would not be long before the whole earth would quake with the coming of God.　Why in most churches nine-tenths of the people do not sing, or they sing so feebly the people at their elbows do not know they are singing. People mouth and mumble the praises of God; but there is not more than one out of a hundred who makes "a joyful noise" unto the Rock of our salvation.　Some-times, when the congregation forgets itself, and is all absorbed in the goodness of God or the glories of heaven,

I get an intimation of what church music will be a hundred years from now, when the coming generation shall wake up to its duty.

WAKE UP.

I promise a high spiritual blessing to any one who will sing in church, and who will sing so heartly that the people all round can not help but sing. Wake up! all the churches from Bangor to San Fransisco and across Christendom. It is not a matter of preference, it is a matter of religious duty. Oh, for fifty times more volume of sounds. German chorals in German cathedrals surpass us, and yet Germany has received nothing at the hands of God compared with America; and ought the acclaim in Berlin be louder than that in Brooklyn? Soft long drawn out music is appropriate for the drawing room and appropriate for the concert, but St John gives an idea of the sonorous and resonant congregational singing appropriate for churches when, in listening to the temple service of heaven, he says: "I heard a great voice, as the voice of a great multitude, and as the voice of many waters, and as the voice of many thunderings: Hallelujah, for the Lord God omnipotent reigneth."

Join with me in a crusade, giving me not only your hearts but the mighty up lifting of our voices, and I believe we can, through Christ's grace, sing fifty thousand souls into the kingdom of Christ. An argument, they can laugh at, a sermon, they can talk down, but a vast audience joining in one anthem is irresistible. Would that Queen Balkis would drive all her spice laden dromedaries into our church music. "Neither was there any such spice as the Queen of Sheba gave King Solomon."

TRUE RELIGION IS ALL THE SWEET SPICES TOGETHER.

Now, I want to impress this audience with the fact that religion is sweetness and perfume and spinkenard and saffron and cinnamon and cassia and frankincense, and all sweet spices together. "Oh," you say, "I have not looked at it as such. I thought it was a nuisance; it had for me a repulsion; I held my breath as though it were malodor; I have been appalled at its advance; I have said, if I have any religion at all, I want to have just as little of it as is possible to get through with." Oh what a mistake you have made, my brother. The religion of Christ is a present and everlasting redolence. It counteracts all trouble. Just put it on the stand beside the pillow of sickness. It catches in the curtains and perfumes the stifling air. It sweetens the cup of bitter medicine, and throws a glow on the gloom of the turned lattice. It is a balm for the aching side, and a soft bandage for the temple stung with pain.

It lifted Samuel Rutherford into a revelry of spiritual delight while he was in physical agonies. It helped Richard Baxter until, in the midst of such a complication of diseases as perhaps no other man ever suffered, he wrote "The Saint's Everlasting Rest." And it poured light upon John Bunyan's dungeon—the light of the shining gate of the shining city. And it is good for rheumatism, and for neuralgia, and for low spirits, and for consumption; it is the catholicon for all disorders. Yes, it will heal all your sorrows.

Why did you look so sad to-day when you came in?

Alas! for the loneliness and the heartbreak, and the load that is never lifted from your soul.   Some of you go about feeling like Macaulay when he wrote, "If I had another month of such days as I have been spending, I would be impatient to get down into my little narrow crib in the ground like a weary factory child." And there have been times in your life when you wished you could get out of this life.   You have said, "Oh, how sweet to my lips would be the dust of the valley," and wished you could pull over you in your last slumber, the coverlet of green grass and daisies.   You have said, "Oh how beautifully quiet it must be in the tomb.   I wish I was there." I see all around about me widowhood and orphanage and childlessness; sadness, disapointment, perplexity. If I could ask all those to rise in this audience who have felt no sorrow, and been buffeted by no disapointment— if I could ask all such to rise, how many would rise? Not one.

A widowed mother with her little child went west, hoping to get better wages there, and she was taken sick and died.   The overseer of the poor got her body and put it in a box, and put it in a wagon, and started down the street toward the cemetery at full trot.   The little child—the only child—ran after it through the streets barcheaded crying, "Bring me back my mother! bring me back my mother!" And it is said that as the people looked on and saw her crying after that which lay in the box in the wagon—all she loved on earth—it is said the whole village was in tears.   And that is what a great many of you are doing—chasing the dead.   Dear Lord, is there no appeasement for all this sorrow that I see about me? Yes, the thought of resurrection, and re-union, far beyond this scene of struggle and tears. "They shall hunger no more, neither thirst any more, neither shall the sun light on them, nor any heat; for the Lamb which is in the midst of the throne shall lead them to living fountains of water, and God shall wipe away all tears from their eyes."

A SHOWER OF SPICES AND A STORY.

Across the couches of your sick, and across the graves of your dead I fling this shower of sweet spices. Queen Balkis, driving up to the pillared portico of the house of cedar, carried on such pungency of perfume as exhales to-day from the Lord's garden. It is peace. It is sweet-ness. It is comfort. It is infinite satisfaction, this Gospel I commend to you. Some one could not under-stand why an old German Christian scholar used to be always so calm, and happy and hopeful, when he had so many trials, and sickness and ailments. A man secreted himself in the house. He said, "I mean to watch this old scholar and christian;" and he saw the old Christian man go to his room and sit down on the chair beside the stand and open the Bible and begin to read. He reads on, and on, chapter after chapter, hour after hour, until his face was all aglow with tidings from heaven, and when the clock struck twelve, he arose and shut his Bible, and said: "Blessed Lord, we are on the same old terms yet. Good night. Good night."

Oh, you sin parched and trouble pounded, here is comfort, here is satisfaction. Will you come and get it? I cannot tell you what the Lord offers you hereafter, so well as I can tell you now. "It doth not yet appear what we shall be.

Have you heard of the Taj Mahal in India, in some respects the most majestic building on earth? Twenty thousand men were twenty years building it. It cost abont sixteen millions of dollars. The walls are of marble, inlaid with carnelian from Bagdad, and turquois from Thibet, and jasper from the Punjaub, and amethyst from Persia, and all manner of precious stones. A traveler says, that it seems to him like the shining of an enchanted castle of burnished silver. The walls are two hundred and forty-five feet high, and from the top of these springs a dome thirty more feet high, that dome containing the most wonderful echo the world has ever known, so that ever and anon travelers, standing below with flutes, and drums and harps, are testing that echo, and the sounds from below strike up, and then come down, as it were, the voices of angels all around about the building. There is around it a garden of tamarind, and banyan, and palm, and all the floral glories of the ransacked earth.

But that is only a tomb of a dead empress, and it is tame compared with the grandeurs which God has builded for your living and immortal spirit. Oh, home of the blessed! Foundations of gold! Arches of victory! Capstones of praise! And a dome in which there are echoing and re-echoing, the hallelujahs of the ages. And around about that mansion is a garden—the garden of God—and all the springing fountains are the bottled tears of the church in the wilderness, and all the crim. son of flowers is the deep hue that was caught up from the carnage of earthly martyrdoms, and the fragrance is the prayers of all the saints, and the aroma puts into utter forgetfulness the cassia and the spikenard, and the frankincense, and the world renowned spices which the Queen Balkis, of Abyssinia, flung at the feet of King Solomon.

When shall these eyes thy heaven built walls.
And pearly gates behold,
Thy bulwarks, with salvation strong,
And streets of shining gold?

Through obduracy on our part, and through the rejection of that Christ who makes heaven possible, I wonder if any of us will miss that spectacle? I fear! I fear! The queen of the south will rise up in judgment against this generation and condemn it, because she came from the uttermost parts of the earth to hear the wisdom of Solomon, and behold a greater than Solomon is here! May God grant that through your own practical experience you may find that religion's ways are ways of pleasantness, and that all her paths, are paths of peace—that it is perfume now and perfume forever. "And there was an abundance of spice; neither was there any such spice as the Queen of Sheba gave to King Solomon."

PAUL AND BARNABAS AT ANTIOCH.

TOO MUCH THEORY, NOT ENOUGH GOOD WORKS IN CHURCHES.

"Faith without works, is dead." James 11, 26.

The Romam Catholic church has been charged with putting too much stress upon good works, and not enough upon faith. I charge Protestantism with putting not enough stress upon good works as connected with salvation. Good works will never save a man, but if a man have not good works he has no real faith and no genuine religion. There are those who depend upon the fact that they are all right inside, while their conduct is right outside. Their religion, for the part, is made up of talk—vigorous talk; fluent talk, boastful talk, perpetual talk. They will entertain you by the hour in telling you how good they are. They come up to such a higher life that we have no patience with ordinary Christians in the plain discharge of their duty. As near as I can tell, this ocean craft is mostly sail, and very little tonnage. Foretopmast staysail, foretopmast studding sail, maintopmast, mizzentop sail—everything from flying jib to mizzen spanker, but making no useful voyage. Now the world has got tired of this, and it wants a religion that will work into all the circum_ stances of life. We do not want a new religion, but the old religion in all possible directions.

Yonder is a river with steep and rocky banks, and it roars like a young Niagara, as it rolls on over its rough bed. It does nothing but talk about itself all the way

[159]

from its source in the mountain to the place where it empties into the sea. The banks are so steep the cattle cannot come down to drink. It does not run one fertilizing rill into the adjoining field. It has not one grist mill or factory on either side. It sulks in rainy weather with chilly fogs. No one cares when that river is born among the rocks, and no one cares when it dies into the sea. But yonder is another river, and it mosses its banks with the warm tides, and it rocks with floral lullaby the water lillies asleep on its bosom. It invites herds of cattle, and flocks of sheep, and coveys of birds to come there and drink. It has three grist mills on one side and six cotton factories on the other. It is the wealth of two hundred miles of luxuriant farms. The birds of heaven chanted when it was born in the mountains, and the ocean shipping will press in from the sea to hail it as it comes down to the Atlantic coast. The one river is a man who lives for himself, the other river is a man who lives for others.

HOW JERUSALEM IS SAID TO HAVE GOT ITS SITE.

Do you know how the site of the ancient city of Jerusalem was chosen? There were two brothers who had adjoining farms. The one brother had a large family, the other had no family. The brother with a large family said: ''There is my brother with no family; he must be lonely, and I will try to cheer him up, and I will take some of the sheaves from my field in the night time and set them over on his farm and say nothing about it.''

The other brother said, ''My brother has a large family, and it is very difficult for him to support them, and I will help him along, and I will take some of the sheaves from my own farm in the night time and set them over on his farm and say nothing about it."

So the work of transference went on night after night, and night after night, but every morning things seemed to be just as they were, for though sheaves had been subtracted from each farm, sheaves had also been added, and the brothers were perplexed, and could not understand. But one night the brothers happened to meet while making this generous transference, and the spot where they met was so sacred that it was chosen as the site of the city of Jerusalem. If that tradition should prove un-founded, it will nevertheless stand as a beautiful allegory setting forth the idea that wherever a kindly, and generous, and loving act is performed, that is the spot fit for some temple of commemoration.

GOOD WORKS WILL KILL BUSINESS FRAUD.

I have often spoken to you about faith, but now I speak to you about works, for "faith without works is dead." I think you will agree with me in the statement that the great want of the world is more practical religion. We want practical religion to go into all merchandise. It will supervise the labeling of goods. It will not allow a man to say a thing was made in one factory, when it was made in another. It will not allow the merchant to say that watch was manufactured in Geneva, Switzerland, when it was manufactured in Massachusetts. It will not allow the merchant to say that wine came from Madeira, when it came from California. Practical religion will walk along by the store shelves, and tear off all the tags that make misrepresentation. It will not allow the merchant to say that is pure coffee, when da-

delion root, and chicory, and other ingredients go into
it.   It will not allow him to say that is pure sugar, when
there are in it sand and ground glass.

PRACTICAL RELIGION WILL SET THINGS ALL RIGHT IN THE
GROCERY STORE.

When practical religion gets its full swing in the
world it will go down the streets, and it will come to
that shoe store, and rip off the fictitious soles of many a
fine-looking pair of shoes, or show that it is pasteboard,
sandwiched between the sound leather.   And this practical religion will go right into a grocery store, aud it will
pull out the plug of all the adulterated sirups, and it will
dump into the ash barrel in front of the store the cassia
bark that is sold for cinnamon, and the brick dust that
is sold for cayenne pepper, and it will shake out the
Prussian blues from the tea leaves, and it will sift from
the flour plaster of Paris, and bone dust, and soapstone,
and it will by chemical analysis separate the one quart of
Ridgewood water from the few honest drops of cow's
milk, and it will throw out the live animalcules from the
brown sugar.

STARTLING FACTS ABOUT ADULTERATIONS IN FOOD AND
DRUGS.

There has been so much adulteration of articles of
food that it is an amazement to me that there is a healthy
man or woman in America.   Heaven only knows what
they put into the spices, and into the sugars, and into
the butter, and into the apothecary drugs.   But chemical analysis, and the microscope have made wonderful
revelations.   The board of health in Massachusettes
analyzed a great amount of what was called pure coffee,

and they found in it not one particle of coffee. In England there is a law that forbids the putting of alum in bread. The public authorities examined fifty-one packages of bread, and found them all guilty. The honest physician, writing a prescription, does not know but that it may bring death, instead of health, to his patient because there may be one of the drugs weakened by a cheaper article, and another drug may be in full force, and so the prescription may have just the opposite effect intended. Oil of wormwood, warranted pure, from Boston, was found to have 41 per cent of resin and alcohol and chloroform. Scammony is one of the most valuable medical drugs. It is very rare, very precious. It is the sap or the gum of a tree, or a bush, in Syria. The root of the tree is exposed, an incision is made into the root, and then shells are placed at this incision to catch the sap or the gum as it exudes.

It is very precious, this scammony. But the peasant mixes it with cheaper material; then it is taken to Aleppo, and the merchant there mixes it with a cheaper material; then it comes on to the wholesale druggist in London or New York, and he mixes it with a cheaper material; then it comes to the retail druggist, and he mixes it with a cheaper material, and by the time the poor sick man gets it into his bottle, it is ashes, and chalk, and sand, and some of what has been called pure scammony, after analysis, has been found to be no scammony at all.

PRACTICAL RELIGION WILL SETTLE "CORNERS."

Now, practical religion will yet rectify all this. It will go to those hypocritical professors of religion who got a "corner" in corn and wheat in Chicago, and New York, sending prices up, and up, until they were beyond the reach of the poor, keeping these breadstuffs in their own hands, or controlling them until, the prices going up, and up and up, they were after a while ready to sell, and they sold out, making themselves millionaires in one or two years—trying to fix the matter up with the Lord by building a church, or a university, or a hospital—deluding themselves with the idea, that the Lord would be so pleased with the gift, He would forget the swindle.

Now, as such a man may have no liturgy in which to say his prayers, I will compose for him one, which he practically is making.

THE SWINDLER'S PRAYER.

"O Lord, we, by getting a 'corner' in breadstuffs, swindled the people of the United States out of ten million dollars, and made suffering all up and down the land, and we would like to compromise this matter with Thee. Thou knowest it was a scaly job, but then it was smart. Now, here we compromise it. Take one per cent of the profits, and with that one per cent you can build an asylum for these poor miserable ragamuffins of the street, and I will take a yacht and g ￢ Europe, for ever and ever, amen!"

Ah, my friends, if a man hath gotten his estate wrongfully, and he build a line of hospitals and universities from here to Alaska, he cannot atone for it. After a while the man who has been getting a "corner" in wheat dies, and then Satan gets a "corner" on him. He goes into a great, long Black Friday. There is a "break" in the market. According to Wall street parlance, he wiped others out, and now he is himself wiped out. No collaterals on which to make a spiritual loan. Eternal defalcation!

PRACTICAL RELIGION WILL ALSO RECTIFY TOIL.

But this practical religion will not only rectify all merchandise, it will also rectify all mechanism and all toil. A time will come when a man will work as faithfully by the job as he does by the day. You say when a thing is slightingly done, "Oh, that was done by the job!" You can tell by the swiftness or slowness with which a hackman drives whether he is hired by the hour or by the excursion. If he is hired by the excursion he whips up the horses, so as to get around and get another customer. All styles of work have to be inspected. Ships inspected, horses inspected, machinery inspected. Boss to watch the journeymen. Capitalist coming down unexpectdly to watch the boss. Conductor of a city car sounding the punch bell to prove his honesty as a passenger hands him a clipped nickle. All things must be watched and inspected. Imperfections in the wood covered with putty. Garments waranted to last until you put them on the third time. Shoddy in all kinds of clothing. Chromos. Pinchbeck. Diamonds for a dollar and a half. Bookbinding that holds on until you read the third chapter. Spavined horses by skillful dose of jockeys for several days made to look spry. Wagon tires poorly put on. Horses poorly shod. Plastering that cracks wlthout any provocation and falls off. Plumbing that needs to be plumbed. Imperfect car wheel that halts the whole train with a hot box. So little practical religion in the mechanism of the world. I tell you, my friends, the law of man will never rectify these things.

It will be the all pervading influence of the practical religion of Jesus Christ that will make the change for the better.

PRACTICAL RELIGION WILL RECTIFY THE FARMERS WORK.

Yes, this practical religion will also go into agricul ture, which is proverbially honest, but needs to be rectified, and it will keep the farmer from sending to the New York market, veal that is too young too kill, and, when the farmer farms on shares, it will keep the man who does the work from making his half, three-fourths, and it will keep the farmer from building his post and rail fence on his neighbor's premises, and it will make him shelter his cattle in the winter storm, and it will keep the old elder from working on Sunday afternoon in the new ground where nobody sees him. And this practical religion will hover over the house, and over the barn, and over the field, and over the orchard.

AND ALSO HELP THE LAWYER AND PHYSICIAN.

Yes, and this practical religion of which I speak will come into the learned professions. The lawyer will feel his responsibility in defending innocence, and arraigning evil, and expounding the law, and it will keep him from charging for briefs he never wrote, and for pleas he never made, and for percentages he never earned, and from robbing widow and orphan because they are defenseless. Yes, this practical religion will come into the physicians life, and he will feel his responsibility as the conservator of the public health, a profession honored by the fact that Christ himself was a physician. And it will make him honest, and when he does not understand a case he will say so, not trying to cover up lack of diagnosis with ponderous technicalities, or send the patient to a reckless drug store because the apothecary happens to pay a percentage on the prescriptions sent.

AND HELP THE SCHOOL TEACHER.

And this practical religion will come to the school teacher, making her feel her responsibility in preparing our youth for usefulness, and for happiness, and for honor, and will keep her from giving a sly box to a dull head, chastising him for what he cannot help, and sending discouragement all through the after years of a lifetime.

This practical religion will also come to the newspaper men, and it will help them in the gathering of the news, and it will help them in setting forth the best interests of society, and it will keep them from putting the sins of the world in larger type than its virtues, and its mistakes than its achievements.

AND SOCIETY.

Yes, this religion, this practical religion, will come and put its hand on what is called good society, elevated society, successful society, so that people will have their expenditures within their income, and they will exchange the hypocritical "not at home" for the honest explanation "too tired" or "too busy to see you," and will keep innocent reception from becoming intoxicating conviviality.

Yes there is a great opportunity for missionary work in what are called the successful classes of society. It is no rare thing now to see a fashionable woman intoxicated in the street, or the rail car, or the restaurant. The number of fine ladies who drink too much is increasing. Perhaps you may find her at the reception in most exalted company, but she has made too many visits to the wine room, and now her eye is glassy, and after a while, her cheek is unnaturally flushed, and then she falls into fits of excruciating laughter about nothing, and then she offers sickening flatteries, telling some homely man how well he looks, and then she is helped into the carriage, and by the time the carriage gets to her home, it takes the husband and the coachman to get her up the stairs. The report is, she was taken suddenly ill at a german. Ah! no. She took too much champagne and mixed liquors, and got drunk. Th t was all.

SOME MEMBERS OF CHURCHES HAVE TOO MANY WIVES, AND
SOME WIVES TOO MANY HUSBANDS.

Yes, this practical religion will have to come in and fix up the marriage relation in America. There are members of churches who have too many wives and too many husbands. Society needs to be expurgated and washed and fumigated and Christianized. We have missionary societies to reform Elm street, in New York, Bedford street, Philadelphia, and Shoreditch, London, and the Brooklyn docks; but there is need of an organization to reform much that is going on in Beacon street and Madison square, and Rittenhouse square and West End and Brooklyn Heights and Brooklyn Hill. We want this practical religion not only to take hold of what are called the lower classes, but to take hold of what are called the higher classes. The trouble is that people have an idea that they can do all their religion on Sunday with hymn book, and prayer book, and liturgy, and some of them sit in church rolling up their eyes as though they were ready for translation, when their Sabbath is bounded on all sides by an inconsistent life, and while you are expecting to come out from under their arms, the wings of an angel, there come out from their foreheads the horns of a beast.

THERE MUST BE A NEW DEPARTURE IN RELIGION.

There has got to be a new departure in religion. I do not say a new religion. Oh, no; but the old religion brought to new appliances. In our times we have had the daguerreotype, and the ambrotype, and the photograph, but it is thes ame old sun, and their arts are only new appliances of the old sunlight! So this glorious gospel is just what we want to photograph the image of God on one soul, and daguerreotype it on another soul. Not a new gospel, but the old gospel put to new work. In our time we have had the telegraphic invention, and the electric light invention, but they are all the children of old electricity, an element that the philosophers have a long while known much about. So this electric gospel needs to flash its light on the eyes, and ears, and souls of men, and become a telephonic medium to make the deaf hear; a telephonic medium to dart invitation and warning to all nations; an electric light to illumine the eastern and western hemispheres. Not a new gospel, but the old gospel doing a new work.

SPECIMENS OF MODEL DOCTORS.

Now you say, "That is a very beautiful theory, but-is it possible to take one's religion into all the avocations and business of life?" Yes, and I will give you a few specimens. Medical doctors who took their religion into every day life: Dr. John Abercrombie, of Aberdeen, the greatest Scottish physician of his day, his book on

"Diseases of the Brain, and Spinal Cord" no more wonderful than his book on "The Philosophy of the Moral
Feelings," and often kneeling at the bedside of his
patient to commend them to God in prayer.   Dr. John
Brown, of Edinburgh, immortal as an author, dying under
the benediction of the sick of Edinburgh, myself remem-
bering him as he sat in his study, in Edinburgh talking to
me about Christ and his hope of heaven.   And scores of
Christian family physicians in Brooklyn just as good as
they were.

MODEL LAWYERS.

Lawyers who carried their religion into their profession: The late Lord Cairns, the queen's adviser for
many years, the highest legal authority in Great Britain
—Lord Cairns, every summer in his vacation, preaching
as an evangelist among the poor of his country.   John
McLean, judge of the Supreme Court of the United
States and president of the American Sunday School
union, feeling more satisfaction in the latter office than
in the former.   And scores of Christian lawyers as eminent in the Church of God as they are eminent at the
bar.

MODEL MERCHANTS.

Merchants who took their religion into everyday life:
Arthur Tappan, derided in his day, because he established that system by which we come to find out the commercial standing of business men, starting that entire
system derided for it then, himself, as I knew him well,
in moral character, A1.   Monday mornings inviting to a
room in the top of his store-house the clerks of his establishment, asking them about their worldly interests and

their spiritual interests, then giving out a hymn, leading in prayer, giving them a few words of good advice, asking them what church they attended on the Sabbath, what the text was, whether they had any especial troubles of their own. Arthur Tappan; I never heard his eulogy pronounced. I pronounce it now. And other merchants just as good. William E. Dodge in the iron business; Moses H. Grinnell in the shipping business; Peter Cooper in the glue business. Scores of men just as good as they were.

MODEL FARMERS.

Farmers who take their religion into their occupation: Why, this minute their horses and wagons stand around all the meeting houses in America. They began this day by a prayer to God, and when they get home at noon, after they have put their horses up, will offer prayer to God at the table, seeking a blessing, and this summer there will be in their fields not one dishonest head of rye, not one dishonest ear of corn, not one dishonest apple. Worshiping God to-day away up among the Berkshire hills, or away down amid the lagoons of Florida, or away out amid the mines of Colorado, or along the banks of the Passaic and the Raritan, where I knew them better, because I went to school with them.

MODEL MECHANICS.

Mechanics who took their religion into their occupation: James Brindley, the famous millright; Nathaniel Bowditch, the famous ship chandler; Elihu Burritt, the famous blacksmith, and hundreds and thousands of strong arms which have made the hammer, and the saw, and the adze, and the drill, and the ax sound in the grand march of our national industries

Give your heart to God and then fill your life with good works. Consecrate to him your store, your shop, your banking house, your factory and your home. They say no one will hear it. God will hear it. That is enough. You hardly know of any one else than Wellington as connected with the victory of Waterloo; but he did not do the hard fighting. The hard fighting was done by the Somerset cavalry, and the Ryland regiments, and Kempt's infantry, and the Scots Grays and the Life Guards. Who cares if only the day was won!

A BEAUTIFUL EXAMPLE OF A YOUNG CHRISTIAN WIFE.

In the latter part of last century a girl in England became a kitchen maid in a farm house. She had many styles of work, and much hard work. Time rolled on, and she married the son of a weaver of Halifax. They were industrious; they saved money enough after a while to build them a home. On the morning of the day when they were to enter that home the young wife arose at four o'clock, entered the front door yard, knelt down, consecrated the place to God, and there made this solemn vow: "O Lord, if thou wilt bless me in this place, the poor shall have a share of it." Time rolled on and a fortune rolled in. Children grew up around them, and they all became affluent; one, a member of parliament, in a public place declared that his success came from that prayer of his mother in the door yard. All of them were affluent. Four thousand hands in their factories. They built dwelling houses for laborers at cheap rents, and when they were invalid, and could not pay, they had the houses for nothing.

One of these sons came to this country, admired our parks, went back, bought land and opened a great public park, and made it a present to the city of Halifax, England. They endowed an orphanage, they endowed two almhouses. All England has heard of the generosity and good works of the Crossleys. Moral—Consecrate to God your small means and humble surroundings, and you will have larger means and grander surroundings. "Godliness is profitable to all things, having promise of the life that now is and of that which is to come." Have faith in God by all means, but remember that faith without works is dead."

THE DEFRAUDER, LIBERTINE, AND ASSASSIN.

"He shall be buried with the burial of an ass." Jeremiah, xxii., 19.

ehoiakim sat for ten years on a throne. Plenty of gold—plenty of sycophants—plenty of chariots. When he rode, I think he rode with four horses; and when he wore diamonds, I think he wore them as big as a walnut. If there had been a railroad so early in the history of the world, he would have stolen it. He wallowed in sin until a sudden change in public affairs, and then he died in shame, and was kicked out of public contempt: Buried with the burial of an ass."

After a life of private or public iniquity, a man's death is not deplored. The obsequies may be pretentious—there may be flags, and wreaths, and catafalques, and military processions; but the world feels that a nuisance has been abated; he is cast forth by reason of the scorn and contempt of men; and figuratively, if not literally, he is "buried with the burial of an ass."

Urged by recent events, I address young men to-night upon the romance of crime, and I want to show them that, though crime may be gilded and fascinating, the end is ruin here, and damnation hereafter.

THE ROMANCE OF FRAUD.

First, There is the romance of fraud. The heroes of this country are fast getting to be those who have most skill in swallowing "trust-funds;" banks, stocks, and moneyed institutions. Our young men are dazzled by the quick success, and say, "That is the way to do it.

ABUSED.

He was a country peddler a few years ago, now see what
a gorgeous turn-out!"   Theft on Wall Street is measured
by a different standárd from that which takes its spoils
through Rat Alley.   He who steals a vest from a second-
hand clothing-store gets a ride in the city van without
the opportunity of looking out of the window, but he who
swallows a moneyed institution astonishes Central Park
with his equipage.

By a kind of irresistible instruction, our young men
learn that the poorest way to get money is to earn. it.
"What!" says the young man of flaunting cravat to the
young man of humble apparel, "you only get eight hundred dollars a year! Why, that would hardly keep me
in pin money! I spend five thousand dollars a year.'
"Where do you get it?"   "Oh, stocks, enterprises, and
all that kind of thing, you know."   The plain young
man has hard work to pay his board-bill; has to wear a
coat after it is out of fashion; denies himself all luxuries.
After a while he gets tired, and goes to flaunting cravat,
and says, "Tell us how you get into these enterprises."
The plain young man soon learns.   Although he has
quitted the store or shop where he used to work, and
seems to be mostly idle, yet he soon dresses better, trades
off his old silver watch for a gold one with a splendid
chain, sets his hat a little farther over on one side of his
head, and smokes better cigars, and more of them.   He
has his hand in.   And if for three or four years he can
escape the penitentiary, he is not far off from being introduced to the Tweed and the Carnochans, or has something to do with the docks, or harbors, or pavements, or
the inspection of the public buildings.   And after he has

got as far as that, he is safe—for perdition. A man has
to travel some distance up before he gets into the romance of crime. The man who is caught and incarcerated is in the prosaic period. If the sheriffs and con-
stable, have given him a chance to learn the business,
he would have stolen as well as anybody. If he could
not have stolen a railroad, he could, at least, have mas-
tered a load of pig-iron.

I thank God when fortunes thus gathered go to smash.
They are plague-struck, and blast a nation. I like to
have them go to pieces in such a wreck that they can
never again be gathered up. I like to have them made
loathsome and an insufferable stench, so that honest
young men may take warning.

If God should put suddenly into money, or its repre-
sentative, the power to return to its rightful owner, there
is not a bank or safety deposit that would not have its
sides blown out; and parchments would rip, and gold
would shoot, and mortgages would rend, and beggars
would get horses, and stock-gamblers would go to the
alm-house. How much dishonesty in the making of in-
voices, and in oaths at the Custom House, and in plastering of labels, and in the filching of customers of rival
houses, and in false samples, and in the making 'and
breaking of contracts! Hundreds of young men are being indoctrinated in the idea that money must be had
quickly, and that the larger the scale on which they take
it, the more admirable the smartness and legerdemain.

A young man of New York stood behind the counter
selling silks to a lady. After the sale had been made, he
said to the customer:

"I see a flaw in that silk."

The lady recognized it and did not conclude the purchase.

The head man of the firm saw the transaction, and wrote to the father of the young man in the country, saying, "Come down and take your boy home; he will never make a merchant."

The father came down in excitement to see what his boy had been doing.

The employer said, "Your son actually stood at the counter the other dry and pointed out a flaw in one of our silks, so that we lost the sale of the goods."

The father said, "If that is all my boy has done, I am proud of him, and I would not have him stay five minutes more under your bad influence. John, take your hat and come home;" and away they started.

The pressure on our young men in town to-day is awful. Hundreds of them are going down under it for time and for eternity. Others are nobly enduring the pressure. May God help them! The public mind is utterly poisoned and diseased on the subject of money-making, and no wonder that God spoke in thunder last week, not only to New York, but to all the cities of the world saying, "Look out how you get you money. By the hand of death or judgement it shall be wrenched from your grasp. If you get riches by fraud, you will leave them in the midst of your days, and at the end you shall be a fool."

What shall be the eternal destiny of such a man? I leave you to guess. I make you the jury to say what shall be the doom of that Wall Street defrauder who, after the most gigantic dishonesties that were ever prac-

ticed on this planet, died without one seeming word of
repentance or of prayer—in his will giving away the
spoils of the most unprecedented thefts without saying
in that will, ''These are the moneys I got by crime, and
are the plea for my eternal condemnation.''   One minute after a man goes up to judgement, how many steam-
boats does he own?   How many shares of stock in Erie
Railway?   How many opera-houses?   None! ' The poor
boy with a penny in his pocket, who stands on the-cor-
ner as the funeral pageant of the dead cheat passes along,
has more money fn his pocket than the man who, a
few days before, boasted that all the country was afraid
of him.

LIBERTINISM.

Next, I speak of the romance of libertinism.   Society
has severest retribution for the impurity that lurks about
the cellars and alleys of the city.   It cries out against it.
It hurls the indignation of the law at it.   But society
becomes more lenient as impurity rises toward affluence
and high social position, until, finally, it is silent, or dis-
posed to palliate.   Where is the judge, or the sheriff, or
tne police, who dare arraign for indecency the wealthy
villian?   May he not walk the streets, and ride the parks,
and sail the steamers, flaunting his vices in the eyes of
the pure?   Does not the vlle hag of uncleanness look out
from tapestried window, and walk richest carpet, and
rustle finest silk, and roll in most sumptuous carriage?
But where is the law to take these brazen wretches of
''high life'' und put their faces in the iron frame of the
State Prison window?

It seems as if modern society were hastening back toward the days of Herculaneum and Pompeii, which sculpured their vileness on pillar and temple wall, until nothing but the lava of a burning mountain could hide the immensity of the crime.

At what time the Lord God shall begin to purge our cities I know not, nor whether it shall be by flood, or by fire, or by hurricane; but I do not believe the holy God will stand it much longer. I think that the thunderbolts of his indignation are hissing hot, and that when he rises up to scourge these crimes, against which he hath uttered more bitter curses than against any other, the fate of Sodom and Gomorrah will be found to have been more tolerable than that of our modern cities, which knew better, but showed disposition to do worse.

Would God that the romance which flings its fascinations over the bestialities of high life might be gone! Let it be known that uncleanness on Madison Square is as damnable in the sight of God as the uncleanness on the five points. Whether it has canopied couch of eiderdown, or sleep amid the putridity of the low tenementhouse, four families in a room, God's consuming vengeance is after it. "All adulterers and whoremongers shall have their place in the lake that burneth with fire and brimstone." It is hell on earth. It is hell in eternity.

Ever and anon we stand aghast at some exposure of splendid libertinism, as God hurls it upon the public gaze. Such a life ends either in violence or murder, and we hear in the hotel hall or boarding-house parlor the crack of a pistol—a libertine shot by a libertine—or the crime puts its victim into the lazar-house, and lets him horribly

die there.   "He goeth after her straightway, as an ox
goeth to the slaughter, or as a fool to the correction of
the stocks, until the dart strikes through his liver."   "As
a bird hasteneth to a snare, and knoweth not that it is
for his life."   "She hath cast down many wounded; yea,
many strong men have been slain by her."

THE ROMANCE OF ASSASSINATION.

Finally, I speak of the romance of assassination. God
gives life, and he only has a right to take it away; and
that man who assumes this divine prerogative has touched the last depth of crime.   Society is alert for certain
forms of murder.   If a citizen, on his way home at night,
is waylaid and slain of a robber, we are all anxious for
his arraignment and execution.   For garroting, or the
beating out of life with a club, or axe, or slung-shot, the
law has a quick spring and a heavy stroke.   But let a
man come to wealth or social pretension, and then attempt to avenge his wrongs by aiming a pistol at the
head or heart of another, and immediately there are sympathies aroused; and the lawyers plead, and the ladies
weep, and the juries are bribed, and the judge halts; a
new trial is granted, and the case is postponed for witnesses that never come: and after a number of months in
prison, the door is opened and the murderer is out.
call this the romance of assassination.

If capital punishment be right, then let the life of the
polished murderer go with the life of the ignorant and
vulgar assassin.   Let there be no partiality of hemp, no
aristocracy of the gallows.   We are, in our cities, on the
march back toward that state of barbarism where every
man is judge, jury, and executive officer—a state of so-

ciety in which that man has the supremacy who has the sharpest knife, and strongest arm, and stealthiest re-venge, and quickest spring.

He who wilfully and in hate takes the life of another is a murderer, I care not what the provocation or what the ¿ circumstances. A jury may clear him amid the plaudits of the court-room; or the President may send him as an embassador to spain; or modern literature may gild the crime until it looks like courage and heroism; neverthe-less, in God's eye, murder is murder, and the judgement day will so pronounce it.

My advice to all young men is to sell their pistols, and take the knife out of the top of their cane, and depend on God and their own stout arm for defense. A man who does not feel himself safe without deadly weapons is in the wrong kind of association and companionship, and you had better get out of it; for the probability is that either they will kill you or you will kill them—which latter thing, for your soul in eternity, will be the greatest disaster of the two; for "no murderer hath eternal life;" and in the future life there is no romance of assassina-tion.

To the youug men of this country there comes a stout warning from recent events. Within the past few days, as never before within our remembrance, the old Bib.e words ring out on the ear: "Her house is the way to hell, going down to the chambers of death." "The bloody and deceitful man shall not iive out half his days." -

What an unclean net it was over there in New York! Both of the chief actors were defrauders and adulterers.

Many of the sympathizers were partners with them in crime. All the circumstances were appalling, horrid, and overwhelming. The comedy and the farce at which the nation laughed, became the tragedy that made the nation shudder.

Oh young man, take not the manners, and customs, and habits of what is wrongly called "high life" for your example. Do not think sin is less to be hated because it is epauleted and adorned. The brown-stone front can no more keep back the judgements of God than can the cellar door. Behold how God blows up the magnificent wickedness of high places!

There may be some here who are venturing out into sin. The marks of pollution are already upon them. At Long Branch or Cape May, some summer day, you may have stood on the beach, and seen a man go down into the breakers to bathe. He went out farther and farther, until you became anxious about him. You wondered if he could swim. You shouted to him, as he advanced in the water, "Come back! come back! You will be lost! you will be lost!" He turned around, waved his hand, and shouted "No danger," and still went on, until, after a while, a wave, with great undertow, swept him out— his corpse the next day washed up on the beach. So I see young men going into the waves of sin—deeper and deeper, farther from God, and farther; and I stand on the beach to-night, and cry the warning: "Come back! come back! You will be lost! you will be lost!" Some, not heeding the warning, will jeer at the alarm and go ahead, till, after a while, the wave of God's indignation will sweep them off, and sweep them down forever.

There may be some here who have ventured into sin-
'ul courses who would like to return.   You came in here
to-night discouraged, and feel that there is but little hope.
I will tell you of a daughter who went from home into
the paths of sin.   After many months of wandering she
resolved one night to go home to her mother's house.   It
was after midnight when she arrived at the house.   She
supposed that the door would be locked; but, putting
her hand on the latch, the door opened.   She asked her
mother why it was that the door, after midnight, was
unlocked.   Said the mother, "That door has never been
locked since you went away.   I have given orders that,
by day and night, it should be unfastened, for I was sure
that you would come back, and when you came I did
not want you to be hindered a miuute."   So I have to
tell you that the door of God's mercy is ever unlocked.
By day and by night it stands open for your coming.
Though your sins were as scarlet, they shall be as snow;
though they were red as crimsou, they shall be as wool.
Though you may be polluted with all crimes, and
smitten of all leprosies, and fired by the most depraved
passions, and have not heard the Gospel invitation for
twenty years, you may have set upon your brow, hot with
infamous practices and besweated with exhaustive indulgences, the flashing coronet of a Savior's forgiveness.

Who is it that cometh younder?   Methinks I know his
step.   Methinks before this I have seen the rage.   Look.
all ye people of God!   Out of all the windows of heaven
let the angels watch!   A prodigal returning!   Let us go
out and meet him.   Welcome back again to thy long

forsaken home and to thy long-forsaken God.   The dead
is alive again!   The lost is found!

>"Pleased with the news, the saints below
>   In songs their tongue employ;
>Beyond the sky the tidings go,
>   And heaven is filled with joy.

>"Nor angels can their joy contain,
>   But kindle with new fire;
>The sinner lost is found! they sing,
>   And strike the sounding lyre."

COMMON CLOAKS FOR SIN.

"But now they have no cloak for their sin " John xv, 22.

in is always disguised. Decked and glossed and perfumed and masked it gains admittance in places from which it would otherwise be repelled. As silently as when it glided into Eden, and as plausible as when it talked to Christ at the top of the temple, it now addresses men. Could people look upon sin as it always is—an exhalation from the pit, the putrefaction of infinite capacities, the ghastly, loathsome, God smitten monster that uprooted Eden, and killed Christ, and would push the entire race into darkness and pain—the infernal charm would be broken. Before our first parents transgressed, sin appeared to them the sweetness of fruit, and the becoming, as gods, To Absalom it was the pleasure of sitting upon a throne. To men now, sin is laughter and permission to luxurious gratification. Jesus Christ in my text suggests a fact which everybody ought to know, and that sin, to hide its deformity and shame, is accustomed to wearing a cloak; and the Savior also sets forth the truth that God can see straight through all such wrappings and thicknesses. I want now to speak of several kinds of cloaks with which men expect to cover up their iniquities, for the fashion in regard to these garments is constantly changing, and every day beholds some new style of wearing them, and if you will tarry a little while I will show you five or six of the patterns of cloaks.

OFFICE AND POSITION A COMMON CLOAK.

First, I remark that there are those who, being honored with official power, expect to make that a successful cloak for their sin. There is a sacredness in office. God himself is king, and all who hold authority in the world serve under Him. The community has committed a monstrous wrong who has elevated to this dignity persons unqualified either by their ignorance or their immorality. Nations who elevate to posts of authority those not qualified to fill them will feel the reaction. Solomon expressed this thought when he said: "Woe unto thee, O land, when thy king is a child and thy princes drink in the morning." While positions of trust may be disgraced by the character of those who fill them, I believe God would have us respectful to the offices, though we may have no admiration for their occupants. Yet this dignity which office confers can be no apology for transgression. Nebuchadnezzar, and Ahab, and Herod in the day of judgment, must stand on the level with the herdsmen that kept their flocks, and the fishermen of Galilee. Pope, and king, and President, and governor, must give an account to God, and be judged by the same law as that which judges the beggar and the slave. Sin is all the more obnoxious when it is imperial and lordly. You cannot make pride or injustice or cruelty sacred by giving it a throne. Belshazzar's decanters could not keep the mysterious finger from writing on the wall. Ahab's sin literally hurled him from the throne to the dogs. The imperial vestments of wicked Jehoram could not keep

Jehu's arrow from striking through his heart. Jezebel's queenly pretension could not save her from being thrown over the wall. No barricade of thrones can arrest God's justice in its unerring march. No splendor or thickness of official robes can be a sufficient cloak of sin. Henry VIII, Louis XV, Catharine of Russia, Mary of England —did their crowns save them? No ruler ever sat so high that the King of kings was not above him. All victors shall bow before him who on the white horse goeth forth conquering and to conquer.

GOOD MANNERS IS ANOTHER CLOAK.

Again, elegance of manners cannot successfully hide iniquity from the eye of God. That model, gentlemanly apostle, Paul, writes to us: "Be courteous." That man can neither be a respectable worldling nor a consistent Christian who lacks good manners. He is shut out from refined circles, and he certainly ought to be hindered from entering the church. We cannot overlook that in a man which we could hardly excuse in a bear. One of the first effects of the grace of God upon an individual is to make him a gentleman. Gruffness, awkwardness, implacability, clannishness are fruits of the devil, while gentleness, and meekness are fruits of the Spirit. But while these excellences of manner are so important, they cannot hide any deformity of moral character. How often is it that we find attractiveness of person, suavity of manners, gracefulness of conversation, gallantry of behavior, thrown like wreaths upon moral death. The flowers that grow upon the scoriæ of Vesuvius do not make it any less of a volcano. The sepulchers in Christs's time did not exhaust all the whitewash. Some of the biggest scoundrels have been the most fascinating. If there are any depending on outward gracefulness, and attractiveness of demeanor, with any hope that because of that God will forgive the sin of their soul, let me assure them that the divine justice cannot be satisfied with smiles and elegant gesticulation. Christ looks deeper than the skin, and such a ragged cloak as the one in which you are trying to cover yourself will be no hiding in the day of His power. God will not in the judgment, ask how gracefully you walked, nor how politely you bowed, nor how sweetly you smiled, nor how impressively you gestured. The deeds done in the body will be the test, and not the rules of Lord Chesterfield.

PROFESSION OF RELIGION IS OFTEN A CLOAK.

Again, let me say that the mere profession of religion is but a poor wrapping of a naked soul. The importance of making a public profession of religion if the heart be renewed cannot be exaggerated. Christ positively and with the earnestness of the night before His crucifixion commanded it. But it is the result of Christian character, not the cause of it. Our church certificate is but a poor title to heaven. We may have the name; and not the reality. There are those who seems to throw themselves back with complacency upon there public confession of Christ, although they give no signs of renewal. If Satan can induce a man to build on such a rotten foundation as that he has acomplished his object. We cannot imagine the abhorence with which God looks upon such a procedure. What would be the feelings of a shepherd if he saw a wolf in the same fold with his flocks, however quiet he might seem to lie, or a general if among his troops he saw one wearing the appointed uniform who nevertheless really belonged to the opposing host? Thus must the heavenly shepherd look upon those who, though they are not his sheep, have climbed up some other way, and thus must the Lord of hosts look upon those who pretend to be soldiers of the cross while they are his armed enemies. If any of you find yourself deficient in the great test of Christian character, do not, I beg of you, look upon your profession of religion as anything consolitory. If you have taken your present position from a view that you have of Christ and your need of him, rejoice with joy unspeakable and full of glory and clap your hands for gladness; but if you find yourself with nothing but the name of life, while dead in trespasses and sins, arouse before the door is shut. That gilded profession—the world may not be able to see through it, but in the day of divine reckoning, it will be found that you have no cloak for your sin.

OUTWARD MORALITY.

Furthermore, outward morality will be no covering for the hidden iniquity of the spirit. The Gospel of Christ makes no assault upon good works. They are as beautiful in God's eye as in ours. Punctuality, truthfulness, almgiving, affection and many other excellences of life that might be mentioned, will always be admired of God and man, but we take the position that good works cannot be the ground of our salvation. What we do right cannot pay for what we do wrong. Admit that you have all those traits of character which give merely worldly respectability and influence, you must at the same time acknowledge that during the course of your life you have done many things you ought not to have done.

CHRIST IS THE ATONING SAVIOUR.

How are these difficult matters to be settled? Ah, my friends,, we must have an atonement. No Christ, no salvation. The great Redeemer comes in and says: "I will pay your indebtedness." So that which was dark enough before is bright enough now. The stripes that we deserve are fallen upon Christ. On his scourged and bleeding shoulders he carries us up over the mountain of our sins and the hills of our iniquities. Christ's good works accepted are sufficient for us, but they who reject them, depending upon their own, must perish. Traits of character that may make us influential on earth will not necessarily open to us the gate of heaven. The plank that will be strong enough for a house floor would not do for a ships hulk. Mere reality might be enough here, but cannot take you through death's storm into heaven's harbor. Christ has announced for all ages: "I am the way, the truth and the life; him that cometh unto me I will in no wise cast out." But pitable in the day of accounts will be the condition of the man, though he may have given all his estate to benevolent purposes, and passed his life in the visiting of the distressed, and done much to excite the admiration of the good and the great, if he have no intimate relation to Jesus Christ. There is a pride and a depravity in his soul that he has never discovered. A brilliant outside will be no apology for a depraved inside. It is no theory of mine, but an announcement of God, who cannot lie: "By the deeds of the law shall no flesh living be justified." Open the door of heaven and look in. Howard is there. but he

did not secure his entrance by the dunge ns ̩̩̩̩ ̩̩̩̩ed
and the lazzarettos into which he carried the medicinss.
Paul is there, but he did not earn his way in by the shipwrecks and imprisonments and scourgings. On a thronc
overtopping perhaps all other, except Christ's, the old
missionary exclaims; "By the grace of God I am what
I am."

HEAVEN CANNOT BE BOUGHT.

Again, exalted social position will be no cloak for si.r.
Men look through the wicked door of prisons, and seeing
the incarcerated wretches exclaim, "Oh, how much vice
there is in the world!" And they pass through the de-
graded streets of a city, and looking into the doors o.
hovels and the dens of corruption they call them God-
forsaken abodes. But you might walk along the avenues
through which the opulent rolls in their flourishing pomp,
and into mansions elegantly adorned, and find that evci.
in the admired walks of life Satan works mischief and
death. The first temptation Satan wrought in a garden.
and he understands yet most thoroughly how to insinuate
himself into any door of ease and splendor. Men frequently judge of sin by the plaees in which it is committed, but iniqulty in satin is to God as loathscme as
iniquity in rags, and in the Day of Judgment the sins of
Madison avenue and Elm street will all be driven in one
herd.

Men cannot escape at last for being respectably sinful.
You know Dives was clothed in purple and fine linen and
fared sumptuously every day, but his fine clothes and
good dinners did not save him. He might on earth have
drank something as rich as champagne and cognac, but

at last he asked for one drop of water. You cannot trade off your attractive abodes here for a house of many mansions on high, and your elegant shade groves here will not warrant you a seat under the tree of life. When God drove Adam and Eve out of Eden He showed that merely living in a garden of delights and comforts will never save a man or a woman. By giving you so much earthly luxury and refinement He intimated that He would have you enjoy yourselves, but He would not have you wrap yourself up in them as a cloak to hide your sins. God now walks in your garden as He did in Eden, even in the cool of the day, and He stands by your well as He did by a well in Samaria, and He would make your comfort on earth a type of your rapture in heaven.

ORTHODOXY CANNOT HIDE OUR INIQUITY.

Furthermore, mere soundness of religious belief will not hide our iniquities; There are men whose heads are as sound as Jonathan Edwards' or John Wesley's, whose hearts are as rotten as Tom Paine's or Charles Guiteau's. It is important that we be practical Christians. It is utter folly in this day for a man to have no preference for any one form of faith when it is so easy to become conversant with the faith of the different sects.

An intoxicated man staggered into my house one night begging for lodging. He made great pretensions to religion. I asked where he went to church.

He said: ''Nowhere; I belong to liberal Christianity.''

But there are those who never become Christians, because their obstinancy prevents them from ever taking a fair view of what religion is. They are like a brute beast in the fact that their greatest strength lies in their horns.

They are combatant, and all they are ever willing to do for their souls is to enter an ecclesiastical fight. I have met men who would talk all day upon the ninth chapter of Romans, who were thoroughly helpless before the fourteenth chapter of John. But there are those who, having escaped from this condition, are now depending entirely upon their soundness of religious theory. The doctrines of man's depravity, and Christ's atonement, and God's sovereignty, are theoretically received by them. But alas! there they stop. It is only the shell of Christianity containing no evangelical life. They stand looking over into heaven and admire its beauty and its song, and are so pleased with the looks from the outside, that they cannot be induced to enter. They could make a better argument for the truth than ten thousand Christians who have in their hearts received it. If syllogisms and dilemmas, and sound propositions, and logical deductions, could save their souls, they would be among the best of Christians. They could correctly define repentance, and faith, and the Atonement, while they have never felt one sorrow for sin, nor exercised a moment's confidence in the great sacrifice. They are almost immovable in their position. We cannot present anything about the religion ot Christ that they do not know. The Saviour described the fate of such a one in his parable: "And that servant which knew his Lord's will and prepared not himself, neither did according to his will, shall be beaten with many stripes." Theories in religion have a beauty of their own, but if they result in no warmth of Christian iife, it is the beauty of hornblende and feldspar. Do not call such coldness and hardness religion. The

River of Life never freezes over.　Icicles never hang on the eaves of heaven.　Soundness of intellectual belief is a beautiful cloak, well woven and well cut, but in the hour when God shall demand our souls it will not of itself be sufficient to hide our iniquities.

CHRIST'S RIGHTEOUSNESS IS THE TRUE CLOAK THAT SAVES US.

My friends, can it be that I have been unkind, and torn from you some hope upon which you were resting for time and eternity?　Verily, I would be unkind if, having taken away your cloak, I did not offer something better.　This is a cold world and you want something to wrap around your spirit.　Christ offers you a robe to-day. He wove it Himself, and He will now, with his own hand prepare it just to fit your soul.　The righteousness He offers is like the coat he used to wear about Judea, with out seam from top to bottom.　There is a day of doom. Coward would I be if I did not dare tell you this.　It shall be a day of unutterable disappointment to those who have trusted in their official dignity, in their elegant manners, in their outward morality, in their soundness of intellectual belief.　But I see a soul standing before God who once was thoroughly defiled.　Yet look at him, and you cannot find a single transgression anywhere about him.　How is this, you ask.　Was he not once a Sabbath breaker, a blasphemer, a robber, a perjurer, a thief, a murderer?　Yes, but Christ hath cleansed him.　Christ hath lifted him up.　Christ hath rent off his rags.　Christ hath robed him in a spotless robe of righteousness.　That is the reason why you cannot see his former degradation. This glorious hope in Christ's name is proffered to-day.

Wandering and wayward soul, is not this salvation worth coming for, worth striving for? Do you wonder that so many, with bitter weeping, have besought it, and with a very enthusiasm of sorrow, cried for divine compassion? Do you wonder at the earnestness of those who stand in pulpits, beseeching men to be reconciled to God? Nay, do not wonder at the importunity of the Holy Ghost, who now striveth with thy soul? In many of the palaces of Europe the walls are mosaic. Fragments of shells and glass are arranged by artists and aggregated into a pictorial splendor. What! made out of broken shells and broken glass! Oh, yes: God grant that by the transforming power of his Spirit we may all be made a part of the eternal palaces; our broken and fragmentary natures polished, and shaped, and lifted up to make a part of the everlasting splendors of the heavenly temple!

> For sinners, Lord, thou cam'st to bleed,
> And I'm a sinner vile indeed.
> Lord, I believe thy grace is free;
> Oh magnify thy grace in me.

"So the shipmaster came to him, and said unto him, What meanest thou, O sleeper? Arise, call upon thy God, if so be that God will think upon us, that we perish not."—Jonah i., 6.

God told Jonah to go to Nineveh on an unpleasant errand! He would not go. He thought to get away from his duty by putting to sea. With pack under his arm, I find him on his way to Joppa, a seaport. He goes down among the shipping, and says to the men lying around on the docks, "Which of these vessels sails to-day?" The sailors answer, "Yonder is a vessel going to Tarshish. I think, if you hurry, you may get on board her." Jonah steps on board the rough craft, asks how much the fare is, and pays it. Anchor is weighed, sails are hoisted, and the rigging begins to rattle in the strong breeze of the Mediterranean. Joppa is an exposed harbor, and it does not take long for the vessel to get out on the broad sea. The sailors like what they call a "spanking breeze," and the plunge of the vessel from the crest of a tall wave is exhilarating to those at home on the deep. But the strong breeze becomes a gale, the gale a hurricane. The affrighted passengers ask the captain if he ever saw anything like this before. "Oh yes," he says; "this is nothing." Mariners are slow to admit danger to landsmen. But, after a while, crash goes the mast, and the vessel pitches so far "a-beams-end" there is a fear she will not be righted. The captain answers few questions, and orders the throwing out of boxes and bundles, and of so much of the cargo as

IN THE STORM.

they can get at. The captain at last confesses that there is but little hope, and tells the passengers that they had better go to praying. It is seldom that a sea-captain is an Atheist. . He knows that there is a God, for he has seen him at every point of latitude between Sandy Hook and Queenstown. Captain Moody, commanding the Cuba, of the Cunard line, at Sunday service led the music and sang like a Methodist. The captain of this Mediterranean craft, having set the passengers to praying, goes around examining the vessel at every point. He descends into the cabin to see whether, in the strong wrestling of the waves, the vessel has sprung aleak, and he finds Jonah asleep. Jonah had had a wearisome tramp, and had spent many sleepless nights about questions of duty, and he is so sound asleep that all the thunder of the storm and the screaming of the passengers does not disturb him. The captain lays hold of him, and begins to shake him out of his unconsciousness with the cry, "Don't you see that we are all going to the bottom? Wake up, and go to praying, if you have any God to go to. What meanest thou, O sleeper? Arise, call upon thy God, if so be that God will think upon us, that we perish not." The rest of the story I will not rehearse, for you know it well. To appease the sea, they threw Jonah overboard.

HOW THE DEVIL CHEATS YOU.

Learn that the devil takes a man's money and then sets him down in a poor landing-place. The Bible says he paid his fare to Tarshish. But see him get out. The sailors bring him to the side of the ship, lift him over "the guards," and let him drop with a loud splash into

the waves.   He paid his fare all the way to Tarshish, but
did not get the worth of his money.   Neither does any
one who turns his back on his duty and does that which
is not right.

There is a young man who, during the past year, has
spent a large part of his salary in carousal.   What has
he gained by it?   A soiled reputation, a half-starved
purse, a dissipated look, a petulant temper, a disturbed
conscience.   The manacles of one or two bad habits that
are pressing tighter and tighter will keep on until they
wear to the bone.   You paid your fare to Tarshish, but
you have been set down in the midst of a sea of disquietude and perplexity.

Ohe hundred dollars for Sunday horse-hire!

One hundred dollars for wine-suppers!

One hundred dollars for cigars!

One hundred dollars for frolics that shall be nameless!

Making four hundred dollars for his damnation!

Instead of being in Tarshish to-night, he is in the middle of the Mediterranean.

A LITERARY JONAH.

Here is a literary man, tired of the faith of his fathers,
who resolved to launch out into what is called Free-think-
ing.   He buys Theodore Parker's works for twelve dollars; Renan's Life of Christ for one dollar and fifty cents;
Andrew Jackson Davis's works for twenty dollars.   Goes
to hear infidels talk at the clubs, and to see spiritualism
at the table-rapping.   Talks glibly of David, the Psal-
mist, as an old libertine; of Paul as a wild enthusiast;
and of Christ as a decent kind of a man—a little weak in
some respects, but almost as good as himself.   Talks

smilingly of Sunday as a good day to put a little extra blacking on one's boots; and of Christians as, for the most part, hypocrites; and of eternity as "the great to be," "the everlasting now," or "the infinite what is it." Some day he gets his feet very wet, and finds himself that night chilly. The next morning has a hot mouth and is headachy. Sends word over to the store that he will not be there to-day. Bathes his feet; has mustard-plasters; calls the doctor. The medical man says aside, "This is going to be a bad case of congestion of the lungs." Voice fails. Children must be kept down stairs, or sent to the neighbors, to keep the house quiet? You say, "Send for the minister." But no; he does not believe in ministers. You say, "Read the Bible to him." No; he does not believe in the Bible. A lawyer comes in, and sitting by his bedside, writes a document that begins, "In the name of God, Amen. I, being of sound mind, do make this my last will and testament." It is certain where the sick man's body will be in less than a week. It is quite certain who will get his property. But what will become of his soul? It will go into "the great to be," or "the everlasting now," or "the infinite what is it." His soul is in deep waters, and the wind is "blowing great guns." Death cries, "Overboard with the unbeliever!" A splash! He goes to the bottom. He paid five dollars for his ticket to Tarshish when he bought the infidel books. He landed in perdition!

SATAN SINKS YOUR CAPITAL.

Every farthing you spend in sin Satan will swindle you out of. He promises you shall have thirty per cent or a great dividend. He lies. He will sink all the capital. .

You may pay full fare to some sinful success, but you will never get to Tarshish.

SLEEPING IN THE MIDST OF DANGER.

Learn how soundly men will sleep in the midst of danger. The worst sinner on shipboard, considering the light he had, was Jonah. He was a member of the Church, while they were heathen The sailors were engaged in their lawful calling, following the sea. The merchants on board, I suppose, were going down to Tarshish to barter; but Jonah, notwithstanding his Christian profession, was flying from duty. He was sound asleep in the cabin. He had been motionless for hours · — his arms and feet in the same posture as when he lay down—his breast heaving with deep respiration. Oh! how could the sinner sleep! What if the ship struck a rock! what if it sprang aleak! what if the clumsy Oriental craft should capsize! What would become of Jonah?

So men sleep soundly now amid perils infinite. In almost every place, I suppose, the Mediterranean might be sounded, but no line is long enough to fathom the profound beneath every impenitent man. Plunging a thousand fathoms down, you cannot touch bottom. Eternity beneath him, before him, around him! Rocks close by, and whirlpools, and hot-breathed Levanters: yet sound asleep! We try to wake him up, but fail. The great surges of warning break over the hurricane-deck—the gong of warning sounds through the cabin—the bell in the wheel-house rings. "Awake!" cry a hundred voices; yet sound asleep in the cabin.

A SHIP FULL OF DEAD MEN.

In the year 1775, the captain of a Greenland whaling

vessel found himself at night surrounded by icebergs, and "lay to" until morning, expecting every moment to be ground to pieces. In the morning he looked about, and saw a ship near by. He hailed it. No answer. Getting into a boat with some of the crew, he pushed on for the mysterious craft. . Getting near by, he saw through the port-hole a man at a stand, as though keeping a log-book. He hailed him. No answer. He went on board the vessel, and found the man sitting at the log-book, frozen to death. The log-book was dated 1762, showing that the vessel had been wandering for thirteen years among the ice. The sailors were found frozen among the hammocks, ·and others in the cabin. For thirteen years this ship had been carrying its burden of corpses.

So from this Gospel craft to-night I descry voyagers for eternity. I cry, "Ship ahoy! ship ahoy!" No answer. . They float about, tossed and ground by the icebergs of sin, hoisting no sail for heaven. I go on board. I find all asleep. · It is a frozen sleep. O that my Lord Jesus would come aboard, and lay hold of the wheel, and steer the craft down into the warm Gulf Stream of his mercy! Awake, thou that sleepest! Arise from the dead, and Christ shall give thee life.

AROUSED BY UNEXPECTED MEANS.

Again: Notice that men are aroused by the most unexpected means. If Jonah had been told one year before that a heathen sea-captain would ever awaken him to a sense of danger, he would have scoffed at the idea; but here it is done. So now, men in strangest ways are aroused from spiritual stupor. A profane man is brought to conviction by the shocking blasphemy of a comrade.

A man attending church, and hearing a sermon from
the text, "The ox knoweth his owner." etc., goes home
unimpressed; but, crossing his barn-yard, an ox comes
up and licks his hand, and he says, "There it is now—
'the ox knoweth his owner, and the ass his master's crib,
but I do not know God." The careless remark of a
teamster has led a man to thoughtfulness and heaven.
The child's remark, "Father, they have prayers at uncle's
house—why don't we have them?" has brought salvation
to the dwelling.

Some man came in here to-night hardly knowing why
he came. He had heard that Talmage is an odd man,
and has come to see whether it is true. . But before this
service is done that man will begin to think about his
soul. He has been upon his last spree. He has made
his last visit to that bad house. His children will to-
morrow morning notice the change. This moment he
starts heavenward; and for all eternity he will bless God
for this visit to the Brooklyn Tabernacle.

By strangest way and in most unexpected manner men
are awakened. The gardener of the Countess of Hunt-
ingdon was convicted of sin by hearing the countess on
the opposite side of the wall talk about Jesus. ·John
Hardoak was aroused by a dream, in which he saw the
last day, and the Judge sitting, and heard his own name
called with terrible emphasis: "John Hardoak, come to
judgment!" The Lord has a thousand ways of waking
up Jonah. Would that the messengers of mercy might
this night find their way down into the sides of the ship,
and that many who are unconsciously rocking in the
awful tempest of their sin might hear the warning.

"What meanest thou, O sleeper? Arise, and call upon thy God!"

WE MAY WAKE UP TOO LATE.

Again: Learn that a man may wake up too late. If instead of sleeping, Jonah had been on his knees confessing his sins from the time he went on board the craft, I think that God would have saved him from being thrown overboard. But he woke up too late. The tempest is in full blast, and the sea, in convulsion, is lashing itself, and nothing will stop it now but the overthrow of Jonah.

So men sometimes wake up too late. The last hour has come. The man has no more idea of dying than I have of dropping down this moment. The rigging is all white with the foam of death. How chill the night is! "I must die," he says, "yet not ready. I must push out upon this awful sea, but have nothing with which to pay my fare, The white caps! the darkness! the hurricane! How long have I been sleeping? Whole days, and months, and years. I am quite awake now. I see every thing, but it is too late." Invisible hands take him up. He struggles to get loose. In vain. They bring his soul to the verge. They let it down over the side. The wind howls. The sea opens its frothing jaws to swallow. The lightnings hold their torches at the soul's burial. The thunders toll their bells as he drops. Eternal death catches him. He has gone forever. And while the cavass cracked, and the yards rattled, and the ropes thumped, the sea took up the funeral dirge, playing, with open diapason of midnight storm, "Because I have called, and ye refused; I have stretched out my hand, and no man regarded; but ye have set at naught all my counsel, and would none of my reproof; I also will laugh at your calamity: I will mock when your fear cometh."

WE MAY NOT WAKE UP AT ALL.

But sometimes men do not wake up even in the last hour of life. Men often die in sickness with befogged brain, and while the friends stand weeping, the dying man looks around and wonders what it all means, or is too stupid to notice the weeping. Now the pulse of the sick man is up to 110! It gets feebler: 90, 80, 60, 50— pulse all gone! The gates of the body open, and the soul passes out, and, for the first time wakes up. "What is this?" it cries—"These sounds, these terrors?" Wide awake now, but what is it? A voice sounds through the darkness: "This is not the Mediterranean on which thou sailest, nor the Euroclydon which has come upon thee. It is the boundless ocean of Eternity, and this battle of wind and wave is an everlasting storm. Voyagers upon this sea sail on forever, yet get to no port. The ship that staggers in these troughs of death rises not upon the crest save to plunge to deeper depths?

The needle of the compass points to no star, but wanders in the box after light, but finding only darkness. They who run up the ratlines to reef the sail are frozen fast in the rigging. He who commands this ship hath an iron face, and wrings his hands, and wishes they might founder and be at rest; and curses the night, and curses the wind, and curses the wave. His name is Despair. The boatswain's whistle is a shriek; and the white-cheeked lay hold of the ropes and pull altogether, their cry is, 'Haul away, lads, the harvest is past! Haul away, lads, the summer is ended!' No glimpse of light-house, or merry dance of light-ship outside of the harbor. No star in the black flag above the top-gallants. Taking their bearings, they find themselves at infinite distance from the shore of earth, and at infinite distance from the shore of heaven. The log-book tells of millions of miles past, but still voyaging, Ages on ages? Sailing on, sailing on! Eternally, eternally! No hammock in that forecastle in which to rest; no striking of eight bells to show that the watch is out. They wake up at last—too late forever!"

ARISE, CALL UPON THY GOD.

Now, lest any of you should make this mistake, I ad-dress you in the words of the Mediterranean sea-captan: "What meanest thou, O sleeper? Arise, call upon thy God, if so be that God will think upon us, that we perish not." If you have a God, you had better call upon him. Do you say "I have no God?" Then you had better call upon your father's God. When your father was in trouble, who did he fly to? You heard him, in his old days, tell about some terrible exposure in a snow-storm, or at sea, or in battle, or among midnight garroters. and how he escaped. Perhaps twenty years before you were born, your father made sweet acquaintance with God.

There is something in the worn pages of the Bible he used to read which makes you think your father had a God. In the old religious books lying around the house, there are passages marked with a lead-pencil—passages that make you think your father was not a godless man, but that, on that dark day when he lay in the back room dying, he was ready—all ready. But perhaps your father was a bad man—prayerless, and a blasphemer, and you never think of him now without a shudder. He worshipped the world or his own appetites. Do not then, I beg of you, call upon your father's God, but call on your mother's God, I think she was good.

You remember when your father came home drunk late on a cold night, how patient your mother was. You often heard her pray. She used to sit by the hour meditating, as though she were thinking of some good, warm place, where it never gets cold, and where the bread does not fail, and staggering steps never come. You remember her now, as she sat, in cap and spectacles, reading her Bible Sunday afternoons. What good advice she used to give you! How black and terrible the hole in the ground looked to you when, with two ropes, they let her down to rest in the graveyard! Ah! I think from your looks that I am on the right track. Awake, O sleeper, and call upon thy mother's God.

But perhaps both your father and mother were depraved. Perhaps your cradle was rocked by sin and shame, and it is a wonder that from such a starting you have come to respectability. Then don't call upon the God of either of your parents, I beg of you.

But you have children. You know God kindled those bright eyes, and rounded those healthy limbs, and set beating within their breast an immortality. Perhaps in the belief that somehow it would be for the best, you have taught them to say an evening prayer, and when they kneel beside you, and fold their little hands, and look up, their face all innocence and love, you know that there is a God somewhere about in the room.

I think I am on the right track at last. Awake, O
sleeper, and call upon the God of thy children. May
he set these little ones to pulling at thy heart until they
charm thee to the same God to whom to-night they have
said their little prayer!

But, alas! alas! some of these men and women are
unmoved by the fact that their father had a God, that
their mother had a God, and their children have a God,
but they have no God. All pious example to them for
nothing. All the divine goodness for nothing. All
warning for nothing. They are sound asleep in the side
of the ship, though the sea and the sky are in mad wrestle.
O my God, wake them up! Drop a thunderbolt upon
their coffin-lid and wake them up!

STORY OF A WRECKED HUSBAND.

Some years ago, a man, leaving his family in Massachusetts, sailed from Boston to China, to trade there.

On the coast of China, in the midst of a night of storm,
he made shipwreck. The adventurer was washed up on
the beach senseless—all his money gone. He had to beg
in the streets of Canton to keep from starving. For two
years there was no communication between himself and
family. They supposed him dead. He knew not but
that his family were dead.

He had gone out as a captain. He was too proud to
come back as a private sailor. But after awhile he
choked down his pride and sailed for Boston. Arriv-
ing there, he took an evening train for the centre of the
state where he had left his family. Taking the stage from
the depot, and riding a score of miles; he got home.
He says that, going up in front of the cottage in the **bright**

moonlight, the place looked to him like heaven. **He** rapped on the window, and the affrighted servant let him in. He went to the room where his wife and child were sleeping. He did not dare to wake them for fear of the shock. Bending over to·kiss his child's cheek, a tear fell upon the wife's face, and she wakened, and he said "Mary!" and she knew his voice, and there was an indescribable scene of welcome, and joy, and thanksgiving to God.

To-night I know that many of you are sea-tossed, and driven by sin in a worse storm than that which came down on the coast of China, and yet I pray God that you may, like the sailor, live to get home. In the house of many mansions your friends are waiting to meet you· They are wondering why you do not come. Escaped from the shipwrecks of earth, may you at last go in! It will be a bright night—a very bright night as you put your thumb on the latch of that door. Once in, you will find the old family faces sweeter than when you last saw them, and there it will be found that He who was your father's God, and your mother's God, and your children's God, is your own most blessed Redeemer, to whom be glory in the Church throughout all ages, world without end. **Amen.**

JESUS QUESTIONING THE DOCTORS.

THE BATTLE OF CREEDS.

"He that passeth, by and meddleth with strife belonging not to him, is like one that taketh a dog by the ears."   Proverbs xxvi, 17.

Solomon here deplores the habit of rushing in between contestants; of taking part in the antagonisms of others; of joining in, fights which they ought to shun. They do no good to others, and get damage for themselves. He compares it to the experiment of taking a dog by the ears. Nothing so irritates the canines as to be clutched by the lugs. Take them by the back of the neck and lift them and it does not seem to hurt or offend, but you take the dog by the ear, and he will take you with his teeth. In all the history of kennels no intelligent or spirited dog will stand that. "Now," says Solomon, you go into quarrels or controversies that are not yours and you will get lacerated and torn and bitten. "He that passeth by and meddleth with strife belonging not to him is like one that taketh a dog by the ears."

THIS IS A TIME OF CHURCH QUARRELS!

This is a time of resounding ecclesiastical quarrels. Never within your memory, or mine, has the air been so full of missiles.

The Presbyterian Church has on hand a controversy so great that it finds it prudent to postpone its settlement for at least one more year, hoping that something will turn up. Somebody might die, or a new General

Assembly may have grace to handle the exciting ques·
tions.

The Episcopal Church has cast out some recalcitrants,
and its digestive organs are taxed to the utmost in trying
to assimilate others.

"Shall women preach?" or "be sent as delegates to
Conference?" are questions that have put many of our
Methodist brethern on the anxious seat.

And the waters in some of the great baptistries are
troubled waters.   Because of the controversies throughout Christendom the air is now like an August afternoon
about 5 o'clock, when it has been steaming hot all day,
and clouds are gathering and there are lions of thunder
with grumbling voices and flashing eyes coming forth from
their cloudy lairs, and people are waiting for the full
burst of the tempest.   I am not much of a weather
prophet, but the clouds look to me mostly like wind
clouds.   It may be a big.blow, but I hope it will soon be
over.

RELIGIOUS CONTROVERSY IS DAMMAGING.

In regard to the battle of the creeds I am every day asked
what I think about it.   I want to make it so plain this
morning what I think, that no one will ever ask again.
Let those who are jurymen in the case (I mean those
who in the different ecclesiastical courts have the questions put directly before them) weigh and decide.   Let
the rest of us keep out.   The most damaging thing on
earth is religious controversy.   No one ever comes out
of it as good a man as he goes in.   Some of the ministers, in all denominations,   who, before the present
acerbity were good and kind and useful, now seem

almost swearing mad. These brethern, I notice, always open their violent meetings with prayer before devouring each other, thus saying grace before meat. They have a moral hydrophobia that makes us think they have taken a dog by the ears. They never read the imprecatory psalms of David with such zest as since the Briggs, and Newton, and McQueary, and Bridgman, and Brooks questions got into full swing. May the rams of the sheep fold soon have their horns sawed off. Before the controversies are settled a good many ministers will, through what they call liberalism, be landed into practical infidelity. And others through what they call conservatism, will shrink up into bigots, tight and hard as the mummies of Egypt, which got through their controversies 3,000 years ago.

INSPIRED OF SATAN.

This trouble throughout Christendom, was directly inspired of Satan. He saw that too much good was being done. Recruits were being gathered by the hundreds of thousands to the gospel standard. The victories for God and the truth were too near together. Too many churches were being dedicated. Too many ministers were being ordained. Too many philanthropies were being fostered. Too many souls were being saved. It had been a dull time in the nether world, and the arrivals were too few. So Satan one day rose upon his throne, and said: "Ye powers of darkness, hear!"

And all up and down the caverns the cry was: Hear! Hear!

Satan said: "There is that American Board of Commissioners for Foreign Missions. It must either be demolished or crippled, or the first thing you know they will have all nations brought to God.

Apollyon the Younger! You go up to Andover and get the Professors discussing whether the heathen can be saved without the gospel. Divert them from the work of missions and get them in angry convention in a room at Young's hotel, Boston, and by the time they adjourn, the cause of foreign missions will be gloriously and magnificently injured.

Diabolus the Younger! You go up and get Union Theological Seminary of New York, and the General Assembly of the Presbyterian Church at Detroit, at swords' points, and diverted from the work of making earnest ministers of religion, and turn that old Presbyterian Church, which has been keeping us out of customers for hundreds of years, into a splendid pandemonium on a small scale.

Abaddon the Third! You go up and assault the old Episcopal Church, which has been storming the heavens for centuries with the sublimest prayers that were ever uttered—church of Bishop Leighton, Bishop White, and Bishop McIlvaine, and get that denomination discussing men instead of discussing the eternities.

Abaddon IV.! You go up to that old Methodist Church, which has through her revivals, sent millions to heaven, which we would otherwise have added to our population, The church of the Wesley, and Matthew Simpson, against which we have an especial grudge, and get them so absorbed in discussing whether women shall take part in her conference, that they shall not have so much time to discuss how many sons and daughters she will take to glory."

SPLITTING UP THE CHURCHES.

What amazes me most is that all people do not see that the entire movement at this time all over Christendom is Satanic. Many of the infernal attacks are sly, and hidden, and strategic, and so ingenious that they are not easily discovered. But here is a bold and uncovered attempt of the powers of darkness to split up the churches, to get ministers to take each other by the throat, to make religion a laughing stock of earth and hell, to leave the Bible with no more respect, or authenticity, than an old almanac of 1822, which told us what would be the change of weather six months ahead and in what quarter of the months is best to plant turnips. In a word, the effort is to stop the evangelization of the world. It seems to me very much like this: There has been a railroad accident and many are wounded and dying.

There are several drug stores near the scene of casualty. All the doctors and druggists are needed, and needed right away. Bandages, stimulants, anæsthetics, medicines of all sorts. What are the doctors and druggists doing? Discussing the contents of some old bottles on the top shelf, bottles of medicine which some doctors and druggists mixed 200, or 300 years ago. "Come, doctors! come druggists!" cry the people, "and help these wounded and dying that are being brought from beneath the timbers of the crushed rail train. In a little while it will be too late. Come for God's sake! Come right away!" "No," says the doctor, "not until we have settled whether the medicine on that top shelf was

rightly mixed. I say there were too many drops of laud-
anum in it and this other man says there were too many
of camphor, and we must get this question settled before
we can attend to the railroad accident." And one doctor takes another doctor by the collar, and pushes him
back against the counter, and one of the doctors says:
"If you will not admit that I am right about that one
bottle, I will smash every bottle in your apothecary
store," and he proceeds to smash. Meanwhile, on the
lower shelf, plainly marked and within easy reach, are
all the medicines needed for the helping of the sufferers.

AND THE DOCTORS ALL FIGHTING.

By the accident, and in that drawer, easily opened,
are bandages and splints, for the lack of which fifty people are dying outside the drug store. Before I apply
this thought every one sees its application. Here is this
old world, and it is off track. Sin and sorrow have col-
lided with it. The groan of agony is fourteen hundred
million voiced. God has opened for relief, and cure a
great Sanitarium, a great House of Mercy, and all its
shelves are filled with balsams, with catholicons, with
help, glorious help, tremendous help, help so easily administered that you need not get upon any step-ladder to
reach it. You can reach it on your knees, and then
hand it to all the suffering, and the sinning, and the
dying. Comfort for all the troubled! Pardon for all
the guilty! Peace for all the dying! But while the
world is needing the relief and perishing for lack of it,
what of the church? Why, it is full of fighting doctors!

On the top shelf are some old bottles, which, several
hundred years ago, Calvin, or Arminius or the mem-

bers of the Synod of Dort, or the farmers of the Nicene creed, filled with holy mixtures, and until we get a revision of these old bottles, and find out whether we must take a teaspoonful, and whether before or after meals, let the nations suffer and groan, and die. Save the bottles by all means, if you cannot save any thing else!

TAKE NO PART IN THE CONTROVERSY.

Now what part shall you and I take in this controversy which is filling all Christendom with clangor? My advice is; take no part.

In time of riot all mayors of cities advise good citizens to stay at home or in their places of business, and in this time of religious riot I advise you to go about your regular work of God. Leave the bottles on the higher shelves for others to fight about and take the two bottles on the shelf within easy reach; the two bottles which are all this dying world needs; the one filled with a portion which is for the cleansing of all sin, the other filled with a portion which is for the soothing of all suffering.

Two Gospel bottles! Christ mixed them out of his own tears and blood. in them is no human admixture, spend no time on the mysteries! You, only a man five or six feet high, ought not to try to wade an ocean 1,000 feet deep. My own experience has been vivid. I devoted the most of my time for years in trying to understand God's Eternal Decrees, and I was determined to find out why the Lord let sin come into the world; and I set out to explore the doctrine of the Trinity, and with a yard-stick to measure the throne of the infinite. As with all my predecessors, the attempt was a dead failure.

For the last thirty years I have not spent two minutes
in studying the controverted points of theology, and if I
live thirty-five years longer I will not spend the thousand-
the part of a second in such exploration. I know two
things that I will devote all the years of my life in pro-
claiming, God will through Jesus Christ pardon sin,
and He will comfort in trouble.

A FOGGY COAST FOR THEOLOGICAL STUDENTS.

Creeds have their uses, but just now the churches are
creeded to death. The young men entering ministry
are going to be launched in the thickest fog that ever
settled on the coasts. As I am told that in all our
services, students of Princeton, and Union and Drew
and other theological seminaries, are present and as
these words will come to thousands of young men who
are soon to enter the ministry, let me say to such, and
through them to their associates, keep out of the be-
wildering, belittling, destroying, and angry controversies
abroad. The questions our Doctors of Divinity are trying to settle will not be settled until the day after the
Day of Judgment. It is such a poor economy of time
to spend years and years in trying to fathom the unfath-
omable, when in five minutes in heaven, we will know
all that we want to know.

WAIT TILL WE GET OUR THRONE.

Wait until the light of eternity flashes upon our newly
ascended spirits. It is useless for ants on different sides
of a mole-hill to try to discuss the comparative heights
of Mont Blanc and Mount Washington. Let me say to
all young men about to enter the ministry, that soon
the greatest novelty in the world will be the unadulter-

ated religion of Jesus Christ. Preach that and you will have a crowd. The world is sick to regurgitation of the modern quacks in religion. The world has been swinging off from the old Gospel, but it will swing back, and by the time you young men go into the pulpits the cry will be coming up from all the millions of mankind: "Give us the bread of life: no sweetened bread, or bread with sickly raisens stuck here and there into it, but good old-fashioned bread as God, our Mother, mixed it, and baked it."

. You see God knew as much when He made the bible, as He knows now. He has not learned a single thing in 6,000 years. He knew at the start that the human race would go wrong and what would be the best means of its restoration and redemption. And the law which was thundered on Mt Sinai, from whose top I had the tables of stone in yonder wall transported, is the perfect law. And the Gospel which Christ announced while dying on that Mount from which I brought that stone in yonder wall, Paul preached on that hill from which I brought yonder granite, is the Gospel that is going to save the world. Young man put on that Gospel armor! No other sword will triumph like that. No other helmet will glance off the battle-axes like that. Our theological seminaries are doing glorious work, but if our theological seminaries shall cease to prepare young men for this plain Gospel advocacy, and shall become mere philosophical schools for guessing about God, and guessing about the Bible, and guessing about the soul, they will cease their usefulness, and young men as in olden times, when they would study or the Gospel ministry, will put themselves under the care of some intelligent and warm hearted pastor, and kneel with him in family prayer at the parsonage, and go with him into the room of the sick and the dying and see what victories the grace of God can gain when the couch of the dying saint is the Marathon.

That is the way the mighty ministers of the Gospel were made in olden times. Oh, for a great wave of revival to roll over our theological seminaries, and our pulpits and our churches, and our ecclesiastical courts, and over all Christendom! That would be the end of controversy. While such a deluge would float the ark of God higher and higher, it would put all the bears and tigers and reptiles of raging ecclesiasticism fifteen cubits under.

WHAT IS THE SIMPLE FACT?

Now, what is the simple fact that you in the pew, and Sabbath-school class, and Reformatory Association, and we in the pulpits have to deal with? It is this: That God has somewhere—it matters not where, but somewhere—provided a great heaven, great for quietness for those who want quiet, great for vast assemblage for those who like multitudes, great for architecture for those who like architecture, great for beautiful landscape for those who like beautiful landscape, great for music for those who like music, great for processions for those who like armies on white horses, and great for anything that one especially desires in such a rapturous dominion; and through the doings of One who was born about five miles south of Jerusalem, and died about ten minutes' walk from its eastern gate, all may enter that great heaven for the earnest and heartfelt asking. That is all. What, then, is your work and mine? Our work is to persuade people to face that way, and start thitherward, and finally go in. But has not religion something to do with this world as well as the next? Oh, yes; but do you not see that if the people start for heaven, on their way there they will do all the good they can? They will at the very start of the journey get so much of the spirit of Christ which is a spirit of kindness and self-sacrifice and generosity and burden-bearing and helpfulness, that every step they take will resound with good deeds. Oh, get your religion off of stilts! Get it down out of the high towers! Get it on a level with the wants and woes of our poor human race! Get it out of the dusty theological books that few people read, and put it in their hearts and lives. Good thing is it to profess religion when you join the Church, but every day somehow we ought to profess religion.

STORY OF A QUILT.

A peculiar patchwork quilt was, during the civil war made by a lady and sent to the hospitals at the front. She had a boy in the army, and was naturally interested in the welfare of soldiers. But what a patchwork quilt she sent! On every block of the quilt was a passage of Scripture or a verse of a hymn. The months and years of the war went by. On that quilt many a wounded man had lain and suffered and died. But one morning the hospital nurse saw a patient under that blanket kissing a figure of a leaf as part of a gown his mother used to wear, and it reminded him of home. "Do you know where this quilt came from?" he asked. The nurse

answered: "I can find out for there was a card pinned
fast to it, and I will find that,"   Sure enough, it confirmed what he thought.   .

Then the nurse pointed to a passage of Scripture in the
block of the quilt, the passage which says: "When he
was yet a great way off, his father saw him and ran and
fell on his neck and kissed him."   "Yes," said the dying
soldier.   "I was a great way off, but God has met me
and had compassion on me.   "Shall I write to your
mother and tell her that the lost one is found and the
dead is alive again?"   He answered: "I wish you would,
if it would not be too much trouble."

GO TO WORK FOR GOD AND HUMANITY.

Do you suppose that woman who made that quilt and
filled it with Scripture passages had any trouble about
who Melchizedec was, or how the doctrine of God's sovereignty can be harmonized with man's free agency, or who
wrote the Pentateuch, or the inconsistencies of the
Nicene creed?   No, no.   Go to work for God and suffering humanity and all your doubts and fears and mysteries
and unbeliefs put together will not be heavy enough to
stir the chemist's scales, which is accustomed to weigh-
ing one fiftieth part of a grain of chamomile flowers.

Why stop a moment to understand the mysteries, when
there are so many certitudes?   Why spend our time exploring the dark garrets and coal-holes of a great palace
which has above ground one hundred rooms flooded with
sunshine?   It takes all my time to absorb what has been
revealed, so that I have no time to upturn and root out
and drag forth what has not been revealed.   The most
of the effort to solve mysteries and explore the inexpli-

cable and harmonize things, is an attempt to help the Lord out of theological difficulties. Good enough intentions, my brother, no doubt; but the Lord is not anxious to have you help Him. He will keep HIs throne without your assistance. Don't be afraid that the Bible will fall apart from inconsistencies. It hung together many centuries before you were born, and your funeral sermon will be preached from a text taken from its undisturbed authenticity.

Do you know that I think that if all ministers in all denominations would stop this nonsense of ecclesiastical strife and take hold the word of God, the only question with each of us being how many souls we can bring to Christ, and in how short a time, the Lord would soon appear for the salvation of all nations?

QUEEN VICTORIA'S VISIT TO SCOTLAND.

When the young Queen of England visited Scotland many years ago, great preparations were made for her reception. The vessel in which she sailed was far out at sea, but every hill in Scotland was illumined with bonfires and torches. The night was set on fire with artificial illumination. The Queen, standing on the ship's deck, knew that Scotland was full of heartiest welcome, and the thunder of the great guns of Glasgow and Edinburgh castle woke up all the echoes. Boom! they sounded up among the hills.

Do you know that I think that our King would land if we were only ready to receive Him. Why not call to Him from all our churches, from all our hospitals, from all our homes? Why not all at once light all the torches of Gospel invitation? Why not ring all the bells of welcome? Why not light up the long night of the world's sin and suffering with bonfires of victory? Why not un- limber all the Gospel batteries and let them boom across the earth and boom into the parting heavens. The King is ready to land if we are ready to receive Him. Why can not we who are now living see His descent? Must it all be postponed to later ages? Has not our poor world groaned long enough in mortal agonies? Have there not been martyrs enough, and have not the lakes of tears and the rivers of blood been deep enough?

OH, CHRIST! WHY TARRIEST THOU?

Why cannot the final glory roll in now? Why can not this dying century feel the incoming tides of the oceans of heavenly mercy? Must our eyes close in death and our ears take on the deafness of the tomb, and there hearts beat their last throb before the day comes in? Oh, Christ! Why tarriest Thou? Wilt Thou not, before we go the way of all the earth, let us see Thy scarred feet under some noonday cloud coming this way? Before we die let us behold Thy hands that were spiked, spread out in benediction for a lost race. And why not let us, with our mortal ears, hear that voice which spoke peace as Thou didst go up, speak pardon and emancipation, and love and holiness and joy to all Nations as Thou comest down? But the skies do not part. I hear no rumbling of chariot wheels coming down over the sapphire. There is no swoop of wings. I see no flash of angelic appear- ances. All is still. I hear nothing but the tramp of my own heart as I pause between these utterances. The King does not land because the world is not ready, and the church is not ready. To clear the way for the Lord's coming let us devote all our energies of body, mind and soul. A Russian General riding over the battleffeld; his horse treading amid the dying and dead, a wounded soldier asked him for water, but the officer did not understand his language and knew not what the poor fellow wanted. Then the soldier cried out, "Christos," and that word meant sympathy and help, and the Russian officer dismounted and put to the lips of the sufferer a cooling draught.

THE CHARMED WORD.

Be that the charmed word with whicn we go forth to do our whold duty. In many languages it has only a little difference of termination. Christos! It stands for sympathy. It stands for help. It stands for pardon. It stands for hope. It stands for heaven. Christos! In that name we were baptized. In that name we took our first sacrament. That will be the battle-shout that will win the whole world for God. Christos! Put it on our banners when we march! Put it on our lips when we die! Put it in the funeral psalms at our obsequies! Put it on the plain slab over our grave! Christos! Blessed be His glorions name forever! Amen!

THE HAUNTS OF VICE IN THE CITIES,

AS SEEN BY DR. TALMAGE AND COMPANIONS DURING A VISIT TO THESE PLACES.

"When said he unto me, Son of man, dig now in the wall; and when I had digged in the wall, behold a door. And he said unto me, Go in and behold the wicked abominations that they do here. So I went in and saw; and behold every form of creeping things and abominable beasts. -- Ezekiel, viii: 8, 9, 10.

So this minister of religion, Ezekiel, was commanded to the exploration of the sin of his day. He was not to stand out side the door guessing what it was, but was to go in and see for himself. He did not in vision say: "O Lord, I don't want to go in; I dare not go in; if I go in I might be criticised; O Lord, please let me off?" When God told Ezekiel to go in, he went in, "and saw, and behold all manner of creeping things and abominable beasts."

I, as a minister of religion, felt I had a Divine commission to explore the iniquities of our cities. I did not ask counsel of my session, or my Presbytery, or of the newspapers, but asking the companionship of three prominent police officials and two of the elders of my church, I unrolled my commission, and it said; "Son of man, dig into the wall; and when I had digged into the wall, behold a door; and he said, Go in and see the wicked abominations that are done here; and I went in, and saw, and behold!" Brought up in the country and

THE DANCE HALL.

surrounded by much parental care, I had not until this
autumn seen the haunts of iniquity.   By the grace of
God defended, I had never sowed any "wild oats."   I
had somehow been able to tell from various sources
something·about the iniquities of the great cities, and to
preach against them; but I saw, in the destruction of a
great multitude of the people, that there must be an infatuation and a temptation that had never been spoken
about, and I said, "I will explore."   I saw tens of
thousands of men going down, and if there had been a
spiritual percussion answering to the physical percussion,
the whole air would have been full of the rumble, and
roar, and crack, and thunder of the demolition, and this
moment, if we should pause in our service, we should
hear the crash, crash!   Just as in the sickly season you
sometimes hear the bell at the gate of the cemetery ringing almost incessantly, so I found that the bell at the
gate of the cemetery where lost souls are buried was toll-
ling by day and tolling by night.

I said, "I will explore."   I went as a physician goes
into a small-pox hospital, or a fever lazzaretto, to see
what practical and useful information I might get.   That
would be a foolish doctor who would stand outside the
door of an invalid writing a Latin prescription.   When
the lecturer in a medical college is done with his lecture
he takes the students into the dissecting room, and he
shows them the reality.   I am here this morning to report a plague, and to tell you how sin dissects the body,
and dissects the mind, and dissects the soul.

, 'Oh!" say you, "are you not afraid that in conse-
quence of your exploration of the inquities of the city

other persons may make exploration, and do themselves damage?"

CRITICISMS.

I reply; "If, in company with the Commissioner of Police, and the Captain of Police, and the Inspector of Police, and the company of two Christian gentlemen, and not with the spirit of curiosity, but that you may see sin in order the better to combat it, then, in the name of the eternal God, go? But, if not, then stay away.

Wellington, standing in the battle of Waterloo when the bullets were buzzing around his head, saw a civilian on the field. He said to him, "Sir, what are you doing here? Be off!"

"Why," replied the civilian, "there is no more danger here for me than there is for you."

Then Wellington flushed up and said, "God and my country demand that I be here, but you have no errand here."

Now I, as an officer in the army of Jesus Christ, went on this exploration, and on to this battle-field. If you bear a like commission, go; if not, stay away.

But you say, "Don't you think that somehow your description of these places will induce people to go and see for themselves?"

I answer, yes, just as much as the description of the yellow fever at Grenada would induce people to go down there and get the pestilence. It was told us there were hardly enough people alive to bury the dead, and I am going to tell you a story in these Sabbath morning sermons of places where they are all dead or dying. And I shall not gild iniquities. I shall play a dirge and not an

anthem, and while I shall not put faintest blush on
fairest cheek, I will kindle the cheeks of many a man
into conflagration, and I will make his ears tingle. But
you say, "Don't you know that the papers are criticising you for the position you take?" I say, yes; and do
you know how I feel about it! There is no man who is
more indebted to the newspaper press than I am. My
business is to preach the truth, and the wider the audience
the newspaper press gives me, the wider my field is. As
the secular and religious press of the United States and
the Canadas, and of England and Ireland and Scotland
and Australia and New Zealand, are giving me every
week nearly three million souls for an audience, I say I
am indebted to the press anyhow. Go on! To the day
of my death I cannot pay them what I owe them. So
slash away, gentlemen. The more the merrier. If there
is anything I despise, it is a dull time. Brisk criticism
is a course Turkish towel, with which every public man
needs every day to be rubbed down, in order to keep
healthful circulation. Give my love to all the secular
and religious editors, and full permission to run their
steel pens clear through my sermons, from introduction
to application.

DANTE'S INFERNO.

It was ten o'clock of a calm, clear, star-lighted night
when the carriage rolled with us from the bright part of
the city down into the region where gambling and crime
and death hold high carnival. When I speak of houses
of dissipation, I do not refer to one sin, or five sins, but
to all sins. As the horses halted, and, escorted by the
officers, of the law, we went in, we moved into a world of

which we were as practically ignorant as though it had
swung as far off from us as Mercury is from Saturn.   No
shout of revelry, no guffaw of laughter, but comparative
silence.   Not many signs of death, but the dead was
there.   As I moved through this place I said,   "This is
the home of lost souls."   It was a Dante's Inferno;
nothing to stir the mirth, but many things to fill the eyes
with tears of pity.   Ah! there were moral corpses.   There
were corpses on the stairway, corpses in the gallery,
corpses in the gardens.   Leper met leper, but no ban-
daged mouth kept back the breath.   I felt that I was
sitting on the iron coast against which Euroclydon had
driven a hundred dismasted hulks—every moment more
blackening hulks rolling in.   And while I stood and
waited for the going down of the storm and the lull of the
sea, I bethought myself, this is an everlasting storm, and
these billows always rage, and on each carcass that
strewed the beach already had alighted a vulture—the
long-beaked, filthy vulture of unending despair—now
picking into the corruption, and now on the black wing
wiping the blood off a soul!   No lark, no robin, no chaf-
finch, but vultures, vultures, vultures.

BITTEN BY A SERPENT.

I was reading of an incident that occurred in Pennsylvania a few weeks ago, where a naturalist had presented
to him a deadly serpent, and he put it in a bottle and
stood it in his studio, and one evening, while in the
studio with his daughter, a bat flew in the window, extinguished the light, struck the bottle containing the
deadly serpent, and in a few minutes there was a shriek
from the daughter, and in a few hours she was dead.

She had been bitten of the serpent. Amid these haunts of death, in that midnight exploration I saw that there were lions and eagles and doves for insignia; but thought to myself how inappropriate. Better the insignia of an adder and a bat.

WHAT I SAW IN THE COSTLIEST HAUNT OF VICE.

First of all, I have to report as a result of this midnight exploration that all the sacred rhetoric about the costly magnificence of the haunts of iniquity is apocryphal. We were shown what was called the costliest and most magnificient- specimen. I had often heard that the walls were adorned with masterpieces; that the fountains were bewitching in the gaslight; that the music was like the touch of Thalberg or a Gottschalk; that the upholstery was imperial; that the furniture in some places was like the throne-room of the Tuilleries. It is all false. Masterpieces! There was not a painting worth five dollars, leaving aside the frame. Great daubs of color that no intelligent mechanic would put on his wall. A cross-breed between a chromo and a splash of poor paint! Music! Some of the homliest creatures I ever saw squawked discord, accompanied by pianos out of tune! Upholstery! Two characteristics; red and cheap. You have heard so much about the wonderful lights—blue and green and yellow and orange flashing across the dancers and the gay groups. Seventy-five cents' worth of chemicals would produce all that in one night. Tinsel gewgaws, tawdriness, frippery, seemingly much of it bought at a second-hand furniture store and never paid for! For the most part, the inhabitants were repulsive. Here and there a soul on whom God had put the crown of beauty, but nothing comparable with the Christian lovliness and purity which you may see any pleasant afternoon on any of the thoroughfares of our great cities.

Young man, you are a stark fool if you go to places of dissipation to see pictures, and hear music, and admire beautiful and gracious countenances. From Thomas's, or Dodworth's, or Gilmore's Band, in ten minutes you will hear more harmony than in a whole year of the racket and bang of the cheap orchestras of the dissolute. Come to me, and I will give you a letter of introduction to any one of five hundred homes in Brooklyn and New · York, where you will see finer pictures and hear more beautiful music—music and pictures compared with which there is nothing worth speaking of in houses of dissipation. Sin, however pretentious, is almost always poor. Mirrors, divans, Chickering grand she cannot keep. The sheriff is after it with uplifted mallet, ready for the vendue. "Going! going! gone!

INFERIOR MUSIC AND GOOD MUSIC.

But, my friends, I noticed in all the haunts of dissipation that there was an attempt at music, however poor. The door swung open and shut to music; they stepped to music; they danced to music; they attempted nothing without music, and I said to myself, "If such inferior music has such power, and drum, and fife, and orchestra are enlisted in the service of the devil, what multipotent power there must be in music! and is it not high time that in all our churches and reform associations we tested how much charm there is in it to bring men off the wrong road to the right road?" Fifty times that night ᵧ said within myself, "If poor music is so powerful in a

bad direction, why cannot good music be almost omnipotent in a good direction?" Oh! my friends, we want
to drive men into the kingdom of God with a musical
staff. We want to shut off the path of death with a
musical bar. We want to snatch all the musical instruments from the service of the devil, and with organ, and
cornet, and base viol, and piano and orchestra praise the
Lord. .

Good Richard Cecil when seated in the pulpit, said
that when Doctor Wargan was at the organ, he, Mr.
Cecil, was so overpowered with the music that he found
himself looking for the first chapter of Isaiah in
the prayer book, wondering he could not find it. Oh!
holy bewilderment. Let us send such men as Phillip
Phillips, the Christian vocalist, all around the world,
and Arbuckle, the cornetist, with his "Robin Adair" set to
Christian melody, and George Morgan with his Hallelujah Chorus, and ten thousand Christian men with uplifted hosannas to capture this whole earth for God. Oh!
my friends, we have had enough minor strains in the
church; give us major strains. We have had enough
dead marches in the church; play us those tunes which
are played when an army is on a dead run to overtake an
enemy. Give us the double-quick. We are in full
gallop of cavalry charge. Forward, the whole line!
Many a man who is unmoved by Chistian argument
surrenders to a Christian song.

THE CONVERTED DRUNKARD.

Many a man under the power of Christian music has
had a change take place in his soul and in his life equal
to that which took place in the life of a man in Scotland,

who for fifteen years had been a drunkard.   Coming
home late at night, as he touched the doorsill, his wife
trembled at his coming.   Telling the story afterward,
she said:

"I didn't dare go to bed lest he violently drag me
forth.   When he came home there was only about one
half inch of the candle left in the socket.   When he
entered, he said:

"Where are the children?"

I said, "They are up stairs in bed."

He said' "Go and fetch them."

I went up and I knelt down and I prayed God to defend me and my children from their cruel father.   And
then I brought them down.   He took up the eldest in
his arms and kissed her and said,

"My dear lass, the Lord hath sent thee a father home
to-night."   And so he did with the second, and then he
took up the third of the children and said, 'My dear boy,
the Lord hath sent thee home a father to-night.'   And
then he took up the babe and said, 'My darling babe,
the Lord hath sent thee home a father to-night.'   And
then he put his arms around me and kissed me, and said,
'My dear lass, the Lord hath sent thee home a husband
to-night.'   Why, sir' I had na' heard anything like that
for fourteen years.   And he prayed and he was comforted, and my soul was restored, for I didn't live as I ought
to have lived, close to God.   My trouble had broken me
down."   Oh! for such a transformation in some of the
homes of Brooklyn to-day.   By holy conspiracy, in the
last song of the morning, let us sweep every prodigal into the kingdom of our God.   Oh! ve chanters above

Bethlehem, come and hover this morning and give us a snatch of the old tune about "good will to men."

SOMETHING THAT AMAZED ME.

But I have, also to report of that midnight exploration, that I saw something that amazed me more than I can tell. I do not want to tell it, for it will take pain to many hearts far away, and I cannot comfort them. But I must tell it.

In all these haunts of iniquity I found young men with the ruddy color of country health on their cheek, evidently just come to town for business, entering stores, and shops, and offices. They had helped gather the summer grain. There they were in haunts of iniquity, the look on their cheek which is never on the cheek except when there has been hard work on the farm and in the open air. Here were these young men who had heard how gayly a boat dances on the edge of a maelstrom, and they were venturing. O God! will a few weeks do such on awful work for a young man? O Lord! hast thou forgotten what transpired when they knelt at the family altar that morning when he came away, and how father's voice trembled in the prayer, and mother and sister sobbed as they lay on the floor?

THE YOUNG MAN'S FIRST NIGHT THERE.

I saw that young man when he first confronted evil. I saw it was the first night there. I saw on him a defiant look, as much as to say, "I am mightier than sin." Then I saw him consult with iniquity. Then I saw him waver and doubt. Then I saw going over his countenance the shadow of sad reflections, and I knew from his looks there was a powerful memory stirring his soul. I think there was a whisper going out from the gaudy upholstery, saying, "My son, go home." I think there was a hand stretched out from under the curtains —a hand tremulous with anxiety, a hand that has been worn with work, a hand partly wrinkled with age, that seemed to beckon him away, and so goodness and sin seemed to struggle in that young man's soul; but sin triumphed, and he surrendered to darkness and to death —an ox to the slaughter. Oh! my soul, is this the end of all the good advice? Is this the end of all the prayers that have been made? Have the clusters of the country vineyard been thrown into this great wine-press where Despair and Anguish and Death trample, and the vintage is a vintage of blood? I do not feel so sorry for that young man who, brought up in city life, knows beforehand what are all the surrounding temptations; but God pity the country lad unsuspecting and easily betrayed. Oh? young man from the farmhouse among the hills, what have your parents done that you should do this against them? Why are you bent on killing with trouble her who gave you birth? Look at her fingers—what makes them so distort? Working for you. Do you prefer to that honest old face the berouged cheek of sin? Write home to-morrow morning by the first mail, cursing your mother's white hair, cursing her stooped shoulder, cursing her old arm-chair, cursing the cradle in which she rocked you. "Oh!" you say, "I can't, I can't." You are doing it already.

THE BLOOD OF A MOTHER'S BROKEN HEART.

There is something on your hands, on your forehead, on your feet. It is red. What is it? The blood of a mother's broken heart! When you were threshing the harvest apples from that tree at the corner of the field last summer, did you think you would ever come to this? Did you think that the sharp sickle of death would cut you down so soon? If I thought I could break the infatuation I would come down from the pulpit and throw my arms around you and beg you to stop. Perhaps I am a little more sympathetic with such because I was a country lad. It was not until fifteen years of age that I saw a great city. I remember how stupendous New York looked as I arrived at Cortlandt Ferry. And now that I look back and remember that I had a nature all awake to hilarities and amusements, it is a wonder I escaped. I was saying this to a gentleman in New York a few days ago, and he said, ''Ah! sir, I guess there were some prayers hovering about.'' When I see a young man coming from the tame life of the country and going down in the city ruin, I am not surprised. My only surprise is that any escape, considering the allurements.

I was a few days ago on the St. Lawrence river, and I said to the captain, ''What a swift stream this is.'' ''Oh!'' he replied, ''seventy-five miles from here it is ten' times swifter. Why, we have to employ an Indian pilot, and we give him $1,000 for his summer's work, just to conduct our boats through between the rocks and the islands, so swift are the rapids.'' Well, my friends, every man that comes into New York and Brooklyn life comes into the rapids, and the only question is whether he shall have safe or unsafe pilotage. Young man your bad habits will be reported at the homestead. You cannot hide them.

There are people who love to carry bad news, and there will be some accursed old gossip who will wend her infernal step toward the old homestead, and she will sit down, and after she has awhile wriggled in the chair, she will say to your old parents, "Do you know your son drinks?"

YOU KILLED HER.

Then your dear parents will get white about the lips, and the mother will ask to have the door set a little open for the fresh air, and before that old gossip leaves the place she will have told your parents all about the places where you are accustomed to go. Then your mother will come out, and she will sit down on the steps where you used to play, and she will cry and cry. Then she will be sick, and the gig of the country doctor will come up the country lane, and the horse will be tied at the swing-gate, and the prescription will fail, and she will get worse and worse, and in her delirium she will talk about nothing but you. Then the farmers will come to the funeral, and tie the horses at the rail fence about the house, and they will talk about what ailed the one that died, and one will say it was intermitten, and the other will say it was congestion; and another will say it was premature old age; but it will be neither intermitten, nor congestion, nor old age. In the ponderous book of Almighty God it will be recorded for everlasting ages to read, that you killed her. Our language is very fertile in describing different kinds of crime. Slaying a man is homicide. Slaying a brother is fratricide. Slaying a father is patricide. Slaying a mother is matricide It takes two words to describe your crime—patricide and matricide.

I must leave to other Sabbath mornings the unrolling of the scroll which I have this morning only laid on your table. We have come only to the vestibule of the subject. I have been treating of generals. I shall come to specifics. I have not told you of all the styles of people I saw in the haunts of iniquity. Before I get through with these sermons and next Sabbath morning I will answer the question everywhere asked me, why does municipal authority allow these haunts of iniquity?

I will show all the obstacles in the way. Sirs, before I get through with this course of Sabbath morning sermons, by the help of the eternal God, I will save ten thousand men! And in the execution of this mission I defy all earth and hell.

A THRILLING INCIDENT.

But I was going to tell you of an incident. I said to the officer, "Well, let us go; I am tired of this scene;" and as we passed out of the haunts of iniquity into the fresh air, a soul passed in. What a face that was! Sorrow only half covered up with an assumed joy. It was a woman's face. I saw as plainly as on the page of a book the tragedy. You know that there is such a thing as somnambulism, or walking in one's sleep. Well, in a fatal sonambulism, a soul started off from her father's house. It was very dark, and her feet were cut of the rocks; but on she went until she came to the verge of a chasm, and she began to descend from bowlder to bowlder down over the rattling shelving—for you know while walking in sleep people will go where they would not go when awake.   Further on down, and further, where no owl of the night or hawk of the day would venture.   On down until she touched the depth of the chasm.   Then, in walking sleep, she began to ascend the other side of the chasm, rock above rock, as the roe boundeth. Without having her head to swim with the awful steep, she scaled the height.   No eye but the sleepless eye of God watched her as she went down one side the chasm and came up the other side the chasm.

FATAL AWAKENING OF THE SOMNAMBULIST.

It was an August night, and a storm was gathering, and a loud burst of thunder awoke her from her somnambulism, and she said, ''Whither shall I fly?'' and with an affrighted eye she looked back upon the chasm she had crossed, and she looked in front, and there was a deeper chasm before her. She said,   ''What shall I do? Must I die here?''   And as she bent over the one chasm, she heard the sighing of the past; and as she bent over the other chasm, she heard the portents of the future. Then she sat down on the granite crag, and cried: ''O! for my father's house!   O! for the cottage, where I might die amid embowering honeysuckle!   O! the past! O! the future! O! father! O! mother! O! God!''   But the storm that had been gathering culminated, and wrote with finger of litghtning on the sky just above the horizon, ''The way of the transgressor is hard.'' And then thunderpeal after thunder-peal uttered it: ''Which forsaketh the guide of her youth and forgetteth the covenant of her God.   Destroyed without remedy!''   And the cavern behind echoed it,   ''Destroyed without remedy!'' And the chasm before echoed it, ''Destroyed without remedy!''

There she perished, her cut and bleeding feet on the edge of one chasm, her long, locks washed of the storm dripping over the other chasm.

And by this time the carriage had reached the curbstone of my dwelling, and I awoke and behold it was a dream.

THE LEPERS OF HIGH LIFE.

"Policeman, what of the night?"—-Isaiah, xxi, 11.

The orignal of the text may be translated either "watchman" or "policeman." I have chosen the latter word. The olden-time cities were all thus guarded.

There were roughs, and thugs, and desperadoes in Jerusalem, as well as there are in New York and Brooklyn. The police headquarters of olden time was on top of the city wall. King Solomon, walking incognito through the streets, reports in one of his songs that he met these officials. King Solomon must have had a large posse of police to look after his royal grounds, for he had twelve thousand blooded horses in his stables, and he had millions of dollars in his palace, and he had six hundred wives, and, though the palace was large, no house was ever large enough to hold two women married to the same man; much less could six hundred keep the peace. Well, the eight was divided into three watches, the first watch reaching from sundown to ten o'clock; the second watch from ten o'clock to two in the morning; the third watch from two in the morning to sunrise. An Idumean, anxious about the prosperity of the city, and in regard to any danger that might threaten it, accosts an officer just as you might any night upon our streets, saying, "Policeman, what of the night?" Policemen, more than any other people, understand a city. Upon them

(240)

are vast responsibilities for small pay. The police officer of your city gets $1,100 salary, but he may spend only one night of an entire month in his family. The detective of your city gets $1,500 salary, but from January to January there is not an hour that he may call his own. Amid cold and heat and tempest, and amid the perils of the bludgeon of the midnight assassin, he does his work. The moon looks down upon nine-tenths of the iniquity of our great cities. What wonder, then, that a few weeks ago, in the interest of morality and religion, I asked the question of the text, ''Policeman, what of the night?''

GOOD ADVICE TO THEOLOGICAL SEMINARIES.

In addition to this powerful escortage, I asked two elders of the church to accompany me; not because they were any better than the other elders of the church, but because they were more muscular, and I was resolved that in any case where anything more than spiritual defense was necessary, to refer the whole matter to their hands! I believe in muscular Christianity. I wish that our theological seminaries, instead of sending out so many men with dyspepsia and liver complaint and all out of breath by the time they have climbed to the top of the pulpit stairs, would, through gymnasiums and other means, send into the pulpit physical giants as well as spiritual athletes. I do wish I could consecrate to the Lord two hundred and fifty pound avoirdupois weight? But, borrowing the strength of others, I started out on the midnight exploration. I was preceded in this work by Thomas Chalmers, who opened every door of iniquity in Edinburgh before he established systematic amelioration, and preceded by Thomas Guthrie. who explored all the squalor of the city before he established the ragged schools, and by every man who has done anything to balk crime, and help the tempted and the destroyed. Above all, I followed in the footsteps of Him who was derided by the hypocrites and the sanhedrims of the day, because he persisted in exploring the deepest moral slush of his time, going down among demoniacs and paupers and adulteresses, never so happy as when he had ten lepers to cure. Some of you may have been surprised that there was a great hue and cry raised before these sermons were begun, and sometimes the hue and cry was made by professors of religion. I was not surprised. The simple fact is that in all our churches there are lepers who do not want their scabs touched, and they foresaw that before I got through with this series of sermons I would show up some of the wickedness and rottenness of what is called the upper class. The devil howled because he knew I was going to hit him hard! Now, I say to all such men, whether in the church or out of it, ''Ye hypocrites, ye generation of vipers, how can ye escape the damnation of.hell?''

HAUNTS OF SIN ARE SUPPORTED BY MEN OF WEALTH.

I notice in my midnight exploration with these high officials that the haunts of sin are chiefly supported by men of means and men of wealth. The young men recently come from the country, of whom I spoke last Sabbath morning, are on small salary, and they have but little money to spend in sin, and if they go into luxuriant iniquity the employer finds it out by the inflamed eye and the marks of dissipation, and they are discharged.

The luxuriant places of iniquity are supported by men, who come down from the. fashionable avenues of New York, and cross over from some of the finest mansions of Brooklyn. Prominent business men from Boston, Philadelphia, and Chicago, and Cincinnati patronize these places of crime. I could call the names of prominent men in our cluster of cities who patronize these places of iniquity, and I may call their names before I get through this course of sermons, though the fabric of New York and Brooklyn society tumble into wreck. Judges of courts, distinguished lawyers, officers of the church, political orators standing on Republican and Democratic and Greenback platforms talking about God and good morals until you might suppose them to be evangelists expecting a thousand converts in one night. Call the roll of dissipation in the haunts of iniquity any night, and if the inmates will answer, you will find there, stock-brokers from Wall street, large importers from Broadway, iron merchants, leather merchants, cotton merchants, hardware merchants, wholesale grocers, representatives from all the commercial and wealthy classes.

PUTREFACTIONS COVERED WITH CAMEL'S-HAIR SHAWLS.

Talk about the heathenism below canal street! There is a worse heathenism above canal street. I prefer that kind of heathenism which wallows in filth and disgusts the beholder rather than that heathenism which covers up its walking putrefaction with camel's-hair shawl and point lace, and rides in turnouts worth $3,000, liveried driver ahead and rosetted flunky behind. We have been talking so much about the gospel for the masses; now let us talk a little about the gospel for the lepers of society, for the millionaire sots, for the portable lazzarettos of upper-tendom. It is the iniquity that comes down from the higher circles of society that supports the haunts of crime, and it is gradually turning our cities into Sodoms and Gomorrahs waiting for the fire and brimstone tempest of the Lord God who whelmed the cities of the plain. We want about five hundred Anthony Comstocks to go forth and explore and expose the abomination of high life.

A NEW YORK BROWN STONE HELL.

For eight or ten years there stood within sight of the most fashionable New York drive a Moloch temple, a brown-stone hell on earth, which neither the Mayor, nor the judges, nor the police dared touch, when Anthony Comstock, a Christian man of less than average physical stature, and with cheek scarred by the knife of a desperado whom he had arrested, walking into that palace of the damned on Fifth avenue, and in the name of God put an end to it, the priestess presiding at the orgies retreating by suicide into the lost world, her bleeding corpse found in her own bath-tub. May the eternal God have mercy on our cities. Gilded sin comes down from these high places into the upper circles of iniquity, and then on gradually down, until in five years it makes the whole pilgrimage, from the marble pillar on the brilliant avenue clear down to the cellars on Wall street. The officer on that midnight exploration said to me:

"Look at them now, and look at them three years from now when all this glory has departed; they'll be a heap of rags in the station-house!" Another of the officers said to me:

"That is the daughter of one of the wealthiest families on Madison square!"

THE MAN AND THE WOMAN ALIKE GUILTY.

But I have something more amazing to tell you than that the men of means and wealth support these haunts of iniquity, and that is, that they are chiefly supported by heads of families—fathers and husbands, with the awful perjury of broken marriage vows upon them, with a niggardly stipend left at home for the support of their families, going forth with their thousands for the diamonds and wardrobe and equipage of iniquity.

In the name of heaven, I denounce this public iniquity. Let such men be hurled out of decent circles.   If they will not repent, overboard with them!

I lift one-half the burden of malediction from the unpitied head of offending woman, and hurl it on the blasted pate of offending man!

Society needs a new division of its anathema.   By what law of justice does burning excoriation pursue offending woman down off the precipices of destruction, while offending man, kid-gloved, walks in refined circles, invited up if he have money, advanced into political recognition, while all the doors of high life open at the first rap of his gold-headed cane?

I say, if you let one come back, let them both come back.   If one must go down, let them both go down.

I give you as my opinion that the eternal perdition of all other sinners will be a heaven compared with the punishment everlasting of that man who, turning his back upon her whom he swore to protect and defend until death, and upon his children, whose destiny may be decided by his example, goes forth to seek affectional alliances elsewhere. For such a man the portion will be fire, and hail, and tempest, and darkness, and blood, and anguish, and despair forever, forever, forever!

HEADS OF FAMILIES SUPPORT THE HAUNTS OF VICE.

My friends, there has got to be a reform in this matter, or American society will go to pieces. Under the head of "incompatibility of temper," nine-tenths of the abomination goes on.

What did you get married for if your dispositions are incompatible?

"Oh!" you say, I rushed into it without thought."

Then you ought to be willing to suffer the punishment for making a fool of yourself! Incompatibility of temper! You are responsible for at least a half of the incompatibility. Why are you not honest and willing to admit either that you did not control your temper, or that you had already broken your marriage oath? In nine hundred and ninety-nine cases out of the thousand, incompatibility is a phrase to cover up wickedness already enacted.

I declare in the presence of this city and in the presence of the world that heads of families are supporting these haunts of iniquity.

I wish there might be a police raid lasting a great while, that they would just go down through these places of sin and gather up all the prominent business men of the city, and march them down through the street followed by about twenty reporters to take their names and put them in full capitals in the next day's paper!

Let such a course be undertaken in our cities, and in

six months there would be eighty per cent off your public crime.

It is not now that the young men and the boys that need so much looking after; it is their fathers and mothers.

Let heads of families cease to patronize places of ini-, quity, and in a short time they would crumble to ruin.

BROOKLYN A WELL REGULATED CITY.

But you meet me with the question, "Why don't the city authorities put an end to such places of iniquity?"

I answer in regard to Brooklyn, the work has already been done. Six years ago there were in the radius of your City Hall thirty-eight gambling saloons. They are all broken up. The ivory and wooden "chips" that came from the gambling-hells into the Police Headquarters came in by the peck. How many inducements were offered to our officials, such as: "This will be worth a thousand dollars to you if you will let it go on." "This will be worth five thousand if you will let it go on." But our commissioners of police, mightier than any bribe, pursued their work until, while beyond the city limits there may be exceptions, within the city limits of Brooklyn there is not a gambling-hell, or policy-shop, or a house of death so pronounced. There are under-ground iniquities and hidden scenes, but none so pronounced.

HOW IT WAS DONE.

Every Monday morning all the captains of the police make reports in regard to their respective precincts. When the work began, the police in authority at that time said:

"O! it can't be done; we can't get into these places of

iniquity to see them, and hence we can't break them up."

"Then," said the commissioners of police, "break in the doors;" and it is astonishing how soon after the shoulders of a stout policeman goes against the door, it gets off its hinges. Some of the captains of the police said:

"This thing has been going on so long, it cannot be crushed."

"Then," said the commissioners of police, "we'll get other captains of police." The work went on until now, if a reformer wants the commissioners of police to show him the haunts of iniquity in Brooklyn, there are none to show him. If you know a single case that is an exception to what I say, report it to me at the close of this service at the foot of this platform, and I will warrant that within two hours after you report the case Commissioner Jourdan, Superintendent Campbell, Inspector Waddy, and as many of the twenty-five detectives and of the five hundred and fifty policemen as are necessary will come down on it like an Alpine avalanche. If you do not report it, it is because you are a coward, or else because you are in the sin yourself, and you do not want it shown up. You shall bear the whole responsibility, and it shall not be thrown on the hard-working and heroic detective and police force. But you say: "How has this general clearing out of gambling-hells and places of iniquity been accomplished?" Our authorities have been backed up by a high public sentiment.

In a city which has on its judicial bench such magnificent men as Neilson, and Reynolds, and McCue, and Moore, and Pratt, and others whom I am not fortunate

enough to know, there must be a mighty impulse up-
ward toward God and good morals.   We have in the
high places of this city men not only with great heads,
but with great hearts.

THE PRODIGAL SON OVER AGAIN.

A young man disappeared from his father's house about
the time the Brooklyn Theatre burned, and it was supposed that he had been destroyed in that ruin.   The
father, broken-hearted, sold his property in Brooklyn, and
in desolation left the city.   Recently the wanderer came
back. ·   He could not find his father, who, in departing,
had given no idea of·his destination.   The case was reported to a man high in official position, and he sat down
and wrote a letter to all the chiefs of police in the United
States, in order that he might deliver that prodigal son
into the arms of his broken-hearted father.   A few days
ago it was found that the father was in California.   I
understand that son is now on his way to meet him, and
it will be the parable of the prodigal son over again when
they embrace each other, and the father says: "Rejoice
with me, for this my son was dead and is alive again,
was lost and is found."   I have forgotten the name of
the father, I have forgotten the name of the son; but I
have not forgotten the name of the officer whose sympathetic heart beats so loud under his badge of office.   It
was Patrick Campbell, Superintendent of the Brooklyn
police.

I do not mention these things as a matter of city pride,
nor as a matter of exultation, but of gratitude to God
that Brooklyn to-day stands foremost among American

cities in its freedom from places of iniquity.   But Brooklyn has a large share of sin.

Where do the people of Brooklyn go when they propose to commit abomination?   To New York.

I was told in the midnight exploration in New York
with the police that there are some places almost entirely
supported by men and women from Brooklyn.   We are
one city after all—one now before the bridge is completed, to be more thoroughly one when the bridge is
done.

WHY NEW YORK IS SO BAD.

Well, then, you press me with another question:
"Why don't the public authorities of New York extirpate
these haunts of iniquity?"   Before I give you a definite
answer I want to say that the obstacles in that city are
greater than in any city on this continent.   It is so vast.
It is the landing-place of European· immigration.   Its
wealth is mighty to establish and defend places of iniquity.   Twice a year there are incursions of people from
all parts of the land coming on the spring and fall trade.
It requires twenty times the municipal energy to keep
order in New York that it does in any city from Portland
to San Francisco.   But still you pursue me with the
question, and I am to answer it by telling you that there
is infinite fault and immensity of blame to be divided between three parties.   First, the police of New York city·
So far as I know .them they are courteous gentlemen.
They have had great discouragement, they tell me, in the
fact that when they arrest crime and bring it before the
courts the witnesses will not appear lest they criminate
themselves.   They tell me also that they have been dis-·

couraged by the fact that so many suits have been brought against them for damages. But after all, my friends, they must take their share of blame.

POLICE IN COMPLICITY WITH CRIME.

I have come to the conclusion, after much research and investigation, that there are captains of police in New York who are in complicity with crime—men who make thousands of dollars a year for the simple fact that they will not tell, and will permit places of iniquity to stand month after month, and year after year.

I am told that there are captains of police in New York who get a percentage on every bottle of wine sold in the haunts of death, and that they get a revenue from all the shambles of sin. What a state of things this is!

In the twenty-ninth precinct of New York there are one hundred and twenty-one dens of death. Night after night, month after month, year after year, untouched.

In the west Twenty-sixth street there are whole blocks that are pandemonium. There are between five and six hundred dens of darkness in the city of New York, where there are 2,500 policemen.

Not long ago there was a masquerade ball in which the masculine and feminine offenders of society were the participants, and some of the police danced in the masquerade and distributed the prizes!

There is the grandest opportunity that has ever opened, for any American, open now. It is for that man in high official position who shall get into his stirrups and say, "Men, follow?" and who shall in one night sweep around and take all of these leaders of iniquity, whether on suspicion or on positive proof saying, "I'll take the respon-

sibility, come on!   I put my private property and my
political aspirations and my life into this crusade against
the powers of darkness."   That man would be Mayor of
the city of New York.   That man would be fit to be President of the United States.

But the second part of the blame I must put at the
door of the District Attorney of New York.   I understand he is an honorable gentleman, but he has not time
to attend to all these cases.   Literally, there are thousands of cases unpursued for lack of time.   Now, I say,
it is the business of New York to give assistants, and
clerks, and help to the District Attorney until all these
places shall go down in quick retribution.

CHRISTIANS ARE MUCH TO BLAME.

But the third part of the blame, and the heaviest part
of it, I put on the moral and Christian people of our
cities, who are guilty of most culpable indifferences on
this whole subject.   When Tweed stole his millions,
large audiences were assembled in indignation, Charles
O'Conor was retained, committees of safety and investigation were appointed, and a great stir made; but night
by night there is a theft and a burglary of city morals as
much worse than Tweed's robberies as his were worse
than common shop-lifting, and it has very little opposition.   I tell you what New York wants; it wants indignation meetings in Cooper Institute and Academy of
Music and Chickering and Irving Halls to compel the
public authorities to do their work and to send the police,
with clubs and lanterns and revolvers, to turn off the
colored lights of the dance-houses, and to mark for confiscation the trunks and wardrobes and furniture and

scenery, and to gather up all the keepers, and all the inmates, and all the patrons, and march them out to the Tombs, fife and drums sounding the Rogue's March.

RAGING VOLCANOES BENEATH OUR CITIES.

While there are men smoking their cigarettes, with their feet on Turkish divans, shocked that minister of religion should explore and expose the iniquity of city life, there are raging underneath our great cities a Cotopaxi, a Stromboli, a Vesuvius, ready to bury us in ashes and scoria deeper than that which overwhelmed Pompeii and Herculaneum. Oh! I wish the time would come for the plowshare of public indignation to push through and rip up and turn under those parts of New York which are the plague of the nation. Now is the time to hitch up the team to this plowshare. In this time, when Mr. Cooper is Mayor, and Mr. Kelly is Comptroller, and Mr. Nichols is Police Commissioner, and Superintendent Walling wears the badge of office, and there is on the judicial benches of New York an array of the best men that have ever occupied these positions since the foundation of the city—Recorder Hackett, Police Magistrates Gilbreth, Wandell, Morgan and Duffy; such men as Gildersleeve, and Sutherland, and Davis, and Curtis; and on the United States Court bench in New York such men as Benedict, and Blatchford, and Choate—now is the time to make an extirpation of iniqnity. Now is the time for a great crusade, and for the people of our cities in great public assemblages to say to police authority: "Go ahead, and we will back you with our lives, our fortunes, and our sacred honor."

I must adjourn until next Sabbath morning much of

what I wanted to say abont certain forms of iniquity which I saw rampant in the night of my exploration with the city officials. But before I stop this morning I want to have one word with a class of men with whom people have so little patience that they never get a kind word of invitation. I mean the men who have forsaken their homes. Oh! my brother, return. You say:

RE-ESTABLISH YOUR HOME.

"I can't; I have no home; my home is broken up."

Re-establish your home. It has been done in other cases, why may it not be done in your case?

"Oh," you say, "we parted for life; we have divided our property; we have divided our effects."

I ask you, did you divide the marriage ring on that bright day when you started life together?

Did you divide your family Bible? If so, where did you divide it? Across the Old Testament, where the Ten Commandments denounce your sin, or across the New Testament, where Christ savs: "Blessed are the pure in heart?" Or did you divide it between the Old and the New Testament, right across the family record of weddings and births and deaths?

Did you divide the cradle in which you rocked your first born?

Did you divide the little grave in the cemetery, over which you stood with linked arms, looking down in awful bereavement?

Above all, I ask you, aid you divide your hope for heaven, so that there is no full hope left for either of you? Go back! There may be a great gulf between you and once happy domesticty; but Christ will bridge that gulf. It may be a bridge of sighs. Turn toward it. Put your foot on the over-arching span. Hear it! It is a voice unrolling from the throne: "He that overcometh shall inherit all things, and I will be unto him a God, and he shall be my son; but the unbelieving, and the sorcerers, and whoremongers, and the adulterers, and the idolators, and all liars shall have their part in the lake which burneth with fire and brimstone—which is the second death!"

THE GATES OF HELL.

"The gates of hell shall not prevail against it."—St. Mathew, xvi, 18.

It is only ten o'clock, said the officer of the law, as we got into the carriage for the midnight exploration—"it is only ten o'clock, and it is too early to see the places that we wish to see, for the theaters have not yet let out."

I said, "What do you mean by that?"

"Well, he said, "the places of iniquity are not in full blast until the people have time to arrive from the theaters."

So we loitered on, and the officer told the driver to stop on a street where is one of the costliest and most brilliant gambling-houses in the city of New York.

A GAMBLING HOUSE DESCRIBED.

As we came up in front all seemed dark. The blinds were down; the door was guarded; but after a whispering of the officer with the guard at the door, we were admitted into the hall, and thence into the parlors, around one table finding eight or ten men in mid-life, well dressed—all the work going on in silence, save the noise of the rattling "chips" on the gambling table in one parlor, and the revolving ball of the roulette table in the other parlor. Some of these men, we were told, had served terms in prison; some were ship-wrecked bankers, and brokers, and money-dealers, and some were going their first rounds of vice—but all intent upon the table, as large or small fortunes moved up and down before them.

[256]

Oh!.there was something awfully solemn in the silence—
the intent gaze, the suppressed emotion of the players.
No one looked up.   They all had money in the rapids,
and I have no doubt some saw, as they sat there, horses
and carriages, and houses and lands, and home and family
rushing down into the vortex.   A man's life would not
have been worth a farthing in that presence had he not
been accompanied by the police, if he had been supposed
to be on a Christian errand of observation.   Some of
these men went by private key, some went in by careful
introduction, some were taken in by patrons, of the
establishment.   The officer of the law told me: ''None
get in here except by police mandate, or by some letter
of a patron."   While we were there a young man came
in, put his money down on the roulette-table, and lost;
put more money down on the roulette-table, and lost;
put more money down on the roulette-table, and lost;
then feeling in his pockets for more money, finding none,
in severe silence he turned his back upon the scene and
passed out.

All the literature about the costly magnificence of such
places is untrue.   Men kept their hats on and smoked,
and there was nothing in the upholstery or the furniture
to forbid.   While we stood there men lost their property
and lost their souls.   O! merciless place.   Not once in
all the history of that gambling-house has there been
one word of sympathy uttered for the losers at the game.

DEATH AND THE GAMBLERS.

Sir Horace Walpole said that a man dropped dead in
front of one of the club-houses of London; his body was
carried into the club-house, and the members of the club

began immediately to bet as to whether he were dead or alive, and when it was proposed to test the matter by bleeding him, it was only hindered by the suggestion that it would be unfair to some of the players! In these gaming-houses of our cities, men have their property wrung away from them, and then they go out, some of them to drown their grief in strong drink, some to ply the counterfeiter's pen, and to restore their fortunes, some resort to the suicide's revolver, but all going down, and that work proceeds day by day, and night by night, until it is estimated that every day in Christendom eighty million dollars pass from hand to hand through gambling practices, and every year in Christendom one hundred and twenty-three billion, one hundred million dollars change hands in that way.

"But," I said, "it is eleven o'clock, and we must be off." We passed out into the hallway and so into the street, the burly guard slamming the door of the house after us, and we got into the carriage and rolled on toward the gates of hell. You know about the gates of heaven. You have often heard them preached about. There are three to each point of the compass. On the north, three gates; on the south, three gates; on the east, three gates; on the west, three gates; and each gate is of solid pearl. Oh! gate of heaven; may we all get into it. But who shall describe the gates of hell spoken of in my text? These gates are burnished until they sparkle and glisten in the gas-light. They are mighty, and set in sockets of deep and dreadful masonry. They are high, so that those who are in may not clamber over and get out. They are heavy, but they swing easily in to let those go in who are to be destroyed. Well, my friends, it is always safe to go where God tells you to go, and God had told me to go through these gates of hell, and explore and report, and, taking three of the high police authorities and two of the elders of my church, I went in, and I am here this morning to sketch the gates of hell.

I remember, when the Franco-German war was going on, that I stood one day in Paris looking at the gates of the Tuilleries, and I was so absorbed in the sculpturing at the top of the gates—the masonry and the bronze— that I forgot myself, and after awhile, looking down, I saw that there were officers of the law scrutinizing me, supposing, no doubt, I was a German, and looking at those gates for adverse purposes. But, my friends, we shall not stand looking at the outside of the gates of hell. Through this midnight exploration I shall tell you of both sides, and I shall tell you what these gates are made of. With the hammer of God's truth I shall pound on the brazen panels, and with the lantern of God's truth I shall flash a light upon the shining hinges.

GATE OF IMPURE LITERATURE.

Gate the first: Impure literature. Anthony Comstock seized twenty tons of bad books, plates, and letter-press, and when our Professor Cochran, of the Polytechnic Institute, poured the destructive acids on those plates, they smoked in the righteous annihilation. And yet a great deal of the bad· literature of the day is not gripped of the law. It is strewn in your parlors; it is in your libraries. Some of your children read it at night after they have retired. the gas-burner swung as near as

possible to their pillow.   Much of this literature is under
the title of scientific information.

A book agent with one of these infernal books, glossed
over with scientific nomenclature, went into a hotel and
sold in one day a hundred copies, and sold them all to
one woman!   It is appalling that men and women who
can get through their family physician all the useful information they may need, and without any contamination, should wade chin deep through such accursed literature under the plea of getting useful knowledge, and
that printing presses, hoping to be called decent, lend
themselves to this infamy.   Fathers and mothers, be not
deceived by the title, "medical works."   Nine-tenths of
those books come hot from the lost world, though they
may have on them the names of the publishing-houses of
New York and Philadelphia.

Then there is all the novelette literature of the day
flung over the land by the million.   As there are good
novels that are long, so I suppose there may be good
novels that are short, and so there may be a good novel
ette, but it is the exception.   No one—mark this—no
one systematically reads the average novelette of this
day and keeps either integrity or virtue.   The most of
these novelettes are written by broken-down literary men
for small compensation, on the principle that, having
failed in literature elevated and pure, they hope to succeed in the tainted and the nasty.   Oh! this is a wide
gate of hell.   Every panel is made out of a bad book or
newspaper.   Every hinge is the interjoined type of a corrupt printing-press.   Every bolt or lock of that gate is
made out of the plate of an unclean pictorial.   In other

words, there are a million men and women in the United States to-day reading themselves into hell.

A BAD BOOK SLEW HER.

When in your own beautiful city a prosperous family fell into ruins through the misdeeds of one of its members, the amazed mother said to the officer of the law: "Why, I never supposed there was anything wrong. I never thought there could be anything wrong." Then she sat weeping in silence for some time, and said: "Oh! I have got it now! I know, I know! I found in her bureau after she went away a bad book. That's what slew her."

THE LEPROUS BOOK SELLERS.

These leprous booksellers have gathered up the catalogues of all the male and female seminaries in the United States, catalogues containing the names and the residences of all the students, and circulars of death are sent to every one, without any exception. Can you imagine anything more deathful? There is not a young person, male or female, or an old person, who has not has offered to him or her a bad book or a bad picture. Scour your house to find out whether there are any of these adders coiled on your parlor center-table, or coiled amid the toilet set on the dressing-case. I adjnre you before the sun goes down to explore your family libraries with an inexorable scrutiny. Remember that one bad book or bad picture may do the work for eternity. I want to arouse all your suspicions about novelettes. I want to put you on the watch against everything that may seem like surreptitious correspondence through the post-office. I want you to understand that impure literature is one of the broadest, highest, mightiest gates of the lost.

Gate the second: The dissolute dance. You shall not divert me to the general subject of dancing. Whatever you may think of the parlor dance, or the methodid motion of the body to sounds of music in the family or the social circle, I am not now discussing that question. . I want you to unite with me this morning in recognizing the fact that there is a dissolute dance. You know of what I speak. It is seen not only in the low haunts of death, but in elegant mansions. It is the first step to eternal ruin for a great multitude of both sexes. You know, my friends, what postures, and attitudes, and figures are suggested of the devil.

They who glide into the dissolute dance glide over an inclined plane, and the dance is swifter and swifter, wilder and wilder, until with the speed of lightning they whirl off the edges of a decent life into a fiery future. This gate of hell swings across the Axminister of many a fine parlor, and across the ball-room of the summer watering-place. You have no right, my brother, my my sister—you have no right to take an attitude to the sound of music which would be unbecoming in the absence of music. No Chickering grand of city parlor or fiddle of mountain picnic can consecrate that which God hath cursed.

Gate the third: Indiscreet apparel. The attire of the woman for the last four or five years has been beautiful and graceful beyond anything I have known; but there are those who will always carry that which is right into the extraordinary and indiscreet. I am told that there is a fashion about to come in upon us that is shocking to all righteousness. I charge Christian women, neither by style of dress nor adjustment of apparel, to become administrative of evil.

Perhaps none else will dare to tell you, so I will tell you that there are multitudes of men who owe their eternal damnation to the boldness of womanly attire. Show me the fashion-plates of any age between this and the time of Louis XVI., of France, and Henry VIII., of England, and I will tell you the type of morals or immorals of that age or that year. No exception to it. Modest apparel means a righteous people. Immodest apparel always means a contaminated and depraved society. You wonder that the city of Tyre was destroyed with such a terrible destruction. Have you ever seen the fashion-plate of the city of Tyre? I will show it to you:

"Moreover. the Lord saith, because the daughters of Zion are haughty and walk with streched-forth necks and wanton eyes, walking and mincing as they go, and making a tinkling with their feet, in that day the Lord will take away the bravery of their tinkling ornaments about their feet, and their cauls, and their round tires like the moon, the rings and nose jewels, the changeable suits of apparel, and the mantels, and the wimples, and the crisping-pins."

That is the fashion-plate of ancient Tyre. And do you wonder that the Lord God in His indignation blotted out the city, so that fishermen to-day spread their nets where that city once stood.

GATE OF ALCHOLIC BEVERAGE.

Gate the fourth: Alcoholic beverage. In our mid-'

night exploration we saw that all the scenes of wickedness were under the enchantment of the wine-cup. That
was what the waitress carried on the platter. That was
what glowed on the table. That was what shone in
illumined gardens. That was what flushed the cheeks of
the patrons who came in. That was what staggered the
step of the patrons as they went out. Oh! the wine-cup
is the patron of impurity. The officers of the law that
night told us that nearly all the men who go into the
shambles of death go in intoxicated, the mental and the
spiritual abolished, that the brute may trumph. Tell
me that a young man drinks, and I know the whole story.
If he becomes a captive of the wine-cup, he will become
a captive of all other vices; only give him time. No one
ever runs drunkenness alone. That is a carrion-crow
that goes in a flock, and when you see that beak ahead,
you may know the other beaks are coming. In other
words, the wine-cup unbalances and dethrones one's
better judgement, and leaves one the prey of all evil appetites that may choose to alight upon his soul.

There is not a place of any kind of sin in the United
States to-day that does not find its chief abettor in the
chalice of inebriacy. There is either a drinking-bar before, or one behind, or one above, or one underneath.
The officers of the law said to me that night: "These
people escape legal penalty because they are all licensed
to sell liquor." Then I said within myself, "The courts
that license the sale of strong drink, license gambling
houses, license libertinism, license disease, license death,
license all sufferings, all crimes, all despoliations, all
disasters, all murders, all woe. It is the courts and the

Legislatures that are swinging wide open these grinding, creaky, stupendous gate of the lost."

But you say, "You have described these gates of hell and shown us how they swing in to allow the entrance of the doomed. Will you not, please, before you get through the sermon, tell us how these gates of hell may swing out to allow the escape of the penitent?"

I reply, but very few escape. Of the thousand that go in nine hundred and ninety-nine perish. Suppose one of these wanderers should knock at your door, would you admit her?

BUT FEW DARE TO HELP THESE FALLEN SOULS.

Suppose you knew where she came from, would you ask her to sit down at your dining-table?

Would you ask her to become the governess of your children?

Would you introduce her among your acquaintance-ships?

Would you take the responsibility of pulling on the outside of the gate of hell while she pushed on the inside of that gate trying to get out?

You would not, not one of a thousand of you that would dare to do it. You write beautiful poetry over her sorrows and weep over her misfortunes, but give her practical help you never will.

There is not one person out of a thousand that will—there is not one out of five thousand that has come so near the heart of the Lord Jesus Christ as to dare to help one of these fallen souls.

But you say, "Are there no ways by which the wanderer may escape?"

Oh, yes; three or four. The one way is the sewing girl's garret, dingy, cold, hunger-blasted.

But you say, "Is there no other way for her to escape?"

THE SAD WAYS FOR ESCAPE.

Oh, yes. Another way is the street that leads to the East River, at midnight, the end of the city dock, the moon shining down on the water making it look so smooth she wonders if it is deep enough. It is. No boatman near enough to hear the plunge. No watchman near enough to pick her out before she sinks the third time.

No other way? Yes. By the curve of the Hudson River Railroad at the point where the engineer of the lightning express train cannot see a hundred yards ahead to the form that lies across the track. He may whistle "down brakes," but not soon enough to disappoint the one who seeks her death.

But you say, "Isn't God good, and won't He forgive?"

Yes; but man will not, woman will not, society will not. The church of God says it will, but it will not. Our work, then, must be prevention rather than cure. Standing here telling this story to-day, it is not so much in the hope I will persuade one who has dashed down a thousand feet over the rocks to crawl up again, into life and light, but it is to alarm those who are coming too near the edges. Have you ever listened to hear the lamentation that rings up from those far depths?

"Once I was pure as the snow, but I fell.
Fell like a snowflake, from heaven to hell;
Fell, to be trampled as filth of the street;
Fell, to be scoffed at, be spit on, and beat.

Pleading, cursing, begging to die,
Selling my soul to whoever would buy;
Dealing in shame for a morsel of bread,
Hating the living and fearing the dead."

But you say, "What can be the practical use of this course of sermons?"

I say, much everywhere. I am greatly obliged to those gentleman of the press who have fairly reported what I have said on these occasions, and the press of this city and New York, and of the other prominent cities. I thank you for the almost universal fairness with which you have presented what I have had to say. Of course, among the educated and refined journalists who sit at these tables, and have been sitting here for four or five years, there will be a fool or two that does not understand his business, but that ought not to discredit the grand newspaper printing-press. I thank also, those who have by letters cheered me in this work—letters coming from all parts of the land, from Christian reformers telling me to go on in the work which I have undertaken. Never so many letters in my life have I received. Perhaps one out of the hundred condemnatory, as one I got yesterday from a man who said he thought my sermons would do great damage in the fact that they would arouse the suspicion of domestic circles as to where the head of the family was spending his evenings! I was sorry it was an anonymous letter, for I should have written to that man's wife telling her to put a detective on her husband's track, for I knew right away he was going to bad places!

My friends, you say, "It is not possible to do anything

with these stalwart iniquities; you cannot **wrestle them**
down."

Stupid man, read my text: "The gates of hell shall
not prevail against the church."   Those gates of hell are
to be prostrated just as certainly as God and the Bible
are true, but it will not be done until Christian men and
women, quitting their prudery and squeamishness in this
matter, rally the whole Christian sentiment of the church
and assail these great evils of society.   The Bible utters
its denunciation in this direction again and again, and
yet the piety of the day is such a namby-pamby, emetic
sort of a thing that you cannot even quote Scripture without making somebody restless.   As long as this holy imbecility reigns in the church of God, sin will laugh you to
scorn.

I do not know but that before the church wakes up
matters will grow worse and worse, and that there will
have to be one lamb sacrificed from each of the most
carefully-guarded folds, and the wave of uncleanness
dash to the spire of the villiage church and the top of
the cathedral pillar. Prophets and patriachs, and apostles
and evangelists,   and Christ himself have thundered
against these sins as against no other, and yet there are
those who think we ought to take, when we speak of these
subjects, a tone apologetic.   I put my foot on all the
conventional rhetoric on this subject, and I tell you
plainly that unless you give up that sin your doom is
sealed, and world without end you will be chased by the
anathemas of an incensed God.   I rally you under the
cheertul prophecy of the text; I rally you to a **besiege-
ment** of the **gates of hell.**

We want in this besieging host no soft sentimentalists, but men who are willing to give and take hard knocks. The gates of Gaza were carried off, the gates of Thebes were battered down, the gates of Babylon were destroyed, and the gates of hell are going to be prostrated.

The Christianized printing-press will be rolled up as the chief battering-ram. Then there will be a long list of aroused pulpits, which shall be assailed fortresses, and God's red-hot truth shall be the flying ammunition of the contest; and the sappers and the miners will lay the train under these foundations of sin, and at just the right time God, who leads on the fray, will call, "Down with the gates!" and the explosion beneath will be answered by all the trumpets of God on high celebrating universal victory. But there may be in this house one wanderer that would like to have a kind word calling homeward, and I cannot sit down until I have uttered that word. I have told you that society has no mercy. Did I hint, at an earlier point in this subject, that God will have mercy upon any wanderer who would like to come back to the heart of infinite love?

A cold Christmas night in a farm-house. Father comes in from the barn, knocks the snow from his shoes, and sits down by the fire. The mother sits at the stand knitting. She says to him:

"Do you remember it is anniversary to-night?"

The father is angered. He never wants any allusion to the fact that one has gone away, and the mere suggestion that it was the anniversary of that sad event made him quite rough, although the tears ran down his cheeks. The old house-dog that had played with the wanderer

when she was a child, came up and put his head on the
old man's knee, but he roughly repulsed the dog. He
wants nothing to remind him of the anniversary day.

THE STORY ABOUT "MEG."

The following incident was told me. It was a cold
winter night in a city church. It is Christmas night.
They have been decorating the sanctuary. A lost wanderer of the street, with thin shawl about her, attracted
by the warmth and light, comes in and sits near the door.
The minister of religion is preaching of Him who was
wounded for our transgressions, and bruised for our iniquities, and the poor soul by the door said:

"Why, that must mean me; mercy for the chief of
sinners; bruised for our iniquities; wounded for our transgressions." The music that night in the sanctuary
brought back the old hymn which she used to sing when
with father and mother she worshiped God in the village
church. The service over, the minister went down the
aisle. She said to him:

"Were those words for me? 'Wounded for our transgressions.' Was that for me?"

The man of God understood her not. He knew not
how to comfort a shipwrecked soul, and he passed on and
he passed out. The poor wanderer followed into the
street.

"What are you doing here, Meg?" said the police.
"What are you doing here to-night?"

"Oh!" she replied, "I was in to warm myself;" and
the rattling cough came, and she held to the railing until
the paroxysm was over. She passed on down the street,
falling from exhaustion; recovering herself again, until

after a while she reached the outskirts of the city and passed on into the country road. It seemed so familiar, she kept on the road, and she saw in the distance a light in the window. Ah! that light had been gleaming there every night since she went away. On that country road she passed until she came to the garden gate. She opened it and passed up the path where she played in childhood. She came to the steps and looked in at the fire on the hearth. Then she put her fingers to the latch. Oh! if that door had been locked she would have perished on the threshold, for she was near to death. But that door had not been locked since the time she went away. She pushed open the door. She went in and laid down on the hearth by the fire. The old house-dog growled as he saw her enter, but there was something in the voice he recognized, and he frisked about her until he almost pushed her down in his joy. In the morning the mother came down, and she saw a bundle of rags on the hearth; but when the face was uplifted, she knew it, and it was no more old Meg of the street. Throwing her arms around the returned prodigal, she cried,

"Oh! Maggie."

The child threw her arms around her mother's neck, and said: "Oh! Mother," and while they were embraced a rugged form towered above them. It was the father. The severity all gone out of his face, he stooped and took her up tenderly and carried her to mother's room, and laid her down on mother's bed, for she was dying. Then the lost one, looking up into her mother's face, said:

"Wounded for our transgressions and bruised for our iniquities!" Mother, do you think that means me?"

WHOM I SAW AND WHOM I MISSED.

"And the vale of Siddim was full of slime-pits,"—Genesis xiv, 10.

About six months ago, a gentleman in Augusta, Georgia, wrote me asking me to preach from this text, and the time has come for the subject. The neck of an army had been broked by falling into these half-hidden slime-pits. How deep they were, or how vile, or how hard to get out of, we are not told; but the whole scene is so far distant in the past that we have not half as much interest in this statement of the text as we have in the announcement that our American cities are full of slime-pits, and tens of thousands of people are falling in them night by night.

WHY I EXPLORED THE SLIME-PITTS.

Recently, in the name of God, I explored some of these slime-pits. Why did I do so? In April last, seated in the editorial rooms of one of the chief daily newspapers of New York, the editor said to me:

"Mr. Talmage, you clergymen are at a great disadvantage when you come to battle iniquity, for you don't know what you are talking about, and we laymen are aware of the fact that you don't know of what you are talking; now, if you would like to make a personal investigation, I will see that you shall get the highest official escort."

I thanked him, accepted the invitation, and told him that this autumn I would begin the tour.

The fact was that I had for a long time wanted to say

[273]

some words of warning and invitation to the young men
of this country, and I felt if my course of sermons was
preceded by a tour of this sort I should not only be better acquainted with the subject, but I should have the
whole country for an audience; and it has been a delib-
erate plan of my ministry, whenever I am going to try
to do anything especial for God, or humanity, or the
church, to do it in such a way that the devil will always
advertise it free gratis for nothing! That was the reason
I gave two weeks' previous notice of my pulpit intentions.
The result has been satisfactory.

I SAW BANKERS, BROKERS, AND MERCHANTS AND MEN
OF LEISURE THERE, BUT NOT THE WORKING MEN!

Standing within those purlieus of death, under the
command of the police and in their company, I was as
much surprised at the people whom I missed as at the
people whom I saw.   I saw bankers there, and brokers
there, and merchants there, and men of all classes and
occupations who have leisure, there; but there was one
class of persons that I missed.   I looked for them all up
and down the galleries, and amid the illumined gardens,
and all up and down the staircases of death.   I saw not
one of them.   I mean the hard-working classes, the
laboring classes, of our great cities.   You tell me they
could not afford to go there.   They could.   Entrance,
twenty-five cents.   They could have gone there if they
had a mind to; but the simple fact is that hard work is a
friend to good morals.   The men who toil from early
morn until late at night when they go home are tired
out, and want to sit down and rest, or to saunter out
with their families along the street, or to pass into some

quiet place of amusement where they will not be ashamed to take wife and daughter. The busy population of these cities are the moral populations.

I observed on the night of our exploration that the places of dissipation are chiefly supported by the men who go to business at nine and ten o'clock in the morning and get through at three and four in the afternoon. They have plenty of time to go to destruction in, and plenty of money to buy a through ticket on the Grand Trunk Railroad to perdition, stopping at no depot until they get to the eternal smash-up! Those are the fortunate and divinely-blessed young men who have to breakfast early and take supper late, and have the entire interregnum filled up with work that blisters the hands, and makes the legs ache and the brain weary.

A SLIM CHANCE FOR THE YOUNG MAN OF LEISURE.

There is no chance for the morals of that young man who has plenty of money and no occupation. You may go from Central Park to the Battery, or you may go from Fulton Steeet Ferry, Brooklyn, or to South Bushwick, or out to Hunter's Point, or out to Gowanus, and you will not find one young man of that kind who has not already achieved his ruin, or who is not on the way thereto at the rate of slxty miles the hour. Those are not the favored and divinely-blessed young men who come and go as they will, and who have their pocket-case full of the best cigars, and who dine at Delmonico's, and who dress in the tip-top of fashion, their garments a little tighter or looser or broader striped than others, their mustaches twisted with stiffer cosmetic, and their hair redolent with costly pomatum, and have their **hat set** farthest over on the right ear, and who have boots fitting the foot with exquisite torture, and who have handkerchiefs soaked with musk, and patchouli, and white rose, and new-mown hay, and "balm of a thousand flowers;" but those are the fortunate young men who have to work hard for a living.

Give a young man plenty of wines, and plenty of cigars and plenty of fine horses, and Satan has no anxiety about that man's coming out at his place. He ceases to watch him, only giving directions about his reception when he shall arive at the end of the journey. If, on the night of our exploration, I had called the roll of all the laboring men of these cities, I would have received no answer, for the simple reason they were not there to answer. I was not more surprised at the people whom I saw there than I was surprised at the people whom I missed. Oh! man, if you have an occupation by which you are wearied every night of your life, thank God, for it is the mightiest preservative against evil.

MIDNIGHT IN NEW YORK.

But by that time the clock of old Trinity Church was striking one, two, three, four, five, six, seven, eight, nine, ten, eleven, twelve—midnight! And with the police and two elders of my church we sat down at the table in the galleries and looked off upon the vortex of death. The music in full blast; the dance in wildest whirl; the wine foaming to the lip of the glass Midnight on earth is midnoon in hell. All the demons of the pit were at that moment holding high carnival. The blue calcium light suggested the burning brimstone of the pit. Seated there, at that hour, in that awful place, you ask me as I have frequently been asked, "What were the emotions that went through your heart?"   And I shall give the rest of my morning's sermon to telling you how I felt.

HOW I FELT WHILE THERE.

First of all, as at no death-bed or railroad disaster did I feel an overwhelming sense of pity.   Why were we there as Christian explorers, while those lost souls were there as participators?   If they had enjoyed the same healthful and Chrtstian surroundings which we have had all our days, and we had been thrown amid the contaminations which have destroyed them, the case would have been the reverse, and they would have been the spectators and we the actors in that awful tragedy of the damned.

As I sat there I could not keep back the tears—tears of gratitude to God for his protecting grace—tears of compassion for those who have fallen so low.   The difference in moral navigation has been the difference in the way the wind blew.   The wind of temptation drove them on the rocks.   The wind of God's mercy drove us out on a fair sea.

There are men and women so merciless in their criticism of the fallen that you might think that God had made them in an especial mold, and that they have no capacity for evil, and yet if they had been subjected to the same allurements, instead of stopping at the up-town haunts of iniquity, they would at this hour been wallowing amid the horrors of Arch Block, or shrieking with delirium tremens in the cell of a police station.   Instead of boasting over your purity and your integrity and your sobriety, you had better be thanking God for his grace, lest some time the Lord would let you loose and you find out how much better you are than others naturally. I will take the best-tempered man in this house, the most honest man in this city, and I will venture the opinion in regard to him that, surround him with all the adequate circumstance of temptation, and the Lord let him loose, he would become a thief, a gambler, a sot, a rake, a wharf-rat. Instead of boasting over our superiority, and over the fact that there is no capacity in us of evil, I would rather have for my epitaph that one word which Duncan Matthewson, the Scotch evangelist, ordered chisled on his tombstone, the name, and the one word, "Kept."

I THOUGHT OF THE YOUNG MAN'S MOTHER.

Again: Seated in that gallery of death, and looking out on that maelstrom of iniquity, I thought to myself, "There! that young man was once the pride of the city home. Paternal care watched him; maternal love bent over him; sisterly affection surrounded him. He was once taken to the altar and consecrated in the name of the Father, and of the Son, and of the Holy Ghost; but he went away. This very moment," I thought to myself, "there are hearts aching for that young man's return. Father and mother are sitting up for him." You say, "He has a night-key, and he comes in without their help. Why do not those parents go sound to sleep?" What! Is there any sleep for parents who suspect a son is drifting up and down amid the dissipations of a great city? They may weep, they may pray, they may wring their hands, but sleep they cannot. Ah! they have done and suffered too much for that boy to give him up now. They turn up the light and look at the photograph of him when he was young and untempted. They stand at the window to see if he is coming up the street. They hear the watchman's rattle, but no sound of returning boy.

WHY I DID NOT WARN HIM THEN.

I felt that night as if I could put my hand on the shoulder of that young man, and, with a voice that would sound all through those temples of sin, say to him, "Go home, young man; your father is waiting for you. Your mother is waiting for you. God is waiting for you. All heaven is waiting for you. Go home! By the tears wept over your waywardness, by the prayers offered for your salvation, by the midnight watching over you when you had scarlet fever and diphtheria, by the blood of the Son of God, by the judgement day when you must give answer for what you have been doing here to-night, go home!" But I did not say this, lest it interfere with my work, and I waited to get on this platform, where, perhaps, instead of saving one young man, God helping me, I might save a thousand young men; and the cry of alarm which I suppressed that night, I let loose to-day in the hearing of this people.

Seated in that gallery of death, and looking off upon the destruction, I bethought myself also, "These are the fragments of broken homes," A home is a complete thing, and if one member of it wander off, then the home is broken. And sitting there, I said: "Here they are, broken family altars, broken wedding-rings, broken vows, broken anticipations, broken hearts."

And, as I looked off, the dance became wilder and more unrestrained, until it seemed as if the floor broke through and the revelers were plunged into a depth from which they may never rise, and all these broken families came around the brink and seemed to cry out:

"Come back, father! Come back, mother! Come back, my son! Come back, my daughter! Come back, my sister!"

But no voices returned, and the sound of the feet of the dancers grew fainter and fainter, and stopped, and there was thick darkness.

And I said, "What does all this mean?"

And there came up a great hiss of whispering voices, saying. "This is the second death!"

But seated there that night, looking off upon that scene of death, I bethought myself also "This is only a miserable copy of European dissipations." In London they have what they call the Argyle, the Cremorne, the Strand, the beer-gardens, and a thousand places of infamy, and it seems to be the ambition of bad people in this country to copy those foreign dissipations. Toadyism when it bows to foreign pretense and to foreign equipage and to foreign title is despicable; but toadyism is more despicable when it bows to foreign vice. Why, you might as well steal the pillow-case of a small-pox hospital, or the shovels of a scavenger's cart, or the coffin of a leper, as to make theft of these foreign plagues. If you want to destroy the people, have some originality of destruction; have an American trap to catch the bodies and souls of men, instead of infringing on the patented inventions of European iniquity.

Seated there that night, I also felt that if the good people of our cities knew what was going on in these haunts of iniquity, they would endure it no longer. The foundations of city life are rotten with iniquity, and if the foundations give way the whole structure must crumble.

FUTURE DANGERS.

If iniquity progresses in the next one hundred years in the same ratio that it has progressed in the century now closing, there will not be a vestige of moral or religious influence left. It is only a question of subtraction and addition. If the people knew how the virus was spreading they would stop it. I think the time has come for action. I wish that the next Mayor of New York whether he be Augustus Schell or Edward Cooper, may rise up to the height of this position. Revolution is what we want, and that revolution would begin to-morrow if the moral and Christian people of our cities knew of the fires that slumber beneath them. Once in a while a glorious missionary or reformer like Mr. Brace or Mr. Van Meter tells to a well-dressed audience in church the troubles that lie under our roaring metropolis, and the conventional church-goer gives his five dollars for bread, or gives his fifty dollars to help support a ragged school, and then goes home feeling that the work is done. Oh! my friends, the work will not be accomplished until by the force of public opinion the officers of the law shall be compelled to execute the law.

We are told that the twenty-five hundred police of New York cannot put down the five or six hundred dens of infamy, to say nothing of the gambling-houses and the

unlicensed grog-shops.   I reply, swear me in as a special
police and give me two hundred police for two nights,
and I would break up all the leading haunts of iniquity
in these two cities, and arrest all their leaders and send
such consternation in the smaller places that they would
shut up of themselves!   I do not think I should be afraid
of lawsuits for damages for false imprisonment.   What
we want in these cities is a Stonewall Jackson's raid
through all the places of iniquity.   I was persuaded by
what I saw on that night of my exploration that the
keepers of all these haunts, of iniquity are as afraid as they
are of death of the police star, and the police club, and
the police revolver.   Hence, I declare that the existence
of these abominations are to be charged either to police
cowardice or to police complicity.

At the close of our journey that night, we got in the
carriage, and we came out on Broadway, and as we came
down the street everything seemed silent save the clattering hoofs and the wheels of our own conveyance.   Looking down the long line of gaslights, the pavement seemed
very solitary.   The great sea of metropolitan life had
ebbed, leaving a dry beach! New York asleep! No! no!
Burglary wide awake.   Libertinism wide awake.   Murder wide awake.   Ten thousand city iniquities- wide
awake.   The click of the decanters in the worst hours of
the debauch.   The harvest of death full.   Eternal woe
the reaper.

"GOOD NIGHT?" NO! BLACK NIGHT.

What is that?   Trinity clock striking, one—two.
"Good night," said the officers of the law, and I respond-
ed "good night," for they had been very kind, and very

generous and very helpful to us. "Good night." And yet, was there ever an adjetive more misapplied? Good night! Why, there was no expletive enough scarred and blasted to describe that night. Black night. Forsaken night. Night of man's wickedness and woman's over-throw. Night of awful neglect on the part of those who might help but do not. For many of those whom we had been watching, everlasting night. No hope. No rescue. No God. Black night of darkness forever. As far off as hell is from heaven was that night distant from being a good night. Oh, my friends, what are you going to do in this matter? Punish the people? That is not my theory. Prevent the people, warn the people, hinder the people before they go down. The first philanthropist this country ever knew was Edward Livingstone, and he wrote these remarkable words in 1833:

"As prevention in the diseases of the body is less painful, less expen-sive, and more efficacious than the most skillful cure, so in the moral maladies of society, to arrest the vicious before the profligacy assumes the shape of crime, to take away from the poor the cause or pretense of re-lieving themselves by fraud or theft, to reform them by education, and make their own industry contribute to their support, although difficult and expensive, will be found more effectual in the suppression of of-fenses, and more economical, than the best organized system of punish-ment."

Next Sabbath morning I shall tell you of my second night of exploration. I have only opened the door of this great subject with which I hope to stir the cities. I have begun, and, God helping me, I will go through. Whoever else may be crowded or kept standing, or kept outside the doors, I charge the trustees and the ushers of this church that they give full elbow-room to all these journalists, since each one is another church five times, or ten times, or twenty times larger than this august assemblage, and it is by the printing-press that the Gospel of the Son of God is to be yet preached to all the world. May the blessing of the Lord God come down upon all the editors, and all the reporters, and all the compositors, and all the proof-readers, and all the typesetters!

YOU MAY BECOME A GOOD MAN—COME BACK.

But, my friends, before the iniquities of our cities are closed, my tongue may be silent in death, and many who are here this morning may have gone so far in sin they cannot get back. You have sometimes been walking on the banks of a river, and you have seen a man struggling in the water, and you have thrown off your coat and leaped in for the rescue. So this morning I throw off the robe of pulpit conventionality, and I plunge in for your drowning soul. I have no cross words for you. I have only cross words for those that would destroy you. I am glad God has not put in my hand any one of the thunderbolts of His power, lest I might be tempted to hurl it at those who are plotting your ruin. I do not give you the tip end of the long fingers of the left hand, but I take your hand, hot with the fever of indulgences and trembling with last night's debauch, into both my hands, and give the heartiest grip of invitation and welcome.

"Oh," you say, "you would not shake hands with me if you met me."

I would. Try me at the foot of this platform and see if I will not. I have sometimes said that I would like to die with my hand in the hand of my family and my kindred; but I revoke that wish this morning and say that I would like to die with my hand in the hand of a returning sinner, when, with God's help, I am trying to pull him up into the glorious liberty of the Gospel. I would like that to be my last work on earth. Oh! my brother, come back!

I TAKE YOU BY THE HAND.

Do you know that God made Richard Baxters and John Bunyans and Robert Newtons out of such as you are? Come back! and wash in the deep fountain of a Savior's mercy. I do not give you a cup, or a chalice, or a pitcher with a limited supply, to effect your ablutions. I point you to the five oceans of God's mercy. Oh! that the Atlantic and Pacific surges of divine forgiveness might roll over your soul.

I do not say to you, as we said to the officers of the law when we left them on Broadway, "Good night." Oh, no. But, as the glorious sun of God's forgiveness rides on toward the mid heavens, ready to submerge you in warmth and light and love, I bid you good morning! Morning of peace for all your troubles. Morning of liberation for all your incarcerations. Morning of resurrection for your soul buried in sin. Good morning! Morning for the resuscitated household that has been waiting for your return. Morning for the cradle and the crib already disgraced with being that of a drunkard's child. Morning for the daughter that has trudged off to hard work because you did not take care of home. Morning for the wife who at forty or fifty years has the wrinkled face, and the stooped shoulder, and the white

TALMAGE'S NEW TABRNACLE, BROOKLYN, N. Y.
DESTROYED BY FIRE, 1894.

UNDER THE POLICE LANTERN.

"The destruction of the poor is their poverty."—Poverbs x, 15.

On an island nine miles long by two and a half wide stands the largest city on this continent—a city mightiest for virtue and for vice. Before I get through with this series of Sabbath morning discourses, I shall show you the midnoon of its magnificent progress and phlianthropy, as well as the midnight of its crime and sin.

Twice in every twenty-four hours our City Hall and old Trinity clocks strike twelve—once while business and art are in tull blast, and once while iniquity is doing its uttermost. Both stories must be told. It is pleasanter to put on a plaster than to thrust in a probe; but it is absurd to propose remedies for disease until we have taken a diagnosis of that disease. The patient may squirm and cringe, and fight back, and resist; but the surgeon must go on.

Before I get through with these Sabbath morning sermons, I shall make you all smile at the beautiful things I will say about the grandeur and beneficence of this cluster of cities; but my work now is excavation and exposure.

HOW SOME OF THE CLERGY SCALP OLD SINNERS!

I have as much amusement as any man of my profession can afford to indulge in at any one time, in seeing some of the clerical "reformers" of this day mount their war-charger, dig in their spurs, and with glittering lance dash down upon the iniquities of cities that have been three or four thousand years dead. These men will corner an old sinner of twenty or thirty centuries ago, and scalp him, and hang him, and cut him to pieces, and then say, "Oh! what great things have been done. "With amazing prowess, they threw sulphur at Sodom, and fire at Gomorrah, and worms at Herod, and pitch Jezebel over the wall, but wipe off their gold spectacles, and put on their best kid gloves, and unroll their marocco-covered sermon, and look bashful when they begin to speak about the sins of our day, as though it were a shame even to mention them. The hypocrites! They are afraid of the libertines and the men who drink too much, in their churches, and those who grind the face of the poor.

Better, I say, clear out all our audiences from pulpit to storm-door, until no one is left but the sexton, and he staying merely to lock up, than to have the pulpit afraid of the pew. The time has come when the living Judases and Herods and Jezebels are to be arraigned. There is one thing I like about a big church: a dozen people may get mad about the truth and go off, and you don't know they are gone until about the next year. The cities standing on the ground are the cities to be reformed, and not the Herculaneums buried under volcanic ashes, or the cities of the plain fifty feet under the Dead Sea.

NEW REVELATIONS.

I unroll the scroll of new revelations. With city missionary, and the police of New York and Brooklyn, I have seen some things that I have not yet stated in this series of discourses on the night side of city life. The night of which I speak now is darker than any other,

No glittering chandelier, no blazing mirror adorns it. It is the long, deep exhaustive night of city pauperism. "We won't want a carriage to-night," said the detectives. "A carriage would hinder us in our work; a carriage going through the streets where we are going would only bring out the people to see what was the matter." So on foot we went up the dark lanes of poverty. Everything revolting to eye, and ear, and nostril. Population unwashed, uncombed. Rooms unventilated. Three midnights overlapping each other—midnight of the natural world, midnight of crime, midnight of pauperism. Stairs oozing with filth. The inmates, nine-tenths of the journey to their final doom, traveled. They started in some unhappy home of the city or of the country. They plunged into the shambles of death within ten minutes walk of the Fifth Avenue Hotel, New York, and then came on gradually down until they have arrived at the Fourth Ward. When they move out of the Fourth Ward they will move into Bellevue Hospital; when they move out of Bellevue Hospital they will move to Blackwell's Island; when they move from Blackwell's Island they will move to the Potter's Field; when they move from the Potter's Field they will move into hell! Bellevue Hospital and Blackwell's Island take care of 18,000 patients in one year.

As we passed on, the rain pattering on the street and dripping around the doorways made the night more dismal. I said, "Now let the police go ahead," and they flashed their light, and there were fourteen persons trying to sleep, or sleeping, in one room. Some on a bundle of straw; more with nothing under them and nothing over them.   "Oh!" you say,   this is exceptional.'

It is not.   Thousands lodge in that way.   One hundred and seventy thousand families living in tenement houses, in more or less inconvenience, more or less squalor.   Half a million people in New York City—five hundred thousand people living in tenement-houses; multitudes of these people dying by inches.   Of the twenty-four thousand that die yearly in New York, fourteen thousand die in tenement-houses.   No lungs that God ever made could for a long while stand the atmosphere we breathed for a little while.   In the Fourth Ward, 17,000 people within the space of thirty acres.

You say,   "Why not clear them out?   Why not, as at Liverpool, where 20,000 of these people were cleared out of the city, and the city saved from a moral pestilence, and the people themselves from being victimized?" There will be no reformation from these cities until the tenement-house system is entirely broken up.   The city authorities will have to buy farms, and will have to put these people on those farms, and compel them to work. By the strong arm of the law, by the police lantern conjoined with Christian Charity, these places must be exposed and must be uprooted.

Those places in London which have become historical for crowded populations—St. Giles, Whitechapel, Holborn, the Strand—have their match at last in the Sixth Ward, Eleventh Ward, Fourteenth Ward, Seventh Ward of New York.   No purification for our cities until each family shall have something of the privacy and seclusion of a home circle. As long as they herd like beasts, they will be beasts.

Hark! What is that heavy thud on the wet pavement? Why, that is a drunkard who has fallen, his head striking against the street—striking very hard.   The police try to lift him up.   Ring the bell for the city ambulance. No.   Only an outcast, only a tatterdemallion—a heap of sores and rags.   But look again.   Perhaps he has some marks of manhood on his face; perhaps he may have been made in the image of God; perhaps he has a soul which will live after the dripping heavens of this dismal night have been rolled together as a scroll; perhaps he may have been died for, by a king; perhaps he may yet be a conqueror charioted in the splendors of heavenly welcome.   But we must pass on.

We cross the street, and there, the rain beating in his face, lies a man entirely unconscious.   I wonder where he came from.   I wonder if any one is waiting for him. I wonder if he was ever rocked in a Christian cradle.   I wonder if that gashed and bloated forhead was ever kissed by a fond mother's lips.   I wonder if he is stranded for eternity.   But we cannot stop.

SOMETHING THAT ASTOUNDED ME.

We passed on down, the air loaded with hlasphemies and obscenities, until I heard something that astounded me more than all.   I said, "What is that?"   It was a loud, enthusiastic Christian song, rolling out on the stormy air.   I went up to the window and looked in. There was a room filled with all sorts of people, some standing, some kneeling, some sitting, some singing, some praying, some shaking hands as if to give encouragement, some wringing their hands as though over a wasted life. What was this?   Oh! it was Jerry McAuley's glorious

Christian mission.   There he stood, himself snatched
from death, snatching others from death.   That scene
paid for all the nausea and fatigue of the midnight exploration.   Our tears fell with the rain—tears of sympathy for a good man's work; tears of gratitude to God
that one lifeboat had been launched on that wild sea of
sin and death; tears of hope that there might be lifeboats
enough to take off all the wrecked, and, that, after a
while, the Church of God, rousing from its fastidtous-
ness, might lay hold with both hands of this work, which
must be done if our cities are not to go down in darkness
and fire and blood

5,000,000 FOREIGN POPULATION.

This cluster of cities have more difficulty than any
other cities in all the land.   You must understand that
within the last twenty-eight years five millions of foreign
population have arrived at our port.   The most of those
who had capital and means passed on to the greater
openings at the West.   Many however, stayed and have
become our best citizens, and best members of our
churches; but we know also that, tarrying within our
borders, there has been a vast criminal population ready
to be manipulated by the demagogue, ready to hatch out
all kinds of criminal desperation.   The vagrancy and the
beggary of our cities, augumented by the very worst populations of London and Edinburg, and Glasgow, and
Berlin, and Belfast, and Dublin and Cork.   We had
enough vagabondage, and enough turpitude in our American cities before this importation of sin was dumped at
Castle Garden.   Oh! this pauperism, when will it ever
be alleviated?   How much we saw?   How much we could

ot see! How much none but the eye of Almighty God
ever will see!

Flash the lantern of the police around to that station-
house. There they come up, the poor creatures, tipping
their torn hats, saying, "Night's lodging, sir?" And then
they are waived away into the dormitories. One hundred and forty thousand such lodgers in the city of New
York every year. The atmosphere unbearable. What
pathos in the fact that many families turned out of doors
because they cannot pay their rent, come in here for
shelter, and after struggling for decency, and struggling
for a good name, are flung into a loathsome pool. The
respectable and the reprobate. Innocent childhood and
vicious old age. The Lord's poor and Satan's desperadoes. There is no report of almshouse und missionary
that will ever tell the story of New York and Brooklyn
pauperism. It will take a large book, a book with more
ponderous lids, a book made of paper other than that of
earthly manufacture. The book of God's remembrance!
At my basement door we average between fifty and one
hundred calls every day for help. Besides that, in my
reception room, from seven o'clock in the morning until
ten o'clock at night, there is a continuous procession of
people applying for aid, making a demand with an old-
fashioned silken purse, caught at the middle with a ring,
the wealth of Vanderbilt in one end and the wealth of
William B. Astor in the other end, could not satisfy.
Of course, I speak of those men's wealth while they
lived. We have more money now than they have since
they had their shroud on. But even the shroud and the
grave, we find, are to be contested for. Cursed be the

midnight prowling jackals of St. Mark's Church-yard!

But I must go on with the fact that the story of Brooklyn and New York pauperism needs to be written in ink, black, blue and red—blue for the stripes, red for the blood, black for the infamy.   In this cluster of cities 20,000 people supported by the bureau for the outdoor sick; 20,000 people taken care of by the city hospitals; 70,000 provided for by private charity; 80,000 taken care of by reformatory institutions and prisons.

COME TO THE RESCUE.

Hear it, ye churches, and pour out your benefaction. Hear it, you ministers of religion, and utter words of sympathy for the suffering, and thunders of indignation against the cause of all this wretchedness.

Hear it, mayoralities and judicial bench, and constabularies.

Unless we wake up, the Lord will scourge us as the yellow fever never scourged New Orleans, as the plague never smote London, as the earthquake never shook Carraccas, as the fire never overwhelmed Sodom.   I wish I could throw a bomb-shell of arousal into every city hall, meeting-house and cathedral on the continent.   The factories at Fall River and at Lowell sometimes stop for lack of demand, and for lack of workmen, but this million roomed factory of sin and death never stops, never slackens a band, never arrests a spindle.   The great wheel of that factory keeps on turning, not by such floods as those of the Merrimac or the Connecticut, but crimson floods rushing forth from the grogeries, and the wine-cellars, and the drinking saloons of the land, and the faster the floods rush the faster the wheel turns; and the band of that wheel is woven from broken heart-strings, and every time the wheel turns, from the mouth of the mill come forth blasted estates, squalor, vagrancy, crime, sin, woe—individual woe, municipal woe, national woe —and the creaking and the rumbling of the wheels are the shrieks and the groans of men and women lost for two worlds, and the cry is, "Bring on more fortunes, more homes, more States, more cities, to make up the awful grist of this stupendous mill." "Oh," you say, "the wretchedness and the sin of the city will go out from lack of material after awhile." No, it will not.

ANOTHER FLASH OF THE LANTERN.

The police lantern flashes in another direction. Here comes 15,000 shoeless, hatless, homeless children, of the street, in this cluster of cities. They are the reserve corps of this great army of wretchedness and crime that are dropping down into the morgue, the East river, the Potter's Field, the prison. A philanthropist has estimated that if these children were placed in a great procession, double file, three feet apart, they would make a procession eleven miles long. Oh! what a pale, cough-ing, hunger-bitten, sin-cursed, opthalmic throng—the tigers, the adders, the scorpions ready to bite and sting society, which they take to be their natural enemy. Howard Mission has saved many. Children's Aid Society has saved many. Industrial Schools have saved many.

THE REGIMENT OF BOOTBLACKS.

One of these societies transported 30,000 childred from the streets of our cities, to farms at the West, by a stratagem of charity, turning them from vagrancy into

useful citizenship, and out of 21,000 children thus transported from the cities to farms only twelve turned out
badly. But still the reserve corps of sin and wretchedness marches on. There is the regiment of boot-blacks.
They seem jolly, but they have more sorrow than many
an old man has had. All kinds of temptation. Working on, making two or three dollars a week. At fifteen
years of age sixty years old in sin. Pitching pennies at
the street corners. Smoking fragments of castaway
cigars. Tempted by the gamblers. Destroyed by the
top gallery in the low playhoues. Blacking shoes their
regular business. Between times blackening their
morals.

"Shine your boots, sir?" they call out with merry voices,
but their is a tremor in their accentuation.

Who cares for them?

You put your foot thoughtlessly on their stand, and
you whistled or smoked, when God knows you might
have given them one kind word. They never had one.

Whoever prayed for a bootblack?

Who, finding the wind blowing under the short jacket,
or reddening his bare neck, ever asked him to warm?

Who, when he is wronged out of his ten cents, demands justice for him?

God have mercy on the bootblacks.

THE SMART YOUNG NEWSBOYS.

The newsboys, another regiment—the smartest boys
in all the city. At work at four o'clock in the morning.
At half-past three, by unnatural vigilance, awake themselves, or pulled at by rough hands In the dawn of the
day standing before the folding-rooms of the great news-

papers, taking the wet, damp sheets over their arms, and
against there chests already shivering with the cold.
Around the bleak ferries, and up and down the streets on
the cold days, singing as merrily as though it were a
Cnristmas carol; making half a cent on each paper, some
of them working fourteen hours for fifty cents! Nine
thousand of these newsboys applied for aid at the News-
boy's Lodging-house on Park place, New York in one
year. About one thousand of them laid up in the savings
bank connected with that institution, a little more than
$3,000. But still this great army marches on, hungry,
cold, sick, toward an early grave, or a quick prison. I
tell you there is nothing that so moves my compassion
as on a cold winter morning to see one of these newsboys, a fourth clad, newspapers on his arm that he cannot seem to sell, face or hands bleeding from a fall, or
rubbing his knee to relieve it from having been hit on
the side of a car, as some "gentleman," with furs around
his neck and gauntlets lined with lamb's wool, shoved
him off, saying, "You miserable rat!" Yet hawking the
papers through the streets, papers full of railroad acci-
dents and factory explosions, and steamers foundering at
sea in the last storm, yet saying nothing, and that which
is to him worse than all the other calamities and all the
other disasters, the calamity that he was ever born at
all.

Flash the police lantern around, and let us see these
poor lads cuddled up under the stairway. Look at them!
Now for a little while they are unconscious of all their
pains and aches and of the storm and darkness, once in
awhile struggling in their dreams as though some one

were trying to take the papers away from them. Standing there I wondered if it would be right to wish that
they might never wake up. God pity them!

There are other regiments in this reserve corps—regiments of rag-pickers, regiments of match-sellers, regiments of juvenile vagrants. Oh! if these lads are not
saved, what is to become of our cities?

THE POLICE STRATEGEM AND THE PREACHER.

But I said to the detective, "I have had enough of
this to-night; let us go." But by that time I had lost
the points of the compass, for we had gone down stai
ways and up stairways, and wandered down through this
street and that street, and all I knew was that I was
bounded on the north by want, and on the south by
squalor, and on the east by crime, and on the west by
despair. The fact was that everything had opened before us; for these detectives pretended to be searching
for a thief, and they took me along as the man who had
lost the property. The stratagem was theirs, not mine.

But I thought coming home that rainy night, I wished
I could make pass before my congregation, as in a pan-
orama, all that scene of suffering, that I might stir their
pity and arouse their beneficence, and make them the
everlasting friends of city evangelization.

"Why," you say, "I had no idea things were so bad.
Why, I get in my carriage at forty-fifth street and I ride
clear down to my banking-house in wall street, and I
don't see anything."

No, you do not want to see! The King and the Parlia
ment of England did not know that there were thirty-six
barrels of gunpowder rolled into the vaults under the

Parliament House.   They did not know Guy Fawkes had
his touchwood and matches all ready—ready to dash the
government of England into atoms.   The conspiracy was
revealed, however.

I tell you I have explored the vaults of city life, and
I am here this morning to tell you that there are death
ful and explosive influences under all our cities, ready to
destroy us with a great moral convulsion.   Some men
say: "I don't see anything of this, and I am not interested in it."   You ought to be.

You remind me of a man who has been shipwrecked
with a thousand others.   He happens to get up on the
shore, and the others are all down in the surf.   He goes
up in a fisherman's cabin, and sits down to warm himself.   The fisherman says: "Oh! this won't do.   Come
out and help me to get these others out of the surf."

"Oh, no!" says the man;   "it's my business now to
warm myself."

"But," says the fisherman, these men are dying; are
you not going to give them help?"

"Oh, no! I've got ashore myself, and I must warm
myself!"

That is what people are doing in the church to-day.
A great multitude are out in the surf of sin and death,
going down forever; but men sit by the fire of the church,
warming their Christian graces, warming their faith,
warming their hope for heaven, and I say,   "Come out,
and work to-day for Christ."

"Oh, no," they say;   "my sublime duty is to warm
myself?"

Such men as that will not come within ten thousand

miles of heaven! Help foreign missions. Those of my own blood are toiling in foreign lands with Christ's Word. Send a million dollars for the salvation of the heathen—that is right—but look after the heathen also around the mouths of the Hudson and East rivers. Send missionaries if you will to Borioboola-gha, but send missionaries also through Houston street, Mercer street, Greene street, Navy street, Fulton street, and all around about Brook-lyn Atlantic Docks. If you will, send quilted coverlets to Central Africa to keep the natives warm in summer-time, and send ice-cream freezers to Greenland, but do have a little common sense and practical charity, and help these cities here that want hats, want clothes, want shoes, want fire, want medicines, want instruction, want the Gospel, want Christ.

I must adjourn to another Sabbath morning much of what I have to say in regard to this midnight exploration, and also the proposing of remedies; for I am not the man to stand here Sabbath by Sabbath talking of ills when I have no panacea. There is an almighty rescue for the city, and in due time I will speak of these things.

THE TWO MAGIC LANTERNS.

You have seen often a magic lantern. You have seen the room darkened, and then the magic lantern throwing a picture on the canvas. Well, this morning I wish I could darken these three great emblazoned windows, and have all the doors darkened, and then I could bring out two magic lanterns—the magic lantern of the home, and the magic lantern of the police.

Here is the magic lantern of the home. Look now upon the canvas. Mother putting the little children to

bed, trying to hush the frisky and giggling group for the
evening prayèr; their foreheads against the counterpane,
they are trying to say their evening prayer; their tongue
is so crooked that none but God and the mother can understand it.   Then the children are lifted into bed, and
they are covered up to the chin.   Then the mother gives
them a warm good-night kiss, and leaves them to the
guardian angels that spread wings of canopy over the
trundle-bed.

Midnight lantern of the police.   Look now on the
canvas.   A boy kennelled for the night underneath the
stairway in a hall through which the wind sweeps, or
lying on the cold ground.   He has no parentage.   He
was pitched into the world by a merciless incognito.   He
does not go to bed; he has no bed.   His cold fingers
thrust through his matted hair his only pillow.   He did
not sup last night; he will not breakfast to-morrow.   An
outcast; a ragamuffin.   He did not say his prayers when
he retired; he knows no prayer; he never heard the name
of God or Christ, except as something to swear by.   The
wings over him, not the wings of angels, but the dark,
bat-like wings of penury and want.

Magic lantern of the home.   Look now on the canvas.
Family gathered around the argand burner.   Father,
feet on ottoman, mother sewing a picturesque pattern.
Two children pretending to study, but chiefly watching
other children who are in unrestrained romp, so many
balls of fun and frolic in full bounce from room to room.
Background of pictures and upholstery and musical instrument, from which jeweled fingers sweep "Home,
Sweet Home."

Magic lantern of the police. Look now on the canvas. A group intoxicated and wrangling, cursing God, cursing each other; the past. all shame, the future all suffering. Children fleeing from the missile flung by a father's hand. Fragments of a chair propped against the wall. Fragments of a pitcher standing on the mantle. A pile of refuse wood brought in from some kitchen, torn by the human swine plunging into the trough.

Magic lantern of the home. Look now upon the canvas. A Christian daughter has just died. Carriages rolling up to the door in sympathy. Flowers in crowns and anchors and harps covering the beautiful casket, the silver plate marked, "aged 18." Funeral services intoned amid the richly-shawled and gold-bracleted. Long procession going out this way to unparralled Greenwood to the beautiful family lot where the sculptor will raise the monument of burnished Aberdeen with the inscription, "She is not dead, but sleepth." Oh! blessed is that home which has a consecrated Christian daughter, whether on earth or in heaven.

Magic lantern of the police. Look now on the canvas. A poor waif of the street has just expired. Did she have any doctor?

No.

Did she have any medicine?

No.

Did she have any hands to close her eyes and fold her arms in death?

No.

Are there no garments in the house fit to wrap her in for the tomb? None.

Those worn-out shoes will not do for these feet in their last journey.   Where are all the good Christians?

Oh! some of them are rocking-chaired, in morning gowns, in tears over Bulwer Lytton's account of the last days of Pompeii; they are so sorry for that girl that got petrified!   Others of the Christians are in church, kneeling on a soft rug, praying for the forlorn Hottentots! Come, call in the Coroner—call in the Charity Commissioner.

The carpenter unrolls the measuring-tape, and decides she will need a box five and a half feet long.   Two men lift her into the box, lift the box into the wagon, and it srarts for the Potter's Field.   The excavation is not large enough for the box, and the men are in a hurry, and one of them gets on the lid and cranches it down to its place in the ground.

Stop! Wait for the city missionary until he can come and read a chapter, or say, "Ashes to ashes, dust to dust."

"No," says the men of the spade, "we have three or four more cases just like this to bury before night."

"Well", I say, "how, then, is the grave to be filled up?"

Christ suggests a way.   Perhaps it had better be filled up with stones.   "Let those who are without sin come and cast a stone at her," until the excavation is filled.

THE CHRIST OF MARY MAGDALEN.

Then the wagon rolls off, and I see a form come slowly across the Potter's Field.   He walks very slowly, as his feet hurt.   He comes to that grave, and there he stands all day and all night, and I come out and accost him, and I say, "Who art thou!" And he says, "I am the Christ of Mary Magdalen!" And then I thought that perhaps there might have been a dying prayer, and that there might have been penitential tears, and around that miserable spot at the last there may be more resurrection pomp than when Queen Elizabeth gets out of her mausoleum in Westminster Abbey.

But I must close the two lanterns.

CLUB-HOUSES—GOOD AND BAD.

"Let the young men now arise and play before us."—II Samuel ii. 14

There are two armies encamped by the pool of Gibeon. The time hangs heavily on their hands. One army proposed a game of sword-fencing. Nothing could be more healthful and innocent. The other army accepts the challenge. Twelve men against twelve men, the sport opens. But something went adversely. Perhaps one of the swordsmen got an unlucky clip, or in some way had his ire aroused, and that which opened in sportfulness ended in violence, each one taking his contestant by the hair, and then with the sword thrusting him in the side; so that that which opened in innocent fun ended in the massacre of all the twenty-four sportsmen.

Was there ever a better illustration of what was true then, and is true now, that that which is innocent may be made destructive?

In my exploration of the night side of city life, I have found out that there is legitimate and an illegitimate use of the club-house. In the one case it may become a healthful recreation, like the contest or the twenty-four men in the text when they began their play; in the other case it becomes the massacre of body, mind, and soul, as in the case of these contestants of the text when they had gone too far with their sport.

All intelligent ages have had their gatherings for political, social, artistic, literary purposes—gatherings characterized by the blunt old Anglo-Saxon designation of "club." If you have read history, you know that there was a King's Head Club, a Ben Johnson Club; a Brother's Club, to which Swift and Bolingbroke belonged; a Literary Club, which Burke and Goldsmith and Johnson and Boswell made immortal: a Jacobin Club, a Benjamin Franklin Junto Club. Some of these to indicate justice, some to favor the arts, some to promote good manners, some to despoil the habits, some to destroy the soul.

If one will write an honest history of the clubs of England, Ireland, Scotland, France, and the United States for the last one hundred years, he will write the history of the world.

ORIGIN OF THE CLUB.

The club was an institution born on English soil, but it has thrived well in American atmosphere. We have in this cluster of cities a great number of them, with seventy thousand members, so called, so known; but who shall tell how many belong to that kind of club where men put purses together and open house, apportioning the expense of caterer and servants and room, and having a sort of domestic establishment—a style of club-house which in my opinion is far better than the ordinary hotel or boarding-house?

THE DIFFERENT KINDS OF CLUBS.

But my object now is to speak of club-houses of a different sort, such as the Union League, which was established during the war, having patriotic purposes, which has now between thirteen and fourteen hundred members, which is now also the head-quarters of Republicanism;

likewise the Manhattan, with large admission fee, four
or five hundred members, the headquarters of the Demo-
cracy, like the Union Club, established in ' 1836, when
New York had only a little over three hundred thousand
inhabitants, their present building having cost $250,000
—they have a membership of between eight and nine
hundred people, among them some of the leading merchant princes of the land; like the Lotos, where journalists, dramatists, sculptors, painters and artist,, from
all branches, gather together to discuss newspapers,
theatres, and elaborate art; like the Americus, which
camps out in summer time, dimpling the pool with its
hook, and arousing the forest with its stag hunt; like the
Century Club, which has its large group of venerable
lawyers and poets; like the Army and Navy Club, where
those who engaged on warlike service once on the land or
the sea now come together to talk over the days of carnage; like the New York Yacht Club, with its floating
palaces of beauty upholstered with velvet and paneled
with ebony, having all the advantages of electric bell,
and of gaslight, and of king's pantry, one pleasure-boat
costing three thousand, another fifteen thousand, another
thirty thousand, another sixty-five thousand dollars, the
fleet of pleasure-boats belonging to the club having cost
over two million dollars; like the American Jockey Club,
to which belong men who have a passionate fondness for
horses, fine horses, as had Job when, in the Scriptures,
he gives us a sketch of that king of beasts, the arch of
its neck, the nervousness of its foot, the majesty of its
gait, the whirlwind of its power, crying out:

"Hast thou clothed his neck with thunder?   The glory

of his nostrils is terrible; he paweth in the valley and
rejoiceth in his strength, he saith among the trumpets
ha! ha! and he smelleth the battle afar off, the thunder
of the captains, and the shouting;" like the Travelers'
Club, the Blossom Club, the Palette Club, the Commercial Club, the Liberal Club, the Stable Gang Club, the
Amateur Boat Club, the gambling clubs, the wine clubs,
the clubs of all sizes, the clubs of all morals, clubs as
good as good can be, and clubs as bad as bad can be,
clubs innumerable.

No series of sermons on the night side of city life
would be complete without a sketch of the clubs, which,
after dark are in full blast.

THE CLUB-HOUSE DESCRIBED.

During the day they are comparatively lazy places.
Here and there an aged man reading a newspaper, or an
employee dusting a sofa, or a clerk writing up the accounts; but when the curtain of the night falls on the
natural day, then the curtain of the club-house hoists
for the entertainment. Let us hasten up, now, the marble stairs.   What an imperial hallway!   See! here are
parlors on this side, with the upholstery of the Kremlin
and the Tuilleries; and here are dining-halls that chal-
lange you to mention any luxury that they cannot afford;
and here are galleries with sculpture, and paintings, and
lithographs, and drawings from the best of artists, Crop-
sey, and Bierstadt, and Church, and Hart, and Gifford—
pictures for every mood, whether you are impassioned or
placid; shipwreck, or sunlight over the sea; Sheridan's
Ride, or the noonday party of the farmers under the tree;

foaming deer pursued by the hounds in the Andirondacks, or the sheep on the lawn.

On this side there are reading-rooms where you find all newspapers and magazines.

On that side there is a library, where you can find all books, from hermeneutics to the fairy tale.

Coming in and out there are gentlemen, some of whom stay ten minutes, others stay many hours. Some of these are from luxuriant homes, and they have excused themselves for a while from the domestic circle that they may enjoy the larger sociability of the club-house. These are from dismembered households, and they have a plain lodging somewhere, but they come to this club-room to have their chief enjoyment. One blackball amid ten votes will defeat a man's becoming a member. For rowdyism, for drunkenness, for gambling, for any kind of misdemeanor, a member is dropped out. Brilliant club-house from top to bottom. The chandeliers, the plate, the furniture, the companionship, the literature, the social prestige, a complete enchantment.

THE BAD CLUB-HOUSE.

But the evening is passing on, and so we hasten through the hall and down the steps, and into the street, and from block to block until we come to another style of club-house. Opening the door, we find the fumes of strong drink snd tobacco something almost intolerable. These young men at this table, it is easy to understand what they are at, from the flushed cheek, the intent look, the almost angry way of tossing the dice, or of moving the "chips." They are gambling.

At another table are men who are telling vile stories.

They are three-fourths intoxicated, and between 12 and
1 o'clock they will go staggering, hooting, swearing,
shouting on their way home. That is an only son. On
him all kindness, all care, all culture has been bestowed
He is paying his parents in this way for their kindness.
That is a young married man, who, only a few months
ago, at the altar, made promises of kindness and fidelity,
every one of which he has broken.

Walk through and see for yourself. Here are all the
implements of dissipation and of quick death. As the
hours of the night go away, the conversation becomes
imbecile and more debasing. Now it is time to shut up.
Those who are able to stand will get out on the pavement and balance themselves against the lamp-post,
or against the railings of the fence. The young man
who is not able to stand will have a bed improvised for
him in the club-house, or two not quite so overcome with
liquor will conduct him to his father's house, and they
will ring the door-bell, and the door will open, and the
two imbecile escorts will introduce into the hallway the
ghastliest and most hellish spectacle that·ever enters a
front door—a drunken son.

If the dissipating club-houses of this country would
make a contract with the Inferno to provide it ten thousand men a year and for twenty years, on the condition
that no more should be asked of them, the club-houses
could afford to make that contract, for they would save
homesteads, save fortunes, save bodies, save minds, and
souls. The ten thousand men who would be sacrificed
by that contract would be but a small part of the multitude sacrificed without the contract.

But I make a vast difference between clubs. I have belonged to four clubs: A theological club, a ball club, and two literary clubs. I got from them physical rejuvenation and moral health. What shall be the principles by which you may judge whether the club where you are a member, or the club to which you have been invited, is a legitimate or an illegitimate club-house.

HOW TO TEST THE CLUB-HOUSES—THEIR INFLUENCE ON THE HOMES.

First of all I want you to test the club by its influences on home, if you have a home. I have been told by a prominent gentleman in club life that three-fourths of the members of the great clubs of these cities are married men. That wife soon loses her influence over her husband who nervously and foolishly looks upon all evening absence as an assault on domesticity. How are the great enterprises of art and literature and beneficence and public weal to be carried on if every man is to have his world bounded on one side by his front door-step, and on the other side by his back window, knowing nothing higher than his own attic, or nothing lower than his own cellar? That wife who becomes jealous of her husband's attention to art, or literature, or religion, or charity, is breaking her own sceptre of conjugal power. I know in this church an instance where a wife thought that her husband was giving too many nights to Christian service, to charitable service, to prayer-meetings, and to religious convocation. She systematically decoyed him away until now he attends neither this nor any other church, and he is on a rapid way to destruction, his morals gone, money gone, and, I fear, his soul gone.

Let any Christian wife rejoice when her husband con-secrates evenings to the service of God, or to charity, or to art, or to anything elevated; but let not men sacrifice home life to club life.

GENIAL AS ANGELS AT THE CLUB-HOUSE AND AS UGLY AS SIN AT HOME.

I have the rolls of the members of a great many of the prominent clubs of these cities, and I can point out to you a great many names of men who are guilty of this sacrilege. They are as genial as angels at the club-house, and as ugly as sin at home. They are generous on all subjects of wine suppers, yachts, and fast horses, but they are stingy about the wife's dress, and the chil-dren's shoes. That man has made that which might be a healthful recreation an usurper of his affections, and he has married it, and he is guilty of moral bigamy. Under this process the wife, whatever her features, be-comes uninteresting and homely. He becomes critical of her, does not like the dress, does not like the way she arranges her hair, is amazed that he ever was so unro-mantic as to offer her hand and heart. She is always wanting money, money, when she ought to be discussing Eclipses, and Dexter, and Derby Day, and English drags with six horses, all answering the pull of one "ribbon."

I tell you, there are thousands of houses in Brooklyn and New York being clubbed to death! There are club-houses in these cities where membership always involves domestic shipwreck. Tell me that a man has joined a certain club, tell me nothing more about him for ten years, and I will write his history, if he be still alive. The man is a wine-guzzler, his wife broken-hearted or prematurely old, his fortune gone or reduced, and his home a mere name in a directory.

THE DIFFERFNCE.

Here are six secular nights in the week.

"What shall I do with them?" says the father and the husband. "I will give four of those nights to the improvement and entertainment of my family, either at home or in good neighborhood; I will devote one to charitable institutions; I will devote one to the club."

I congratulate you.

Here is a man who says, "I will make a different division of the six nights. I will take three for the club and three for other purposes."

I tremble.

Here is a man who says, "Out of the six secular nights of the week, I will devote five to the club house and one to the home, which night I will spend in scowling like a march squall, wishing I was out spending it as I had spent the other five."

That man's obituary is written. Not one out of ten thousand that ever gets so far on the wrong road ever stops. Gradually his health will fail, through late hours and through too much stimulus. He will be first-rate prey for erysipelas and rheumatism of the heart.

The doctor coming in will at a glance see it is not only present disease he must fight, but years of fast living.

The clergyman, for the sake of the feelings of th' family, on the funeral day will only talk in religious generalities.

The men who got his yacht in the eternal rapids will

not be at the obsequies. They will have pressing engagements that' day. They will send flowers to the
coffin-lid, and send their wives to utter words of sympathy, but they will have engagements elsewhere. They
never come.

Bring me mallet and chisel, and I will cut on the
tombstone that man's epitaph, "Blessed are the dead
who die in the Lord."

"No," you say, "that would not be appropriate."

"Let me die the death of the righteous, and let my
last end be like his."

"No," you say, "that would not be appropriate."

Then give me the mallet and the chisel, and I will cut
an honest epitaph; "Here lies the victim of a dissipating club-house!"

I think that damage is often done by the scions of some
aristocratic family who belong to one of these dissipating club-houses. People coming up from humbler classes
feel it an honor to belong to the same club, forgetting
the fact that many of the sons and grandsons of the large
commercial establishments of the last generation are
now, as to mind, imbecile; as to body, diseased; as to
morals, rotten. They would have got through their
property long ago if they had had full possession of it;
but the wily ancestors, who got the money by hard
knocks, foresaw how it was to be, and they tied up everything in the will.

Now, there is nothing of that unworthy descendant
but his grandfather's name and roast beef rotundity. And
yet how many steamers there are which feel honored to

lash fast that worm-eaten tug, though it drags them straight into the breakers.

CLUB-HOUSE INFLUENCE ON OCCUPATION.

Another test by which you can find whether your club is legitimate or illegitimate—the effect it has on your secular occupation. I can understand how through such an institution a man can reach commercial successes. I know some men have formed their best business relations through such a channel.

If the club has advantaged you in an honorable calling it is a legitimate club. But has your credit failed?

Are bargain-makers more cautious how they trust you with a bill of goods?

Have the men whose names were down in the commercial agency A 1 before they entered the club, been going down since in commercial standing?

Then look out!

You and I every day know of commercial establishments going to ruin through the social excesses of one or two members. Their fortunes beaten to death with ball-players' bat, or cut amidships by the front prow of the regatta, or going down under the swift hoofs of the fast horses, or drowned in large potations of Cognac and Monongahela. Their club-house was the "Loch Earn" Their business house was the "Ville du Havre." They struck, and the "Ville du Havre" went under. Or, to take illustration from last Monday night's disaster: Their club-house was the "Eilion," and their business house was the "Pommerania." They struck, and the "Pommerania" went under.

A third test by which you may know whether the club

to which you belong, or the club to whose membership you are invited, is a legitimate club or an illegitimate club, is this: What is the effect on your sense of moral and religious obligation?

CLUB INFLUENCE ON RELIGIOUS OBLIGATIONS.

Now, if I should take the names of all the people in this audience this morning, and put them on a roll and then I should lay that roll back of this organ, and a hundred years from now some one should take that roll and call it from A to Z, there would not one of you answer.   I say that any association that makes me forget that fact is a bad association.

When I go to Chicago I am sometimes perplexed at Buffalo, as I suppose many travelers are, as to whether it is better to take the Lake Shore route or the Michigan central, equally expeditious and equally safe, getting at the destination at the same time; but suppose that I hear that on one route the track is torn up, and the bridges are torn down, and the switches are unlocked?   It will not take me a great while to decide which road to take. Now, here are two roads into the future, the Christian and the unchristian, the safe and the unsafe.

Any institution or any association that confuses my idea in regard to that fact is a bad institution and a bad association. I had prayers before I joined the club.   Did I have them after?   I attended the house of God before I connected myself with the club.   Since that union with the club do I absent myself from religious influences?

Which would you rather have in your hand when you come to die, a pack of cards or a Bible?

Which would you rather have pressed to your lips in

the closing moment, the cup of Belshazzarean wassail or the chalice of Christian communion?

Who would you ra.her have for your pall-bearers, the elders of a Christian church, or the companions whose conversation was full of slang and innuendo?

Who would you rather have for your eternal companions, those men who spend their evenings betting, gambling, swearing, carousing, and telling vile stories, or your little child, that bright girl whom the Lord took?

Oh! you would not have been away so much nights, would you, if you had known she was going away so soon?

Dear me; your house has never been the same since.

SHE WILL NEVER GET OVER IT.

Your wife has never been brightened up. She has not got over it; she never will get over it. How long the evenings are, with no one to put to bed, and no one to tell the beautiful Bible story! What a pity it is that you cannot spend more evenings at home trying to help her to bear that sorrow! You can never drown that grief in the wine cup. You can never break away from the little arms that used to be flung around your neck when she used to say, "Papa, do stay home to-night— do stay home to-night." You will never be able to wipe from your lips the dying kiss of your little girl.

The fascination of a dissipating club-house is so great that sometimes a man has turned his back on his home when his child was dying of scarlet fever. He went away. Before he got back at midnight the eyes had been closed, the undertaker had done his work, and the wife, worn out with three weeks watching, lay unconscious in the next room. Then there is a rattling of the

night-key in the door, and the returned father comes up
stairs, and he sees the cradle gone, and the windows up,
and says, "What's the matter?"   In the judgement day
he will find out what was the matter.

A STRANGE, BUT A STRONG ROPE.

Oh! man astray, God help you!   I am going to make
a very stout rope.   You know that sometimes a rope-
maker will take very small threads, and wind them together until, after awhile, they become ship-cable.   And
I am going to take some very small, delicate threads, and
wind them together until they make a very stout rope.
I will take all the memories of the marriage day, a thread
of laughter, a thread of light, a thread of music, a thread
of banqueting, a thread of congratulation, and I twist
them together, and I have one strand.   Then I take a
thread of the hour of the first advent in your house, a
thread of the darkness that preceded, and a thread of
the light that followed, and a thread of the beautiful
scarf that little child used to wear when she bounded out
at eventide to greet you, and then a thread of the beautiful dress in which you laid her away for the resurrection.   And then I twist all these threads together, and
I have another strand.   Then I take a thread of the
scarlet robe of a suffering Christ, and a thread of the
white raiment of your loved ones before the throne, and
a string of the heart cherubic, and a string of the harp
seraphic, and I twist them all together, and I have a
third strand.

"Oh!" you say, "either strand is strong enough to
hold fast a world."

Now I will take these strands, and I will twist them

together, and one end of that rope I will fasten, not to
the communion table for it shall be removed—not to a
pillar of the organ, for that will crumble in the ages, but
I wind it 'round and 'round the cross of a sympathizing
Christ, and having fastened one end of the rope to the
cross I throw the other end to you.

' Lay hold of it! Pull for your life! Pull for heaven!

THE SINS OF SUMMER WATERING PLACES.

"A pool, which is called in the Hebrew tongue Bethesda, having five porches. In these lay a multitude of blind, halt, withered, waiting for the moving of the water,"—John v. 2, 3.

Outside of the city of Jerusalem, there was a sensitive watering-place, the popular resort for invalids. To this day there is a dry basin of rock which shows that there must have been a pool there three hundred and sixty feet long, one hundred and thirty feet wide, and seventy-five feet deep. This pool was surrounded by five piazzas, or porches, or bathing-houses, where the patients tarried until the time when they were to step into the water.

A MINIATURE SARATOGA AND LONG BRANCH.

So far as reinvigoration was concerned, it must have been a Saratoga and a Long Branch on a small scale; a Leamington and a Brighton combined—medical and therapeutic.

Tradition says that at a certain season of the year there was an officer cf the government who would go down to that water and pour in it some healing quality, and after that the people would come and get the medication; but I prefer the plain statement of Scripture, that at a certain season, an angel came down and stirred up, or troubled the water; and then the people came and got the healing.

That angel of God that stirred up the Judean water-

[320]

Ing-place had his counterpart in the angel of healing that, in our day, steps into the mineral waters of Congress, or Sharon, or Sulphur Springs, or into the salt sea at Cape May and Nahant, where multitudes who are worn out with commercial and professional anxieties, as well as those who are afflicted with rheumatic, neuralgic, and splenetic diseases, go, and are cured by the thousands. These Bethesdas are scattered all up and down our country, blessed be God!

OFF FOR A VACATION.

We are at a season of the year when railway trains are being laden with passengers and baggage on their way to the mountains, and the lakes, and the sea-shore. Multitudes of our citizens are packing their trunks for a restorative absence.

The city heats are pursuing the people with torch and fear of sunstroke.   The long silent halls of sumptuous hotels are all abuzz with excited arrivals.

The crystalline surface of Winnipiseogee is shattered with the stroke of steamers laden with excursionists.

The antlers of Adirondack deer rattle under the shot of city sportsman.   The trout make fatal snap at the hook of adroit sportsmen, and toss their spotted brilliance into the game basket.   Soon the baton of the orchestral leader will tap the music-stand on the hotel green, and American life will put on festal array, and the rumbling of the tenpin alley, and the crack of the ivory balls on the green-baized billiard tables, and the jolting of the bar-room goblets, and the explosive uncorking of champagne bottles, and the whirl and the rustle of the ball-room dance, and the clattering hoofs of the race courses,

will attest that the season for the great American watering-places is fairly inaugurated.   Music! Flute, and
drum, and cornet-a-piston, and clapping cymbals, will
wake the echoes of the mountains.

I BELIEVE IN WATERING PLACES.

Glad I am that fagged-out American life, for the most
part, will have an opportunity to rest, and that nerves
racked and destroyed will find a Bethesda.

I believe in watering-places·   I go there sometimes.
Let not the commercial firm begrudge the clerk, or the
employer the journeyman, or the patient the physician,
or the church its pastor, a season of inoccupation.   Luther used to sport with his children; Edmund Burke
used to caress his favorite horse.   Thomas Chalmers, in
the dark hour of the Church's disruption, played kite for
for recreation—so I was told by his own daughter—and
the busy Christ said to the busy apostles: ''Come ye apart
awhile into the desert, and rest yourselves.'' And I have
observed that they who do not know how to rest, do not
know how to work.

But I have to declare this truth to-day, that some of
our fashionable watering-places are the temporal and
eternal destruction of ''a multitude that no man can
number;'' and amid the congratulations of this season,
and the prospect of the departure of many of you for the
country, I must utter a note of warning, plain, earnest,
and unmistakable.

THE FIRST TEMPTATION.

The first temptation that is apt to hover in this direction, is to leave your piety all at home.   You will send
the dog, and cat, and canary-bird to be well cared for

somewhere else; but the temptation will be to leave your religion in the room with the blinds down and the door bolted, and then you will come back in the autumn to find that it is starved and suffocated, lying stretched on the rug, stark dead.

There is no surplus of piety at the watering-places. I never knew any one to grow very rapidly in grace at the Catskill Mountain House, or Sharon Springs, or the Falls of Montmorency. It is generally the case that the Sabbath is more of a carousal than any other day, and there are Sunday walks, and Sunday rides, and Sunday excursions. Elders, and deacons, and ministers of religion, who are entirely consistent at home, sometimes when the Sabbath dawns on them at Niagara Falls, or the White Mountains, take the day to themselves. If they go to the church, it is apt to be a sacred parade, and the discourse, instead of being a plain talk about the soul, is apt to be what is called a crack sermon—that is, some discourse picked out of the effusions of the year as the one most adapted to excite admiration; and in those churches, from the way the ladies hold their fans, you know that they are not so much impressed with the heat as with the picturesqueness of half disclosed features.

Four puny souls stand in the organ loft and squall a tune that nobody knows, and worshippers, with two thousand dollars worth of diamonds on the right hand, drop a cent into the poor-box, and then the benediction is pronounced and the farce is ended. The toughest thing I ever tried to do was to be good at a watering-place.

The air is bewitched with the "world, the flesh, and

devil." There are Christians who, in three or four weeks in such a place, have had such terrible rents made in their Christian robe, that they had to keep darning it until Christmas to get it mended!

The health of a great many people makes an annual visit to some mineral spring an absolute necessity; but, my dear people, take your Bible along with you, and take an hour for secret prayer ever day, though you be surrounded by guffaw and saturnalia. Keep holy the Sabbath, though they deride you as a bigoted Puritan. Stand off from John Morrissey's gambling hell, and those other institutions which propose to imitate on this side the water the iniquities of Baden-Baden. Let your moral and immortal health keep pace with your physical recuperation and remember that all the waters of Hawthorne, and sulphur and chalybeate springs cannot do you so much good as the mineral, healing, perrennial flood that breaks forth from the "Rock of Ages." This may be your last summer. If so, make it a fit vestibule of heaven.

THE HORSE RACING BUSINESS.

Another temptation, however, around nearly all our watering-places, is the horse-racing business. We all admire the horse; but we do not think that its beauty, or speed, ought to be cultured at the expense of human degradation. The horse-race is not of such importance as the human race. The Bible intimates that a man is better than a sheep, and I suppose he is better than a horse, though, like Job's stallion, his neck is clothed with thunder.

Horse races in olden times were under the ban of

Christian people; and in our day the same institution has come up under fictitious names.   And it is called a "Summer Meeting," almost suggestive of postve relig- ious exercises.   And it is called an "Agricultural Fair," suggestive of everything that is improving in the art of farming.   But under these deceptive titles are the same cheating, and the same betting, and the same drunken- ness, and the same vagabondage, and the same abomina- tions that were to be found under the old horse-racing system.

I never knew a man yet who could give himself to the pleasures of the turf for a long reach of time and not be battered in morals.   They hook up their spanking team, and put on their sporting cap, and light their cigar, and take the reins, and dash down the road to perdition!

The great day at Saratoga and Long Branch, and Cape May, and nearly all the other watering-places, is the day of the races.   The hotels are thronged, every kind of equipage is taken up at an almost fabulous price; and there are many respectable people mingling with jockies and gamblers, and libertines, and foul-mouthed men and flashy women.   The bar-tender stirs up the brandy smash.   The bets run high.   The greenhorns, supposing all is fair, put in their money, soon enough to lose it.

Three weeks before the race takes place the struggle, is decided, and the men in the secret know on which steed to bet their money.   The two men on the horses riding around, long before arranged who shall beat. Leaning from the stand or from the carriage, are men and women so absorbed in the struggle of bone and

muscle, and mettle, that they make a grand harvest for
pickpockets who carty off the pocket-book and portmon-
naies.

Men looking on see only two horses with two riders
flying around the ring; but there is many a man on that
stand whose honor, and domestic happiness, and fortune
—white mane, white foot, white flank—are in the ring,
racing with inebriety, and with fraud, and with profanity,
and with ruin—black neck, black foot, black flank. Neck
and neck, they go in that moral Epsom.   White horse
of honor; black horse of ruin.

Death says: "I will bet on the black horse."

Spectator says: "I will bet on the white horse."

The white horse of honor a little way ahead.

The black horse of ruin, Satan mounted, all the time
gaining on him.

Spectator breathless.   Put on the lash.   Dig in the
spurs.   There!   They are past the stand.   Sure.

Just as I expected it.   The black horse of ruin has
won the race, and all the galleries of darkness "huzza!
huzza!" and the devils come in to pick up their wagers.

Ah, my friends, have nothing to do with horse-racing
dissipations this summer.   Long ago the English government got through looking to the turf for the dragoon
and light cavalry horse.   They found the turf depreciates
the stock; and it is yet worse for men.

Thomas Hughes, the member of Parliament, and the
author known all the world over, hearing that a new turf
enterprise was being started in this country, wrote a
letter in which he said: "Heaven help you, then; for of
all the cankers of our old civilization, there is nothing in

this country approaching in unblushing meanness, in ras-
cality holding its head high, to this belauded institution
of the British turf."

Another famous sportsman writes: "How many fine
domains have been shared among these hosts of rapacious
sharks during the last two hundred years; and unless the
system be altered, how many more are doomed to fall in
to the same gulf!"

The Duke of Hamilton, through his horse-racing proclivities, in three years got through his entire fortune of
£70,000; and I will say that some of you are being un-
dermined by it. With the bull-fights of Spain and the
bear-baitings of the pit, may the Lord God annihilate
the infamous and accursed horse-racing of England and
America.

DISSIPATION AND DYSPEPSIA.

I go further and speak of another temptation that
hovers over the watering place; and this is the temptation to sacrifice physical strength. The modern Bethesda, just like this Bethesda of the text, was intended to
recuperate the physical health; and yet how many come
from the watering-places, their health absolutely destroyed.

New York and Brooklyn idiots, boasting of having
imbibed twenty glasses of congress water before breakfast. Families accustomed to going to bed at ten o'clock
at night, gossiping until one or two o'clock in the morning. Dyspeptics, usually very cautious about their
health, mingling ice-creams, and lemons, and lobster-
salads, and cocoanuts until the gastric juices lift up all
their voices of lamentation and protest. Delicate women

and brainless young men chassezing themselves into vertigo and catalepsy. Thousands of men and women coming back from our watering-places in the autumn with the foundations laid for ailments that will last them all their life long. You know as well as I do that this is the simple truth.

In the summer, you say to your good health, "Good-bye; I am going to have a good time for a little while; I will be very glad to see you again in the autumn."

Then in the autumn when you are hard at work in your office, or store, or shop, or counting-room, Good Health will come in and say: "Good-bye; I am going."

You say: "Where are you going?"

"O!" says Good Health, "I am going to take a vacation."

It is a poor rule that will not work both ways, and your good health will leave you choleric, and splenetic, and exhausted. You coquetted with your good health in the summer-time, and your good health is coquetting with you in the winter-time. A fragment of Paul's charge to the jailer would be an appropriate inscription for the hotel register in ever watering-place: "Do thyself no harm."

TEMPTATION TO HASTY MARRIAGES.

Another temptation hovering around the watering-place is to the formation of hasty and life-long alliances. The watering-places are responsible for more of the domestic infelicities of this country than all other things combined. Society is so artificial there that no sure judgment of character can be formed. They who form companionships amid such circumstances, go into a lotterv where there are twenty blanks to one prize. In the severe tug of life you want more than glitter and splash. Life is not a ball-room, where the music decides the step, and bow, and prance, and graceful swing of long trail can make up for strong common sense. You might as well go among the gaily-painted yachts of a summer regatta to find war vessels, as to go among the bright spray of the summer watering-place to find character that can stand the test of the great struggle of human life.

Ah, in the battle of life you want a stronger weapon than a lace fan or a croquet mallet! The load of life is so heavy that in order to draw it you want a team stronger than one made up of a masculine grasshopper and a feminine butterfly.

FOPS WITH THEIR "AHS! OHS! AND HE HES!"

If there is any man in the community that excites my contempt, and that ought to excite the contempt of every man and woman, it is the soft-handed, soft-headed fop, who, perfumed until the air is actually sick, spends his summer in taking killing attitudes, and waving sentimental adieus, and talking infinitesimal nothings, and finding his heaven in the set of a lavendar kid-glove. Boots as tight as an inquisition. Two hours of consummate skill exhibited in the tie of a flaming cravat. His conversation made up of "Ahs!" and "Ohs!" and "He hes!" It would take five hundred of them stewed down to make a teaspoonful of calf's-foot jelly.

There is only one counterpart to such a man as that, and that is the frothy young woman at the watering-place; her conversation made up of French moonshine:

what she had on her head only equalled by what she had
on her back; useless ever since she was born, and to be
useless until she is dead; and what they will do with
her in the next world I do not know, except to set her
up on the banks of the River of Life, for eternity, to
look sweet!　God intends us to admire music, and fair
faces and graceful step; but amid the heartlessness, and
the inflation and the fantastic influences of our modern
watering-places, beware how you make life-long cove-
nants.

Another temptation that will hover over the watering-
place is that to baneful literature.　Almost every one
starting off for the summer takes some reading matter.
It is a book out of the library, or off the book-stand, or
bought of the boy hawking books through the cars.　I
really believe there is more pestiferous trash read among
the intelligent classes in July and August than in all the
other ten months of the year.　Men and women who at
home would not be satisfied with a book that was not
really sensible, I found sitting on hotel piazza, or under
the trees, reading books, the index of which would make
them blush if they knew that you knew what the book
was.

"O," they say, "you must have intellectual recreation."

Yes.　There is no need that you take along into a
watering-place, "Hamilton's Metaphysics," or some
thunderous discourse on the eternal decrees, or Faraday's
Philosophy."　There are many easy books that are good.
You might as well say:

"I propose now to give a little rest to my digestive

organs, and instead of eating heavy meat and vegetables, I will, for a little while, take lighter food—a little strychnine and a few grains of ratsbane."

Literary poison in August is as bad as literary poison in December. Mark that. Do not let the frogs and the lice of a corrupt printing-press jump and crawl into your Saratoga trunk or White Mountain valise. Would it not be an awful thing for you to be struck with lightning some day when you had in your hand one of these paper-covered romances—the hero a Parisian roue, the heroine an unprincipled flirt—chapters in the book that you would not read to your children at the rate of a hundred dollars a line.

Throw out all that stuff from your summer baggage. Are there not good books that are easy to read—books of entertaining travel; books of congenial history; books of pure fun; books of poetry, ringing with merry canto; books of fine engraving; books that will rest the mind as well as purify the heart and elevate the whole life? My hearers, there will not be an hour between this and the day of your death when you can afford to read a book lacking in moral principle.

Another temptation hovering all around our watering-places, is to intoxicating beverage. I am told that it is becoming more and more fashionable for women to drink; and it is not very long ago that a lady of great respectability, In this city, having taken two glasses of wine away from home, became violent, and her friends, ashamed, forsook her, and she was carried to a police station, and afterward to her disgraced home.

I care not how well a woman may dress, if she has

taken enough of wine to flush her cheek and put a glassiness on her eye, she is intoxicated. She may be handed into a 2500 dollar carriage, and have diamonds enough to confound the Tiffany's—she is intoxicated. She may be a graduate of Packer Institute, and the daughter of some man in danger of being nominated for the Presidency—she is drunk. You may have a larger vocabulary than I have, and you may say in regard to her that she is "convivial," or she is "merry," or she is "festive," or she is "exhilarated;" but you cannot with all your garlands of verbiage, cover up the plain fact that it is an old fashioned case of drunk.

Now the watering-places are full of temptations to men and women to tipple.

At the close of the ten-pin or billiard game, they tipple.

At the close of the cotillion, they tipple.

Seated on the piazza cooling themselves off they tipple.

The tinged glasses come around with bright straws, and they tipple.

First, they take "light wines" as they call them; but "light wines," are heavy enough to debase the appetite. There is not a very long road between champagne at five dollars a bottle and whisky at five cents a glass.

Satan has three or four grades down which he takes men to destruction. One man he takes up, and through one spree pitches him into eternal darkness. That is a rare case. Very seldom, indeed, can you find a man who will be such a fool as that.

Satan will take another man to a grade, to a descent at an angle about like the Pennsylvania coal-shute, or the

Mount Washington rail track, and shove him off.   But that is very rare.

ON THE DOWN GRADE.

When a man goes down to destruction, Satan brings him to a plane.   It is almost a level.   The depression is so slight that you can hardly see it.   The man does not actually know that he is on the down grade, and it tips only a little toward darkness—just a little.   And the first mile it is claret, and the second mlle it is sherry, and the third mile it is punch, and the fourth mile it is ale, and the fifth mile it is porter, and the sixth mile it is brandy, and then it gets steeper, and steeper, and steeper, and the man·gets frightened, and says:

"O, let me get off."

"No," says the conductor, "this is an express-train, and it don't stop until it gets to the Grand Central depot of Smashupton!"

Ah, "Look not upon the wine when it is red, when it giveth its color in the cup, when it moveth itself aright. At the last it biteth like a serpent, and stingeth like an adder."   And if any young man of my congregation should get astray this summer in this direction, it will not be because I have not given him fair warning.

My friends, whether you tarry at home—which will. be quite as safe and perhaps quite as comfortable—or go into the country, arm yourself against temptation.   The grace of God is the only safe shelter, whether in town or country.   .There are watering-places accessible to all of us.   You cannot open a book of the Bible without finding out some such watering-place.   Fountains open for sin and uncleanness.   Wells of salvation.   Streams from

Lebanon. A flood struck out of the rock by Moses. Fountains in the wilderness discovered by Hagar. Water to drink and water to bathe in. The river of God which is full of water. Water of which if a man drink, he shall never thirst. Wells of water in the Valley of Baca. Living fountains of water. A pure river of water as clear as crystal from under the throne of God. These are watering-places accessible to all of us. We do not have a laborious packing up before we start—only the throwing away of our transgressions. No expensive hotel bills to pay; it is "without money and without price." No long and dusty travel before we get there; it is only one step away.

In California, in five minutes I walked around and saw ten fountains all bubbling up into eternal life—healing and therapeutic.

A chemist will go to one of these summer watering-places and take the water, and analyze it, and tell you that it contains so much of iron and so much of soda, and so much of lime, and so much of magnesia. I come to this Gospel well, this living fountain, and analyze the water; and I find that its ingredients are peace, pardon, forgiveness, hope, comfort, life, heaven. "Ho, every one that thirsteth, come ye" to this watering-place.

Crowd around this Bethesda this morning. O, you sick, you lame, you troubled, you dying—crowd around this Bethesda. Step in it, oh, step in it! The angel of the covenant this morning stirs the water! Why do you not step in it? Some of you are too weak to take a step in that direction. Then we take you up in the arms of our closing prayer, and plunge you clean under the wave!

hoping that the cure may be as sudden and as radical as with Captain Naaman, who, blotched and carbuncled, stepped into the Jordan, and after the seventh dive came up, his skin roseate complexioned as the flesh of a little child.

THE WOMAN OF PLEASURE.

"She that liveth in pleasure is dead while she liveth."—I, Tim.v, 6

It is a strong way of putting the truth, that a woman who seeks in worldly advantage her chief enjoyment, will come to dissapointment and death.

My friends, you all want to be happy. You have had a great many recipes by which it is proposed to give you satisfaction—solid satisfaction. At times you feel a thorough unrest. You know as well as older people what it is to be depressed. As dark shadows sometimes fall upon the geography of the school-girl as on the page of the spectacled philosopher. I have seen as cloudy days in May as in November. There are no deeper sighs breathed by the grandmother than by the granddaughter.

I correct the popular impression that people are happier in childhood and youth than they ever will be again. If we live aright, the older we are the happier. The happiest woman that I ever knew was a Christian octogenarian; her hair white as white could be; the sunlight of heaven late in the afternoon gilding the peaks of snow. I have to say to a great many of the young people of this church that the most miserable time you are ever to have is just now.

As you advance in life, as you come out into the world and have your head and heart all full of good, honest, practical, Christian work, then you will know what it is to begin to be happy. There are those who would have

us believe that life is chasing thistle-down and grasping bubbles. We have not found it so. To many of us it has been discovering diamonds larger than the Kohinoor, and I think that our joy will continue to increase until nothing short of the everlasting jubilee of heaven will be able to express it.

Horatio Greenough, at the close of the hardest life a man ever lives—the life of an American artist—wrote: "I don't want to leave this world until I give some sign that, born by the grace of God in this land, I have found life to be a very cheerful thing, and not the dark and bitter thing with which my early prospects were clouded."

Albert Barnes, the good Christian, known the world over, stood in his pulpit in Philadelphia, at seventy or eighty years of age, and said: "This world is so very attractive to me, I am very sorry I shall have to leave it."

I know that Solomon said some very dolorous things about this world, and three times declared: "Vanity of vanities, all is vanity." I suppose it was a reference to those times in his career when his seven hundred wives almost pestered the life out of him! But I would rather turn to the description he has given of religion, when he says in another place: "Her ways are ways of pleasantness, and all her paths are peace." It is reasonable to expect it will be so.

The longer the fruit hangs on the tree, the riper and more mellow it ought to grow. You plant one grain of corn, and it will send up a stalk with two ears, each having nine hundred and fifty grains, so that one grain planted will produce ninteen hundred grains. And ought

not the implantation of a grain of Christian principle in
a youthful soul develop into a large crop of gladness on
earth and to a harvest of eternal joy in heaven?   Hear
me, then, this morning, while I discourse upon some of
the mistakes which young people make in regard to happiness, and point out to the young women of this church
what I consider to be the sources of complete satisfaction.

SOCIAL POSITION CANNOT GIVE TRUE HAPPINESS.

And, in the first place, I *advise you not to build your
happiness upon mere social position.   Persons at your
age, looking off upon life, are apt to think that if, by
some stroke of what is called good-luck, you could arrive
in an elevated and affluent position, a little higher than
that in which God has called you to live, you would be
completely happy.   Infinite mistake!   The palace floor
of Ahasuerus is red with the blood of Vashti's broken
heart.   There have been no more scalding tears wept
than those which coursed the cheek of Josephine.

If the sobs of unhappy womanhood in the great cities
could break through the tapestried wall, that sob would
came along your street to-day like the simoon of the
desert.   Sometimes I have heard in the rustling of the
robes on the city pavement the hiss of the adders that
followed in the wake.   You have come out from your
home, and you have looked up at the great house, and
covet a life under those arches, when, perhaps, at that
very moment, within that house, there may have been
the wringing of hands, the start of horror, and the very
agony of hell.   ·

I knew such a one.   Her father's house was plain,

most of the people who came there were plain; but, by a change in fortune such as sometimes comes, a hand had been offered that led her into a brilliant sphere. All the neighbors congratulated her upon her grand prospects; but what an exchange!

On her side it was a heart full of generous impulse and affection.

On his side it was a soul dry and withered as the stubble of the field.

On her side it was a father's house, where God was honored and the Sabbath life flooded the rooms with the very mirth of heaven.

On his side it was a gorgeous residence, and the coming of mighty men to be entertained there; but within it were revelry and godlessness. Hardly had the orange blossoms of the marriage feast lost their fragrance, than the night of discontent began to cast here and there its shadow. The ring on the finger was only one link of an iron chain that was to bind her eternally captive. Cruelties and unkindness changed all those splendid trappings into a hollow mockery. The platters of solid silver, the caskets of pure gold, the head-dress of gleaming diamonds, were there; but no God, no peace, no kind words, no Christian sympathy. The festive music that broke on the captive's ear turned out to be a dirge, and the wreath in the plush was a reptile coil, and the upholstery that swayed in the wind was the wing of a destroying angel, and the bead-drops on the pitcher were the sweat of everlasting despair.

O, how many rivalries and unhappinesses among those who seek in social life their chief happiness! It matters not how fine you have things; there are other people who have it finer.

Taking out your watch you tell the hour of day, some one will correct your time-piece by pulling out a watch more richly chased and jeweled.

Ride in a carriage that cost you eight hundred dollars, and before you get around the park you will meet one that cost two thousand dollars.

Have on your wall a picture by Copley, and before night you will hear of some one who has a picture fresh from the studio of Church or Bierstadt. All that this world can do for you in ribbons, in silver, in gold, in Axminster plush, in Gobelin tapestry, in wide halls, in lordly acquaintanceship, will not give you the ten-thousandth part of a grain of solid satisfaction.

The English lord, moving in the very highest sphere, was one day found seated, with his chin on his hand, and his elbow on the window-sill, looking out, and saying: "O, I wish I could exchange places with that dog." Mere social position will never give happiness to a woman's soul. I have walked through the halls of those who despise the common people; I have sat at their banquets: I have had their friendship; yea, I have heard from their own lips the story of their disquietude; and I tell the young women of this church that they who build on mere social position their soul's immortal happiness, are building on the sand.

BEAUTY CANNOT INSURE HAPPINESS.

I go further, and advise you not to depend for enjoyment upon mere personal attractions. It would be sheer hypocrisy, because we may not have it ourselves, to despise, or affect to despise, beauty in others. When God gives it, He gives it as a blessing and as a means of usefulness.

David and his army were coming down from the mountains to destroy Nabal and his flocks and vineyards. The beautiful Abigail, the wife of Nabal, went out to arrest him when he came down from the mountains, and she succeeded. Coming to the foot of the hill, she knelt. David with his army of sworn men came down over the cliffs, and when he saw her kneeling at the foot of the hill, he cried:

"Halt!" to his men, and the caves echoed it: "Halt! halt!"

That one beautiful woman kneeling at the foot of the cliffs had arrested all those armed troops. A dew-drop dashed back Niagara.

The Bible sets before us the portraits of Sarah and Rebecca, and Abishag, Absalom's sister, and Job's daughters, and says: "They were fair to look upon." By out-door exercise, and by skillful arrangement of apparel, let woman make themselves attractive.

The sloven has only one mission, and that to excite ou loathing and disgust But alas! for those who depen upon personal charms for their happiness. Beauty is such a subtle thing, it does not seem to depend upon facial proportions or upon the sparkle of the eye, or upon the flush of the cheek. You sometimes find it among irregular features It is the soul shining through the face that makes one beautiful. But alas! for those who depend upon mere personal charms. They will come to dissapointment and to a great fret. There are so many different opinions about what are personal charms; and then sickness, and trouble, and age, do make such ravages. The poorest god.that a woman ever worships is her own face.

The saddest sight in all the world is a woman who has built everything on good looks, when the charms begin to vanish. O, how they try to cover the wrinkles and hide the ravages of time! When Time, with iron-shod feet, steps on a face, the hoof-marks remain, and you cannot hide them. It is silly to try to hide them. I think the most repulsive fool in all the world is an old fool!

Why, my friends, should you be ashamed to be getting old? It is a sign—it is prima facie evidence, that you have behaved tolerable well or you would not have lived to this time. The grandest thing, I think, is eternity, and that is made up of countless years. When the Bible would set forth the attractiveness of Jesus Christ, it says: "His hair was white as snow." But when the color goes from the cheek,.and the lustre from the eye, and the spring from the step, and the gracefulness from the gait, alas! for those who have built their time and there eternity upon good looks. But all the passage of years cannot take out of one's face benignity, and kindness, and compassion, and faith. Culture your heart and you culture your face. The brightest glory that ever beamed from a woman's face is the religion of Jesus Christ.

A WAR INCIDENT.

In the last war, two hundred wounded soldiers came to Philadelphia one night, and came unheralded, and they had to extemporize a hospital for them, and the Christian women of my church, and of other churches, went out that night to take care of the poor wounded fellows. That night I saw a Christian woman go through the wards of the hospitals, her sleeves rolled up, ready for hard work, her hair dishevelled in the excitement of the hour. Her face was plain, very plain; but after the wounds were washed and the new bandages were put round the splintered limbs, and the exhausted boy fell off into his first pleasant sleep, she put her hand on his brow, and he started in his dream, and said:

"O, I thought an angel touched me!"

There may have been no classic elegance in the features of Mrs. Harris, who came into the hospital after the "Seven Days" awful fight before Richmond, as she sat down by a wounded drummer-boy and heard him soliloquize:

"A ball through my body, and my poor mother will never again see her boy. What a pity it is!"

And she leaned over him and said: "Shall I be your mother and comfort you?"

And he looked up and said: "Yes, I'll try to think she's here. Please to write a long letter to her, and tell her all about it, and send her a lock of my hair and comfort her. But I would like to have you tell her how much I suffered—yes, I would like you to do that, for she would feel so for me. Hold my hand while I die."

There may have been no classic elegance in her features, but all the hospitals of Harrison's Landing and Fortress Monroe would have agreed that she was beautiful; and if any rough man in all that ward had insulted her, some wounded soldier would have leaped from his couch, on his best foot, and struck him dead with a crutch.

FLATTERY CANNOT GIVE YOU TRUE HAPPINESS.

Again: I advise you not to depend for happiness upon the flatteries of men. It is a poor compliment to your sex that so many men feel obliged in your presence to offer unmeaning compliments. Men capable of elegant and elaborate conversation elsewhere sometimes feel called upon at the door of the drawing-room to drop their common sense and to dole out sickening flatteries. They say things about your dress, and about your appearance, that you know, and they know, are false. They say you are an angel. You know you are not. Determined to tell the truth in office, and store, and shop, they consider it honorable to lie to a woman. The same thing that they told you on this side of the drawing-room three minutes ago they said to some on the other side of the drawing-room. O, let no one trample on your self respect. The meanest thing on which a woman can build her happiness is the flatteries of men.

NOR FASHION.

Again: I charge you not to depend for happiness upon the discipleship of fashion. Some men are just as proud of being out of the fashion as others are of being in it. I have seen men as vain of their old fashioned coat, and their eccentric hat, as your brainless fop is proud of his dangling fooleries. Fashion sometimes makes a reasonable demand of us, and then we ought to yield to it. The daisies of the field have their fashion of color and leaf; the honeysuckles have their fashion of ear-drop; and the snowflakes flung out of the winter heavens have their fashion of exquisiteness. After the summer shower the sky weds the earth with a ring of rainbow. And I do not think we have a right to despise all the elegancies and fashions of this world, especially if they make reasonable demands upon us; but the discipleship and worship of fashion is death to the body, and death to the soul.

I am glad the world is improving. Look at the fashion plates of the seventeenth and eighteenth centuries, and you will find that the world is not so extravagant and extraordinary now as it was then, and all the marvellous things that the granddaughter will do will never equal that done by the grandmother. Go still further back to the Bible times, and you find that in those times fashion wielded a more terrible scepter. You have only to turn to the third chapter of Isaiah.

Only think of a woman having all that on! I am glad that the world is getting better, and that fashion which has dominated in the world so ruinously in other days has for a little time, for a little degree at any rate, relaxed its energies. Oh, the danger of the discipleship of fashion. All the splendors and extravaganza of this world dyed into your robe and flung over your shoulder cannot wrap peace around your heart for a single moment. The gayest wardrobe will utter no voice of condolence in the day of trouble and darkness.

That woman is grandly dressed, and only she, who is wrapped in the robe of a Savior's righteousness. The home may be very humble, the hat may be very plain, the frock may be very coarse; but the halo of heaven settles in the room when she wears it, and the faintest touch of the resurrection angel will change that garment into raiment exceeding white, so as no fuller on earth could whiten it.

I come to you, young woman, to-day, to say that this world cannot make you happy. I know it is a bright world, with glorious sunshine, and golden rivers, and fire worked sunset, and bird orchestra, and the darkest cave, has its crystals, and the wrathiest wave its foam-wreath, and the coldest midnight its flaming aurora; but God will put out all these lights with the blast of his own nostrils, and the glories of this world will perish in the final conflagration

You will never be happy until you get your sins forgiven and allow Christ Jesus to take full posession of your soul.   He will be your friend in every perplexity. He will be in comfort in every trial.   He will be your defender in every strait.

I do not ask you to bring, like Mary, the spices to the sepulcher of a dead Christ, but to bring you all to the feet of a living Jesus.   His word is peace,   His look is love.   His hand is help.   His touch is life.   His smile is heaven.

Oh, come, then, in flocks and groups!   Come, like the south wind over banks of myrrh.   Come, like the morning light tripping over the mountains.   Wreath all your affections for Christ's brow, set all your gems in Christ's coronet, pour all your voices in Christ's song, and let this Sabbath air rustle with the wings of rejoicing angels, and the tower ot God ring out the news of souls saved!

"This world its fancied pearl may crave,   •

'Tis not the pearl for me;
'Twill dim its luster in the grave,
'Twill perish in the sea.
But there's a pearl of price untold,
Which never can be bought with gold;
Oh, that's the pearl for me."

KEEPING BAD COMPANY.

"A companion of fools shall be destroyed."—Proverbs. xiii, 20.

On the night of city exploration I found that hardly any young man came to places of dissipation alone. Each one was accompanied. No man goes to ruin alone. He always takes some one else with him.

"May it please the court," said a convicted criminal, when asked if he had anything to say before sentence of death was passed upon him—"may it please the court, bad company has been my ruin. I received the blessing of good parents, and, in return, promised to avoid all evil associations. Had I kept my promise, I should have been saved this shame, and been free from the load of guilt that hangs around me like a vulture, threatening to drag me to justice for crimes yet unrevealed. I, who once moved in the first circles of society, and have been the guest of distinguished public men, am lost, and all through bad company."

This is but one of the thousand proofs that the companion of fools shall be destroyed. It is the invariable rule. Thers is a well man in the wards of a hospital, where there are a hundred people sick with ship fever, and he will not be so apt to take the disease as a good man would be apt to be smitten with moral distemper, if shut up with iniquitous companions.

In olden times prisoners were herded together in the same cell, but each one learned the vices of all the cul-

[348]

THE MUSIC HALL AND BEER GARDEN.

prits, so that, instead of being reformed by incarceration, the day of liberation turned them out upon society beasts, not men.

We may, in our places of business, be compelled to talk to and mingle with bad men; but he who deliberately chooses to associate himself with vicious people, is engaged in carrying on a courtship with a Delilah, whose shears will clip off all the locks of his strength, and he will be tripped into perdition. Sin is catching, is infectious, is epidemic. I will let you look over the millions of people now inhabiting the earth, and I challenge you to show me a good man who, after one year, has made choice and consorted with the wicked. A thousand dollars reward for one such instance. I care not how strong your character may be. Associate with horse-thieves, you will become a horse-thief. Clan with burglars, and you will become a burglar. Go among the unclean, and you will become unclean. Not appreciating the truth of my text, many a young man has been destroyed. He wakes up some morning in the great city, and knows no one except the persons into whose employ he has entered.

As he goes into the store all the clerks mark him, measure him and discuss him. The upright young men of the store wish him well, but perhaps wait for a formal introduction, and even then have some delicacy about inviting him into their associations. But the bad young men of the store at the first opportunity approach and offer their services. They patronize him. They profess to know all about the town. They will take him anywhere that he wishes to go—if he will pay the expenses.

For if a good young man and a bad young man go to some place where they ought not, the good young man has invariable to pay the charges.   At the moment the ticket is to be paid for, or the champagne settled for, the bad young man feels around in his pockets and says,   "I have forgotten my pocket-book."

In forty-eight hours after the young man has entered the store the bad fellows of the establishment slap him on the shoulder familiarly; and, at his stupidity in taking certain allusions, say, "My young friend, you will have to be broken in;" and they immediately proceed to break him in.

Young man, in the name of God I warn you to beware how you let a bad man talk familiarly with you. If such a one slap you on the shoulder familiarly turn round and give him a withering look, until the wretch crouches in your presence.   There is no monstrosity of wickedness that can stand unabashed under the glance of purity and honor.   God keeps the lightnings of heaven in his own scabbard, and no human arm can wield them; but God gives to every young man a lightning that he may use, and that is the lightning of an honest eye. Those who have been close observers of city life will not wonder why I give warning to young men and say, "Beware of bad company."

SHUN THE SKEPTIC!

First, I warn you to shun the skeptic—the young man who puts his fingers in his vest and laughs at your old-fashioned religion, and turns over to some mystery of the Bible, and says, "Explain that, my pious friend; explain that."   And who says, "Nobody shall scare me;

I am not afraid of the future; I used to believe in such things, and so did my father and mother, but I have got over it " Yes, he has got over it; and if you sit in his company a little longer, you will get over it too.

Without presenting one argument against the Christian religion, such men will, by their jeers and scoffs and caricatures, destroy your respect for that religion, which was the strength of your father in his declining years, and the pillow of your old mother when she lay a-dying.

Alas! a time will come when that blustering young infidel will have to die, and then his diamond ring will flash no splendor in the eyes of Death, as he stands over the couch, waiting for his soul. Those beautiful locks will be uncombed upon the pillow; and the dying man will say:

"I cannot die—I cannot die."

Death standing ready beside the couch says, "You must die; you have only half a minute to live; let me have it right away—your soul."

"No," says the young infidel, "here are my gold rings, and these pictures; take them all."

"No," says Death, "What do I care for pictures!—your soul."

"Stand back," says the dying infidel.

"I will not stand back," says Death, for you have only ten seconds now to live: I want your soul."

The dying man says, "Don't breath that cold air into my face. You crowd me to hard. It is getting dark in the room. O God!"

"Hush," says Death; you said there was no God."

"Pray for me," exclaims the expiring infidel.

"Too late to pray," says Death; "but three more seconds to live, and I will count them off—one—two—three." He has gone!

Where? Where? Carry him out—out, and bury him beside his father and mother, who died while holding fast the Christian religion. They died singing; but the young infidel only said, "Don't-breathe that cold air into my face. You crowd me too hard. It is getting dark in the room.

SHUN THE IDLER!

Again, I urge you to shun the companionship of idlers. There are men hanging around every store, and office and shop, who have nothing to do, or act as if they had not. They are apt to come in when the firm are away, and wish to engage you in conversation while you are engaged in your regular employment. Politely suggest to such persons that you have no time to give them during business hours. Nothing would pleaso them so well as to have you renounce your occupation and associate with them. Much of the time they lounge around the doors of engine houses, or after the dining hour stand upon the steps of a fashionaple hotel or an elegant restaurant wishing to give you the idea that that is the place where they dine. But they do not dine there. They are sinking down lower and lower, day by day. Neither by day nor by night have anything to do with the idlers.

Before you admit a man into your acquaintance ask him politely, "What do you do for a living?" If he says "Nothing, I am a gentleman," look out for him. He may have a very soft hand, and very faultless apparel, and have a high-sounding family name, but his touch is death.   Before you know it, you will in his presence be ashamed of your work dress.   Business will become to you drudgery, and after awhile you will lose your place, and afterward your respectability, and last of all your soul.

Idleness is next door to villainy.   Thieves, gamblers, burglars, shop-lifters and assassins are made from the class who have nothing to do.   When the police go to hunt up and arrest a culprit they seldom go to look in at the busy carriage factory, or behind the counter where diligent clerks are employed, but they go among the groups of idlers.

The play is going on at the theatre, when suddenly there is a scuffle in the top gallery.   What is it?

A policeman has come in, and, leaning over, has tapped on the shoulder of a young man, saying, "I want you, sir."   He has not worked during the day, but somehow has raked together a shilling or two to get into the top gallery.   He is an idler.   The man on his right hand is an idler, and the man on his left hand is an idler.

During the past few years there has been a great deal of dullness in business.   Young men have complained that they have little to do.   If they have nothing else to do they can read and improve their minds and hearts. These times are not always to continue.   Business is waking up, and the superior knowledge that in this interregnum of work you may obtain will be worth fifty thousand dollars of capital.   The large fortunes of the next twenty years are having their foundations laid this winter by the young men who are giving themselves to self-improvement. I went into a store in New York and saw five men, all Christians, sitting around, saying that they had nothing to do. It is an outrage for a Christian man to have nothing to do. Let him go out and visit the poor, or distribute tracts, or go and read the Bible to the sick, or take out his New Testament and be making his eternal fortune. Let him go into the back office and pray.

Shrink back from idleness in yourself and in others, if you would maintain a right position. Good old Ashbel Green, at more than eighty years of age, was found busy writing, and some young man said to him: "Why do you keep busy? It is time for you to rest!" He answered: "I keep busy to keep out of mischief." No man is strong enough to be idle.

Are you fond of pictures? If so I will show you one of the works of an old master. Here it is: "I went by the field of the slothful, and by the vineyard of the man void of understanding; and lo! it was all grown over with thorns, and nettles had covered the face thereof, and the stone wall was broken down. Then I saw and considered well. I looked upon it and received instructions. Yet a little sleep, a little slumber, a litlle folding of the hands to sleep. So shall thy poverty come as one that traveleth and thy want as an armed man." I don't know of another sentence in the Bible more explosive than that. It first hisses softly, like the fuse of a cannon, and at last bursts like a fifty-four pounder. The old proverb was right: "The devil tempts most men, but idlers tempt the devil."

A young man came to a man of ninety years of age

and said to him: "How have you made out to live so long and be so well?" The old man took the youngster to an orchard, and, pointing to some large trees full of apples, said: "I planted these trees when I was a boy, and do you wonder that now I am permitted to gather the fruit of them?" We gather in old age what we plant in our youth. Sow to the wind and we reap the whirlwind. Plant in early life the right kind of a Christian character, and you will eat lucious fruit in old age, and gather these harvest apples in eternity.

AVOID THE PERPETUAL PLEASURE SEEKER.

Again: I urge you to avoid the perpetual pleasure-seeker. I believe in recreation and amusement. I need it as much as I need bread, and go to my gymnasium with as conscientious a purpose as I go to the Lord's Supper; and all persons of sanguine temperament must have amusement and recreation. God would not have made us with the capacity to laugh if he had not intended us sometimes to indulge in it. We will go forth from the festivities of coming holidays better prepared to do our work.

God hath hung in sky, and set in wave, and printed on grass many a roundelay; but he who chooses pleasure-seeking for his life-work does not understand for what God made him. Our amusements are intended to help us in some earnest mission.

The thunder-cloud hath an edge exquisitely purpled, but with voice that jars the earth, it declares, "I go to water the green fields."

The wild-flowers under the fence are gay, but they say, "We stand here to make room for the wheat-field, and to refresh the husbandmen in their nooning."

The stream sparkles and foams, and frolics, and says, "I go to baptize the moss. I lave the spots on the trout. I slake the thirst of the bird.   I turn the wheel of the mill.   I rock in my crystal cradle muckshaw and water-lily."

And so, while the world plays, it works.   Look out for the man who always plays and never works.

You will do well to avoid those whose regular business it is to play ball, skate or go a-boating.   All these sports are fraud in their places.   I never derived so much advantage from any ministerial association, as from ministerial club that went out to play ball every Saturday afternoon in the outskirts of Philadelphia.   These recreations are grand to give us muscle and spirits for our regular toil.   I believe in muscular Christianity. A man is often not so near God with a weak stomach as when he has a strong digestion.   But shun those who make it their life occupation to sport.   There are young men whose industry and usefulness have fallen overboard from the yacht on the Hudson or the Schuylkill.   There are men whose business fell through the ice of the skating pond, and has never since been heard of.   There is a beauty in the gliding of a boat, in the song of skates, in the soaring of a well-struck ball, and I never see one fly but I involuntarily throw up my hands to catch it; and, so far from laying an injunction upon ball-playing, or any other innocent sport, I claim them all as belonging of right to those of us who toil in the grand industries of church and state.

But the life business of pleasure-seeking always makes

in the end a criminal or a sot. George Brummel was smiled upon by all England, and his life was given to pleasure. He danced with peeresses, and swung a round of mirth, and wealth, and applause, until exhausted of purse, and worn out of body, and bankrupt of reputation, and ruined of soul, he begged a biscuit from a grocer, and declared that he thought a dog's life was better than a man's.

Such men will crowd around your anvil, or seek to decoy you off. They will want you to break out in the midst of your busy day to take a ride with them to Coney Island or to Central Park. They will tell you of some people you must see; of some excursion that you must take; of some Sabbath day that you ought to dishonor. They will tell you of exquisite wines that you must take; of costly operas that you must hear; or wonderful dancers that you must see; but before you accept their convoy or their companionship, remember that while at the end of a useful life you may be able to look back to kindnesses done, to honorable work accomplished, to poverty helped, to a good name earned, to Christian influence exerted, to a Savior's cause advanced—these pleasure-seekers on their death-bed have nothing better to review than a torn play-bill, a ticket for the races, an empty tankard, and the cast-out rinds of a carousal· and as in the delirium of their awful death they clutch the goblet, and press it to their lips, the dregs of the cup falling upon their tongue, will begin to hiss and uncoil with the adders of an eternal poison.

Cast out these men from your company. Do not be intimate with them. Always be polite? There is no demand that you ever sacrifice politeness. A young man accosted a Christian Quaker with, "Old Chap, how did you make all your money?" The Quaker replied, "By dealing in an article that thou mayst deal in if thou wilt—civility." Always be courteous, but at the same time firm. Say no as if you meant it. Have it understood in store, and shop, and street that you will not stand in the companionship of the skeptic, the idle, the pleasure-seeker.

Rather than enter the companionship of such, accept the invitation to a better feast. The promises of God are the fruits. The harps of heaven are the music. Clusters from the vineyards of God have been pressed into the tankards. The sons and daughters of the Lord Almighty are the guests. While, standing at one banquet, to fill the cups and divide the clusters, and command the harps, and welcome the guests, is a daughter of God on whose brow are the blossoms of Paradise, and in whose cheek is the flash of celestial summer. Her name is Religion.

"Her ways are ways of pleasantness.
And all her paths are peace."

THE HANDWRITING ON THE WALL.

THE TIDES OF MUNICIPAL SIN.

"He beheld the city, and wept over it."—Luke xix, 41.

The citizens of Old Jerusalem are in the tip-top of excitement. A country man has been doing some wonderful works and asserting very high authority. The police court has issued papers for his arrest, for this thing must be stopped, as the very government is imperilled.

News comes that last night this stranger arrived at a suburban village, and that he is stopping at the house of man whom he has resuscitated after four days' sepulture. Well, the people rush out into the streets, some with the idea of helping in the arrest of this stranger when he arrives, and others expecting on the morrow he will come into the town, and by some supernatural force oust the municipal and royal authorities and take everything in his town hands.

They pour out of the city gates until the procession reaches to the village. They come all around about the house where the stranger is stopping, and peer into the doors and windows that they may get one glimpse of him or hear the hum of his voice.

The police dare not make the arrest because he has, somehow, won the affections of all the people. O, it is a lively night in Bethany. The heretofore quiet village is filled with uproar, and outcry, and loud discussion about the strange acting countryman. I do not think there was any sleep in that house that night where the

[359]

stranger was stopping. Although he came in weary he finds no rest, though for once in his lifetime he had a pillow.

But the morning dawns, the olive gardens wave in the light, and all along the road, reaching over the top of Olivet toward Jerusalem, there is a vast swaying crowd of wondering people. The excitement around the door of the cottage is wild, as the stranger steps out beside an unbroken colt that has never been mounted, and after his friends had strewn their garments on the beast for a saddle, the Saviour mounts it, and the populace, excited, and shouting, and feverish, push on back toward Jerusalem. Let none jeer now or scoff at this rider, or the populace will trample him under foot in an instant.

There is one long shont of two miles, and as far as the eye can reach, you see wavings of demonstrations and approval. There was something in the rider's visage, something in his majestic brow, something in his princely behavior, that stirs up the enthusiasm of the people. They run up against the beast and try to pull off their arms, and carry on their shoulders, the illustrious stranger. The populace are so excited that they hardly know what to do with themselves, and some rush up the road side trees and wrench off branches and throw them in his way: and others doff their garments, what though they be new and costly, and spread them for a carpet for the conqueror to ride over.

"Hosanna!" cry the people at the foot of the hill.

"Hosanna!" cry the people all up and down the mountain.

The procession has now come to the brow of Olivet.

Magnificent prospect reaching out in every direction—
vineyards, olive groves, jutting rock, silvery Siloam, and
above all, rising on its throne of hills, the most highly
honored city of all the earth, Jerusalem. Christ there,
in the midst of the procession, looks off, and sees here
fortressed gates, and yonder the circling wall, and here
the towers blazing in the sun, Phasælus and Mariamne.
Yonder is Hippicus, the king's castle. Looking along
in the range of the larger branch of that olive tree you
see the mansions of the merchant princes. Through this
cleft in the limestone rock you see the palace of the
richest trafficer in all the earth. He has made his
money by selling Tyrian purple. Behold now the Temple! Clouds of smoke lifting from the shimmering roof,
while the building rises up beautiful, grand, majestic,
the architectural skill and glory of the earth lifting themselves there in one triumphant doxology, the frozen
prayer of all nations.

The crowd looked around to see exhilaration and
transport in the face of Christ. O, no! Out from amid
the gates, and the domes, and the palaces there arose a
vision of that city's sin, and of that city's doom, which
obliterated the landscape from horizon to horizon, and
He burst into tears. "He beheld the city, and wept
over it."

Standing in some high tower of the beloved city of
our residence, we might look off upon a wondrous scene
of enterprise, and wealth, and beauty; long streets, faced
by comfortable homes, here and there rising into affluence, while we might find thousands of people who would
be glad to cast palm branches in the way of him who

comes from Bethany to Jerusalem, greeting him with the vociferation: "Hosanna! to the Son of David."

And yet how much there is to mourn over in our cities. passing along the streets to-day are a great multitude. Whither do they go? To church. Thank God for that. Listen, this morning, and you hear multitudinous voices of praise. Thank God for that.

When the evening falls you will find Christian men and women knocking at hovels of povery, and finding no light, taking the matches from their pocket, and by a momentary glance revealing wan faces, and wasted hands, and ragged bed, sending in before morning, candles and vials of medicine, and Bibles and loaves of bread, and two or three flowers from the hot-house. Thank God for that.

But listen again, and you hear the thousand-voiced shriek of blasphemy tearing its way up from the depths of the city. You see the uplifted decanters emptied now but uplifted to fight down the devils they have raised.

Listen to that wild laugh on the street corner, that makes the pure shudder and say: "Poor thing, that's a lost soul!" Hark! to the click of the gambler's dice and the hysteric guffaw of him who has pocketed the last dollar of that young man's estate.

This is the banquet of Bacchus. That young man has taken his first glass. That man has taken down three-fourth of his estate. This man is trembling with last night's debauch. This man has pawned everything save that old coat. This man is in delirium, sitting pale and unaware of anything that is transpiring about him—quiet until after awhile he rises up with a shriek, enough

to make the denizens of the pit clap to the door and put
their fingers in their ears, and rattle their chains still
louder to drown out the horrible outcry.

You say: ''Is it not strange that there should be so-
much suffering and sin in our cities?''

No, it is not strange.

When I look abroad and see the temptations that are
attempting to destroy men for time and eternity, I am
surprised in the other direction that there are any true,
upright, honest, Christian people left. There is but little
hope for any man in these great cities who has not
established in his soul, sound, thorough Christian principle.

COEMERCIAL FRAUDS!

First, look around you and see the temptations to
commercial frauds. Here is a man who starts in business.

He says: ''I'm going to be honest;'' but on the same
street, on the same block, in the same business, are
Shylocks.

Those men, to get the patronage of any one, will break
all understandings with other merchants, and will sell at
ruinous cost, putting their neighbors at great disadvantage, expecting to make up the deficit in something
else. If an honest principle could creep into that man's
soul, it would die of sheer loneliness! The man twists
about, trying to escape the penalty of the law, and de-
spises God, while he is just a little anxious about the
sheriff.

The honest man looks about him and says: ''Well,
this rivalry is awful. Perhaps I am more scrupulous

than I need be.   This little bargain I am about to enter is doubtful; but then they all do it."

EFFECT OF FRAUDULENT COMPETITION.

And so I had a friend who started in commercial life, and as a book merchant, with a high resolve.   He said: "In my store there shall be no book that I would not have my family read."

Time passed on, and one day I went into his store and found some iniquitous books on the shelf, and I said to him: "How is it possible that you can consent to sell such books as these?"

"Oh," he replied: "I have got over those puritanical notions.   A man cannot do business in this day unless he does it in the way other people do it."

To make a long story short, he lost his hope of heaven. and in a little while he lost his morality, and then he went into a mad-house.   In other words, when a man casts off God, God casts him off.

One of the mightiest temptations in commercial life, in all our cities, to-day, is in the fact that many profess-ed Christian men are not square in their bargains.   Such men are in Baptist, and Methodist, and Congregational Churches, and our own denomination is as largely repre-sented as any of them.

Our good merchants are foremost in Christian enter-prises; they are patronizers of art, philanthropic and patriotic.   God will attend to them in the day of His coronation.   I am not speaking of them, but of those in commercial life who are setting a ruinous example to our young merchants.

Go through all the stores and offices in this city, and

tell me in how many of those stores and offices are the principles of Christ's religion dominant?

In three-fourths of them?

No.

In half of them?

No.

In one-tenth of them?

No.

Decide for yourself.

GOD AND THE OIL SWINDLER.

The impression is sbroad, somehow, that charity can consecrate iniquitous gains, and that if a man give to God a portion of an unrighteous bargain, then the Lord will forgive him the rest. The secretary of a benevolent society came to me and said:

"Mr. So-and-So has given a large amount of money to the missionary cause," mentioning the sum.

I said: "I can't believe it."

He said: "It is so."

Well, I went home, staggered and confounded. I never knew the man to give to anything; but after awhile I found out that he had been engaged in the most infamous kind of an oil swindle, and then he proposed to compromise the matter with the Lord, saying:

"Now here is so much for Thee, Lord. Please to let me off!"

. I want to tell you that the Church of God is not a shop for receiving stolen goods, and that if you have taken anything from your fellows, you had better return it to the men to whom it belongs. If, from the nature of the circumstances, that be impossible, you had better get your stove red hot, and when the flames are at their fierciest toss in the accursed spoil. Cod does not want it.

The commercial world to-day is rotten through and through, and many of you know better than I can tell you that it requires great strength of moral character to withstand the temptations of business dishonesties. Thank God a great many of you have withstood the temptations, and are as pure, and upright, and honest as the day when you entered business. But you are the exceptions in the case. God will sustain a man, however, amid all the excitements of business, if he will only put his trust in Him.

HOW HONESTY WAS REWARDED.

In a drug-store, in Philadelphia, a young man was told that he must sell blacking on the Lord's day.

He said to the head man of the firm: "I can't possibly do that. I am willing to sell medicines on the Lord's day, for I think that is right and necessary; but I can't sell this patent blacking."

He was discharged from the place.

A Christian man hearning of it, took him into his employ, and he went on from one success to another, until he was known all over the land for his faith in God and his good works, as well as for his worldly success. When a man has sacrificed any temporal, financial good for the sake of his spiritual interests, the Lord is on his side, and one with God is a majority.

Again: Look around you and see the pressure of political life. How many are going down under this influence. There is not one man out of a thousand that can

stand political life in our cities.   Once in awhile a man
comes and says: ''Now I love my city and my country,
and, in the strength of God, I am going in as a sort of
missionary to reform politics."   The Lord is on his side.
He comes out as pure as when he went in, and, with such
an idea, I believe he will be sustained; but he is the exception.   When such an upright, pure man does step into politics, the first thing, the newspapers take the job
of blackening him all over, and they review all his past
life, and distort everything that he has done, until, from
thinking himself a highiy respectable citizen, he begins
to contemplate what a mercy it is that he has been so
long out of gaol.

The most hopeless, God-for-saken people in all our
cities are those who, not in a missionary spirit, but with
the idea of-sordid gain, have gone into political life.

I pray for the prisoners in gaol, and think they may be
converted to God, but I never have any faith to pray for
an old politician.

Then look around and see the allurements to an impure life.   Bad books. unknown to father and mother,
vile as the lice of Egypt, creeping into some of the best
of families of the community; and boys read them while
the teacher is looking the other way, or at recess, or on
the corner of the street when the groups are gathered.
These books are read late at night.   Satan finds them a
smooth plank on which he can slide down into perdition
some of your sons and daughters.

Reading bad books—one never gets over it.   The
books may be burned, but there is not enough of power
in all the apothecary's preparations to wash out the stain

from the soul.   Father's hands, mother's hands, sister's hands, will not wash it out.   None but the hand of the Lord God can wash it out.   And what is more perilous in regard to these temptations, we may not mention them.   While God in this Bible, from chapter to chapter, thunders His denunciation against these crimes, people expect the pulpit and the printing-press to be silent on the subject, and just in proportion as people are impure are they fastidious on the theme.   They are so full of decay and death they do not want their sepulchres opened.   But I shall not be hindered by them.   I shall go on in the name of the Lord Almighty, before whom you and I must at last come into judgment, and shall pursue that vile sin and thrust it with the two edged-sword of God's truth, though I find it sheltered under the chandeliers of some of your beautiful parlors.

God will turn into destruction all the unclean, and no splendors of surrounding can make decent that which He has smitten.

God will not excuse sin merely because it has costly array, and beautiful tapestry, and palatial residence, any more than He will excuse that which crawls, a blotch of sores, through the lowest cellar. Ever and anon, through some law-suit there flashes upon the people of our great cities what is transpiring in seemingly respectable circles.

You call it ''High Life,'' you call it ''Fast living,'' you call it ''People's eccentricity.''   And while we kick off the sidewalk the poor wretch who has not the means to garnish his iniquity, these lords and ladies, wrapped in purple and fine linen, go unwhipped of public justice.

Ah, the most dreadful part of the whole thing is that there are persons abroad whose whole business it is to despoil the young. Salaried by infamous establishments, these cormorants of darkness, these incarnate fiends, hang around your hotels, and your theatres, and they insinuate themselves among the clerks of your stores, and, by adroitest art, sometimes get in the purest circles. Oh, what an eternity such a man as that will have! As the door opens to receive him, thousands of voices will cry out: "See here what you have done;" and the wretch will wrap himself with fiercer flame and leap into deeper darkness, and the multitudes he has destroyed will pursue him, and hurl at him the long, bitter, relentless, everlasting curse of their own anguish.

If there be one cup of eternal darkness more bitter than another, they will have to drink it to the dregs. If, in all the ocean of the lost world that comes billowing up, there be one wave more fierce than another, it will dash over them. "God will wound the hairy scalp of him who goeth on still in his trespasses."

I think you are persuaded there is but little chance here in Brooklyn, or in New York, or Philadelphia, or Boston, for any young man without the grace of God.

I will even go further and make it more emphatic, and say there is no chance for any young man who has not above him, and beneath him, and before him, and behind him, and on the right of him, and on the left of him, and within him, the all-protecting grace of God.

My word of warning is to those who have recently come to the city; some of them entering our banking institutions, and some of them our stores and shops. Shelter yourselves in God.   Do not trust yourselves an hour without the defences of Christ's religion.

I stood one day at Niagara Falls, and I saw what you may have seen there, six rainbows bending over that tremendous plunge.   I never saw anything like it before or since.   Six beautiful rainbows arching that great cataract!   And so over the rapids and the angry precipices of sin,   where so many have been dashed down,   God's beautiful admonitions hover, a warning arching each peril —six of them, fifty of them—a thousand of them.   Beware! beware! beware!

This afternoon,   young men, while you have time to reflect upon these things, and before the duties of the office and the store, and the shop, come upon you again, look over this whole subject, and after the day has passed, and you hear in the nightfall the voices and the footsteps of the city dying from your ear, and it gets so silent that you can hear distinctly your watch under your pillow going "tick, tick!" then open your eyes and look out upon the darkness, and see two pillars of light, one horizontal, the other perpendicular, but changing their direction until they come together, and your enraptured vision beholds it—THE CROSS!

THE HAPPY HOME.

ASTRAY, BUT RECOVERED.

CHRIST CAN SAVE ALL.

"All we like sheep have gone astray; we have turned every one to his own work; and the Lord hath laid on him the iniquity of us all."—Isaiah Liii, 6.

Within ninety years at the longest all who hear or read this sermon will be in eternity. During the next fifty years you will nearly all be gone. The next ten years will cut a wide swath among the people. The year 1891 will to some be the finality. Such considerations make this occasion absorbing and momentous.

The first half of my text is an indictment. "All we like sheep have gone astray." Some one says: "Can you not drop the first word? That, is too general that sweeps too great a circle." Some man rises in the audience and he looks over on the opposite side of the house and he says, "There is a blasphemer, and I understand how he has gone astray. And there is an impure person, and he has gone astray."

THE TEXT TAKES US ALL IN.

Sit down, my brother and look at home. My text takes us all in. It starts behind the pulpit, sweeps the circuit of the room and comes back to the point where it started when it says, "All we like sheep have gone astray." I can very easily understand why Martin Luther threw up his hands after he had found the Bible and cried out. "Oh! my sins, my sins," and why the publi-

(371)

can, according to the custom to this day in the east when they have any great grief, began to beat himself and cry as he smote upon his breast, "God be merciful to me a sinner."

ILLUSTRATION FROM THE SHEPHARD'S LIFE.

I was, like many of you brought up in the country; and I know some of the habits of sheep and how they get astray, and what my text means when it says, "All we like sheep have gone astray." Sheep get astray in two ways, either by trying to get in other pastures, or from being scared by the dogs. In the former way some of us got astray. We thought the religion of Jesus Christ short commons. We thought there was better pasturage somewhere else. We thought if we could only lie down on the banks or distant streams or under great oaks on the other side of some hill we might be better fed.

We wanted other pasturage than that which God through Jesus Christ gave our soul, and we wandered on and we were lost. We wanted bread and we found garbage. The further we wandered, instead of finding rich pasturage, we found blasted heath and sharper rocks and more stinging nettles. No pasture. How was it in the worldly groups when you lost your child? Did they come around and console you very much? Did not the plain Christian man who came into your house and sat up with your darling child give you more comfort than all worldly associations? Did all the convival songs you ever heard comfort you in that day of bereavement so much as the song they sang to you, perhaps the very song that was sung by your little child the last Sabbath afternoon of her life.

There is a happy land far, far away,
Where saints immortal reign, bright, bright as day.

Did your business associates in that day of darkness, and trouble give you any especial condolence? Business exasperated you, business wore you out, business left you as limp as a rag, business made you mad. You got dollars, but you got no peace. God have mercy on the man who has nothing but business to comfort him. The world afforded you no luxurious pasturage.

AN INCIDENT OF AN ACTOR.

A famous English actor stood on the stage impersonating, and thunders of applause came down from the galleries, and many thought it was the proudest moment of all his life; but there was a man asleep just in front of him, and the fact that that man was indifferent and somnolent spoiled all the occasion for him, and he cried, "Wake up! Wake up!"

Some little annoyance in life has been more pervading to your mind than all the brilliant congratulations and successes. Poor pasturage for your soul you found in this world. The world has cheated you, the world has belied you, the world has misinterpreted you, the world has persecuted you· It never comforted you. Oh! this world is a good rack from which a horse may pick his hay; it is a good trough from which the swine may crunch their mess; but it gives but little food to a soul blood bought and immortal.

WHAT IS A SOUL?

What is a soul? It is a hope high as the throne of

God.   What is a man?   You say, "It is only a man."
It is only a man gone overboard in business life.

What is a man?   The battle grounds of three worlds,
with his hands taking hold of destinies of light or darkness.

A man! No line can measure him. No limit can bound
him.   The archangel before the throne can not outlive
him.   The stars shall die, but he will watch their extinguishment.   The world will burn, but he will gaze on
the conflagration.   Endless ages will march on; he will
watch the procession.

A man! The masterpiece of God Almighty.   Yet you
say, "It is only a man."   Can a nature like that be fed
on husks of the wilderness?

> Substantial comfort will not grow
>   On nature's barren soil;
> All we can boast till Christ we know
>   Is vanity and toil.

THOSE WHO STRAY IN TROUBLE.

Some of you got astray by looking for better pasturage; others by being scared of the dogs.   The hound gets
over into the pasturage field.   The poor things fly in
every direction.   In a few moments they are torn of the
hedges and they are plashed of the ditch, and the lost
sheep never gets home unless the farmer goes after it.

There is nothing so thoroughly lost as a lost sheep.
It may have been in 1857, during the financial panic, or
during the financial stress of 1873, when you got astray.
You almost became an atheist.   You said, "Where is
God, that honest men go down and thieves prosper?"
You were dogged of creditors, you were dogged of the
banks, you were dogged of worldly disaster, and some of

you went into misanthropy, and some of you took to strong drink, and others of you fled out of Christian association, and you got astray. O man! that was the last time when you ought to have forsaken God.

Standing amid the foundering of your earthly fortunes, how could you get along without a God to comfort you, and a God to deliver you, and a God to help you, and a God to save you? You tell me you have been through enough business trouble almost to kill you. , I know it. I cannot understand how the boat could live one hour in that chopped sea. But I do not know by what process you got astray, some in one way and some in another, and if you could really see the position some of you occupy before God this morning, your soul would burst into an agony of tears and you would pelt the heavens with the cry, "God have mercy!" Sinai's batteries have been unlimbered above your soul, and at times you have heard it thunder: "The wages of sin is death." "All have sinned and come short of the glory of God." "By one man sin entered into the world, and death by sin; and so death passed upon all men for that all have sinned." "The soul that sinned it shall die."

THE BOMBARDMENT OF SEBASTOPOL.

When Sebastopol was being bombarded, two Russian frigates burned all night in the harbor throwing a glare upon the trembling fortress, and some of you are standing in the night of your soul's trouble. The cannonade and the conflagration, the multiplication of your sorrows and troubles I think must make the wing of God's hovering angels shiver to the tip.

But the last part of my text opens a door wide enough

to let us all out and to let all heaven in. Sound it on
the organ with all the stops out. Thrum it on the harp
with all the strings atune. With all the melody possible
let the heavens sound it to the earth and let the earth
tell it to the heavens. "The Lord hath laid on him the
iniquity of us all." I am glad that the prophet did not
stop to explain whom he meant by "him." Him of the
manger, him of the bloody sweat, him of the resurrection
throne, him, of the cruciflxion agony. "On him the
Lord hath laid the iniquity of us all."

CHRIST COMES TO THE FALLEN.

"Oh," says some man, "that is not generous, that is
not fair; let every man carry his own burden and pay his
own debts." That sounds reasonable. If I have an
obligation and I have the means to meet it, and I come
to you and ask you to settle that obligation, you rightly
say, "Pay your own debts." If you and I walking down
the street, both hale, hearty and well, I ask you to carry
me, you say, and say rightly, "Walk on your own feet!"
But suppose you and I were in a regimeut and I was
wounded in the battle and I fell unconscious at your
feet with gunshot fractures and dislocations, what would
you do? You would call to your comrades saying,
"Come and help, this man is helpless; bring the ambulance; let us take him to the hospital," and I would be a
dead lift in your arms, and you would lift me from the
ground where I had fallen and put me in the ambulance
and take me to the hospital and have all kindness shown
me. Would there be anything mean in your doing that?
Would there be anything bemeaning in my **accepting**

that kindness? Oh, no. You would be mean not to do it. That is what Christ does.

If we could pay our debts then it would be better to go up and pay them, saying, "Here, Lord, here is my obligation; here are the means with which I mean to settle that obligation; now give me a receipt, cross it all out." The debt is paid. But the fact is we have fallen in the battle, we have gone down under the hot fire of our transgressions, we have been wounded by the sabers of sin, we are helpless we are undone. Christ comes. The cloud clang heard in the sky on that Christmas night was only the bell, the resounding bell, of the ambulance. Clear the way for the Son of God. He comes down to bind up thy wounds, and to scatter the darkness, and to save the lost. Clear the way for the Son of God.

CHRIST PAYS THE DEBT.

Christ comes down to see us, and we are dead lift. He does not lift us with the tips of his fingers. He does not lift us with one arm. He comes down upon his knee, and then with a dead lift he raises us to honor and glory and immortality. "The Lord hath laid on him the iniquity of us all." "Why, then, will no man carry his sins? You cannot carry successfully the smallest sin you ever committed. You might as well put the Apenines on one shoulder and the Alps on the other. How much less can you carry all the sins of your lifetime? Christ comes and looks down in your face and says: "I have come through all the lacerations of these days and through all the tempests of these nights. I have come to bear your burdens, and to pardon your sins, and to pay your debts. Put them on my shoulder; put them on

my heart."   "On him the Lord hath laid the iniquity of
us all."

Sin has almost pestered the life out of some of you.
At times it has made you cross and unreasonable, and it
has spoiled the brightness of your days and the peace of
your nights.   There are men who have been riddled of
sin.   The world gives them no solace.   Gossamer and
volatile the world, while eternity, as they look forward
to it, is as black as midnight.   They writhe under the
stings of a conscience which proposes to give no rest
here and no rest hereafter; and yet they do not repent,
they do not pray, they do not weep. They do not realize
that just the position they occupy is the position occupied by scores, hundreds and thousands of men who
never found any hope.

If this meeting should be thrown open and the people
who are here could give their testimony, what thrilling
experiences we should hear on all sides!

There is a man in the gallery who would say: "I had
brilliant surroundings, I had the best education that one
of the best collegiate institutions of this country could
give, and I observed all the moralities of life, and I was
self righteous, and I thought I was all right before God
as I am all right before men, but the Holy Spirit came
to me one day and said, 'You are a sinner;' the Holy
Spirit persuaded me of the fact.   While I had escaped
the sins against the law of the land I had really committed the worst sin a man ever commits—the driving back
of the son of God from my heart's affections. And I saw
that my hands were red with the blood of the Son of
God, and I began to pray, and peace came to my heart,

and I know by experience that what you say this morning is true, "On him the Lord hath laid the iniquities of us all."

Yonder is a man who would say, "I was the worst drunkard in New York; I went from bad to worse; I destroyed myself, I destroyed my home; my children cowered when I entered the house; when they put up their lips to be kissed I struck them; when my wife protested against the maltreatment, I kicked her into the street. I know all the bruises and all the terrors of a druukard's woe. I went on further and further from God until one day I got a letter saying:

"MY DEAR HUSBAND—I have tried every way, done everything, and prayed earnestly and fervently for your reformation, but it seems of no avail. Since our little Henry died, with the exception of those few happy weeks when you remained sober, my life has been one of sorrow. Many of the nights I have sat by the window, with my face bathed in tears, watching for your coming. I am broken hearted, I am sick. Mother and father have been here frequently and begged me to come home, but my love for you and my hope for brighter days have always made me refuse them. That hope seems now beyond realization, and I have returned to them. It is hard, and I battled long before doing it. May God bless and preserve you, and take from you that accursed appetite and hasten the day when we shall be again living happily together. This will be my daily prayer, knowing that he has said, "Come unto me all ye that labor and are heavy laden, and I will give you rest." From your loving wife, MARY.

"And so I wandered on and wandered on," says that man, "until one night I passed a Methodist meeting house, and I said to myself, "I'll go in and see what they are doing," and I got to the door, and they were singing:

All may come, whoever will,
This man receives poor sinners still.

"And I dropped right there where I was and I said, 'God have mercy,' and he had mercy on me. My home is restored, my wife sings all day long during work, my children come out a long way to greet mé home, and my household is a little heaven. I will tell you what did all this for me. It was the truth that this day you pro-claim, "On him the Lord hath laid the iniquity of us all."

JESUS AND THE PRODIGAL DAUGHTER

Yonder there is a woman who would say: "I wander-ed off from my father's house; I heard the storm that pelts on a 'lost soul; my feet were blistered on the hot rocks. I went on and on, thinking that no one cared for my soul, when one night Jesus met me and he said:

"Poor thing, go home! your father is waiting for you, your mother is waiting for you. Go home, poor thing!"

And, sir, I was too weak to pray, and I was too weak to repent, but I just cried out; I sobbed out my sins and my sorrows on the shoulders of him of whom it is said, "the Lord hath laid on him the iniquity of us all."

There is a young man who would say: "I had a Chris-tian bringing up; I came from the country to city life; I started well, I had a good position, a good commercial position, but one night at the theatre I met some young men who did me no good. They dragged me all through the sewers of iniquity, and I lost my morals and I lost my position, and I was shabby and wretched. I was going down the street, thinking that no one cared for me, when a young man tapped me on the shoulder and said:

'George, come with me and I will do you good.'

I looked at him to see whether he was joking or not. I saw he was in earnest and I said, 'What do you mean, sir?'

'Well,' he replied, 'I mean if you will come to the meeting to-night I will be very glad to introduce you. I will meet you at the door. Will you come?'

Said I, 'I will.'

"I went to the place where I was tarrying. I fixed myself up as well as I could. I buttoned my coat over a ragged vest and went to the door of the church, and the young man met me and we went in; and as I went in I heard an old man praying, and he looked so much like my father I sobbed right out; and they were all around so kind and sympathetic that I just gave my heart to God, and I know this morning that what you say is true; I believe it in my own experience. 'On him the Lord hath laid the iniquity of us all.'"

COME AND BE SAVED.

Oh, my brother, without stopping to look as to whether your hand trembles or not, without stopping to look whether your hand is bloated with sin or not, put it in my hand, let me give you one warm, brotherly, Christian grip, and invite you right up to the heart, to the compassion, to the sympathy, to the pardon of him on whom the Lord had laid the iniquity of us all. Throw away your sins. Carry them no longer. I proclaim emanci-

382

pation this morning to all who are bound, pardon for all sin, and eternal life for all the dead.

CHRIST CAN BEAR AWAY THE SINS OF ALL.

Some one comes here this morning, and I stand aside. He comes up these steps. He comes to this place. I must stand aside. Taking that place he spreads abroad his hands and they were nailed. You see his feet, they were bruised. He pulls aside the robe and shows you his wounded heart.

I say, "Art thou weary?"

"Yes," he says, "weary with the world's woe."

I say, "Whence comest thou?"

He says, "I come from Calvary."

I say, "Who comes with thee?"

He says, "No one; I have trodden the winepress alone!"

I say, "Why comest thou here?"

"Oh," he says, "I came here to carry all the sins and sorrows of the people."

And he kneels and he says, "Put on my shoulders all the sorrows and all the sins." And, conscious of my own sins first, I take them and put them on the shoulders of the son of God. I say, "Canst thou bear any more, O Christ?"

He says, "Yea, more."

And I gather up the sins of all those who serve at these altars, and officers of the Church of Jesus Christ— I gather up all their sins and put them on Christ's shoulders, and I say, "Canst thou bear any more?"

He says, "Yea, more."

Then I gather up the sins of a hundred people in this

house, and I put them on the shoulders of Christ, and I say, "Canst thou bear more?"

He says, "Yea, more."

And I gather up all the sins of this assembly, and I put them on the shoulders of the Son of God, and I say, "Canst thou bear them?"

"Yea," he says. "more."

But he is departing. Clear the way for him, the Son of God. Open the door and let him pass out. He is carrying our sins and bearing them away. We shall never see them again. He throws them down into the abysm, and you hear the long reverbating echo of their fall. Oh him the Lord hath laid the iniquity of us all.'

Will you let him take away yonr sins to-day? Or do you say, "I will take charge of them myself; I will fight my own battles; I will risk eternity on my own accounts?"

A clergyman said in his pulpit one Sabbath, "Before next Saturday night one of this audience will have passed out of life." A gentleman said to another seated next to him: "I don't believe it. I mean to watch, and if it doesn't come true by next Saturday night I shall tell that clergyman his falsehood."

The man seated next to him said, "Perhaps it will be yourself."

"Oh, no," the other replied: "I shall live to be an old man."

That night he breathed his last.

WHOSOEVER WILL, LET HIM COME.

To-day the Saviour calls. All may come. God never destroys anybody. The man jumps off. It is suicide--

soul suicide—if the man perishes, for the invitation is,
'Whosoever will let him come." Whosoever, whosoever,
whosoever!   In this day of merciful visitation, while
many are coming into the kingdom of God, join the procession heavenward.

Seated among us during the service was a man who
came in and said, "I don't know*that there is any God."

That was on Friday night.   I said, "We will kneel
down and find out whether there is any God."   And in
the second seat from the pulpit we knelt.

He said: "I have found him.   There is a God, a par-
doning God.   I feel him here."

He knelt in the darkness of sin.   He arose two
minutes afterwards in the liberty of the Gospel.

While another sitting under the gallery on Friday night
said: "My opportunity is gone; last week I might have
been saved, not now; the door is shut."

And another from the very midst of the meeting, during the week, rushed out of the front door of the Tabernacle, saying, "I am a lost man."

"Behold! the Lamb of God who taketh away the sins of
the world."   "Now is the accepted time.   Now is the
day of salvation."   "It is appointed unto all men once
to die, and after that—the judgment!"

REBUILDING THE CITY.

"Then I went up in the night by the brook, and viewed the wall, and turned back, and entered by the gate of the valley, and so returned."—Nehemiah, ii, 15.

A dead city is more suggestive than a living city—past Rome than present Rome—ruins rather than newly frescoed cathedral. But the best time to visit a ruin is by moonlight. The Coliseum is far more fascinating to the traveler after sundown than before. You may stand by daylight amid the monastic ruins of Melrose Abbey and study shafted oriel, and rosetted stone and mullion, but they throw their strongest witchery by moonlight. Some of you remember what the enchanter of Scotland said in the "Lay of the Last Minstrel:"

> Would'st thou view fair Melrose aright,
> Go visit it by the pale moonlight,
> JERUSALEM IN RUINS.

Washington Irving describes the Andalusian moonlight upon the Alhambra ruins as amounting to an enchantment. My text presents you Jerusalem in ruins. The tower down. The gates down. The walls down. Everything down. Nehemiah on horseback, by moonlight looking upon the ruins. While he rides there are some friends on foot going with him, for they do not want the many horses to disturb the suspicions of the people. These people do not know the secret of Nehemiah's heart, but they are going as a sort of body guard. I hear the clicking hoofs of the horse on which Nehemiah rides as he

[385]

guides it this way and that, into this gate and out of that, winding through that gate amid the debris of once great Jerusalem. Now the horse comes to a dead halt at the tumbled masonry where he cannot pass. Now he shies off at the charred timbers. Now he comes along where the water under the moonlight flashes from the mouth of the brazen dragon after which the gate was named. Heavy hearted Nehemiah! Riding in and out now by his old home desolated, now by the defaced temple, now amid the scars of that city that had gone down under battering ram and conflagation.

The escorting party knows not what Nehemiah means. Is he getting crazy? Have his own personal sorrows, added to the sorrows of the nation, unbalanced his intellect? Still the midnight exploration goes on. Nehemiah on horseback rides through the fish gate, by the tower of the furnaces, by the king's pool, by the dragon well, in and out, in and out, until the midnight ride is completed, and Nehemiah dismounts from his horse, and to the amazed and confounded and incredulous body guard declares the dead secret of his heart when he says.

"Come, now, let us build Jerusalem."

"What! Nehemiah, have you any money?"

"No."

"Have you any kingly authority?"

"No."

"Have you any eloquence?"

"No."

Yet that midnight, moonlight ride of Nehemiah resulted in the glorious rebuilding of the city of Jerusalem.

The people knew not how the thing was to be done, but with great enthusiasm they cried out:.

"Let us rise up now and build the city."

Some people laughed and said it could not be done. Some people were infuriate and offered physical violence, saying the thing should not be done. But the workmen went right on, standing on the wall, trowel in one hand, sword in the other until the work was gloriously completed. At that very time, in Greece, Xenophon was writing a history, and Plato was making philosophy, and Demosthenes was rattling his rhetorical thunder, but all of them together did not do so much for the world as this midnight, moonlight ride of praying, courageous, homesick, close mouthed Nehemiah.

LOVE OF JERUSALEM.

My subject first impresses me with the idea what an intense thing is church affection. Seize the bridle of that horse and stop Nehemiah. Why are you risking your life here in the night? Your horse will stumble over these ruins and fall on you. Stop this useless exposure of your life. No; Nehemiah will not stop. He at last tells us the whole story. He lets us know he was an exile in a far distant land, and he was a servant, a cup bearer in the palace of Artaxerxes Longimanus, and one day while he was handing the cup of wine to the king, the king said to him:

"What is the matter with you? You are not sick. I know you must have some great trouble. What is the matter with you?"

Then he told the king how that beloved Jerusalem was broken down; how that his father's tomb had been desecrated; how that the Temple had been dishonored and defaced; how that the walls were scattered and broken.

"Well," says King Artaxerxes, "what do you want?"

"Well," said the cup bearer Nehemiah, "I want to go home. I want to fix up the grave of my father. I want to restote the beauty of the Temple. I want to rebuild the masonry of the city wall. Besides, I want passports so that I shall not be hindered in my journey. And besides that," as you will find in the context, "I want an order on the man who keeps your forest for just so much timber as I may need for the rebuilding of the city."

"How long shall you be gone?" said the king.

The time of absence is arranged. In hot haste this seeming adventurer comes to Jerusalem, and in my text we find him on horseback in the midnight, riding around the ruins.

LOVE OF THE CHURCH.

It is through the spectacles of this scene that we discover the ardent attachment of Nehemiah for sacred Jerusalem, which in all ages has been the type of the church of God, our Jerusalem, which we love just as much as Nehemiah loved his Jerusalem. The fact is that you love the church of God so much that there is no spot on earth so sacred, unless it is your own fireside. The church has been to you so much comfort and illumination that there is nothing that makes you so irate as to have it talked against. If there have been times when you have been carried into captivity by sickness, you longed for the church, our holy Jerusalem, just as much as Nehemiah longed for his Jerusalem, and the first day you came out you came to the house of the Lord. When the

Temple was in ruins as ours was years ago, like Nehemiah, you walked around and looked at it, and in the moonlight you stood listening if you could not hear the voice of the dead organ, the psalm of the expired Sabbaths.

What Jerusalem was to Nehemiah, the church of God is to you. Skeptics and infidels may scoff at the church as an obsolete affair, as a relic of the dark ages, as a convention of goody goody people, but all the impression they have ever made on your mind against the church of God is absolutely nothing. You would make more sacrifices for it to-day than for any other institution, and if it were needful you would die in its defense. You can take the words of the kingly poet as he said, "If I forget thee, O Jerusalem, let my right hand forget her cunning." You understand in your own experience the pathos, the homesickness, the courage, the holy enthusiasm of Nehemiah in his midnight, moonlight ride around the ruins of his beloved Jerusalem.

EXPLORATION BEFORE RESTORATION.

Again, my text impresses me with the fact that, before reconstruction, there must be an exploration of ruins. Why was not Nehemiah asleep under the covers? Why was not his horse stabled in the midnight? Let the police of the city arrest this midnight rider, out on some mischief. No. Nehemiah is going to rebuild the city, and he is making the preliminary exploration. In this gate, out that gate, east, west, north, south. All through the ruins. The ruins must be explored before the work of reconstruction can begin. The reason that so many people in this day, apparently converted, do not stay converted is because they did not first explore the ruins of their own heart. The reason that there are so many professed Christians who in this day lie and forge and steal, and commit adultery, and go to the penitentiary, is because they first do not learn the ruin of their own heart. They have not found out that "the heart is deceitful above all things, and desperately wicked." They had an idea that they were almost right, and they built religion as a sort of extension, as an ornamental cupola. There was a superstructure of religion built on a substratum of unrepented sins.

CHRIST'S WAY.

The trouble with a good deal of modern theology is that instead of building on the right foundation, it builds on the debris of an unregenerated nature. They attempt to rebuild Jerusalem before, in the midnight of conviction, that they have seen the ghastliness of the ruin. They have such a poor foundation for their religion that the first northeast storm of temptation blows them down. I have no faith in a man's conversion if he is not converted in the old fashioned way—John Bunyan's way, John Wesley's way, John Calvin's way, Paul's way, Christ's way, God's way. A dentist once said to me:

"Does that hurt?"

Said I: "Of course it hurts. It is in your business as in my profession. We have to hurt before we can help."

You will never understand redemption until you understand ruin. A man tells me that some one is a member of the church. It makes no impression on my mind at all. I simply want to know whether he was converted in the old fashioned way, or whether he was converted in the new fashioned way. If he was converted in the old fashioned way he will stand. If he was converted in the new fashioned way he will not stand. That is all there is about it. A man comes to me to talk about religion. The first question I ask him is: "Do you feel yourself to be a sinner?" If he says, "Well I—yes," the hesitancy makes me feel that that man wants a ride on Nehemiah's horse by midnight through the ruins—in by the gate of his affections, out by the gate of this will; and before he has got through with that midnight ride he will drop the reins on the horse's neck, and will take his right hand and smite on his heart and say: "God be merciful to me, a sinner;" and before he has stabled his horse he will take his feet out of the stirrups, and he will slide down on the ground and he will kneel, crying, "Have mercy on me, O God, according to thy loving kindness, according unto the multitude of thy tender mercies; blot out my transgressions, and my sins are ever before thee."

THE TRUE GOSPEL.

"Ah, my. friends, you see this is not a complimentary gospel. That is what makes some people so mad.

It comes to a man of a million dollars and impenitent in his sins, and says, "You're a pauper."

It comes to a woman of fairest cheek, who has never repented, and says, "You're a sinner."

It comes to a man priding himself on his independence, and says "You're bound hand and foot by the devil."

It comes to our entire race and says, "You're a ruin, a ghastly ruin, an illimitable ruin."

Satan sometimes says to me, "Why do you preach that truth? Why don't you preach a gospel with no repentance in it, saying nothing about the ruin, talking all the time about redemption?"

"I say, "Get thee behind me, Satan." I would rather lead five souls the right way than twenty thousand the wrong way.

The redemption of the gospel is a perfect farce if there is no ruin. "The whole need not a physician, but they are sick." "If any one, though he be an angel from heaven, preach any other gospel than this," says the apostle, "let him be accursed." There must be the midnight ride over the ruins before Jerusalem can be built. There must be the clicking of the hoofs before there can be the ring of the trowels.

TRIUMPHANT SADNESS.

Again. My subject gives me a specimen of busy and triumphant sadness. If there was any man in the world who had a right to mope and give up everything as lost, it was Nehemiah. You say: "He was a cup bearer in the palace of Shushan, and it was a grand place." So it was. The hall of that palace was two hundred feet square, and the roof hovered over thirty-six marble pillars, each pillar sixty feet high; and the intense blue of the sky, and the deep green of the forest foliage, and the white of the driven snow, all hung trembling in the upholstery. But, my friends, you know very well that fine architecture will not put down homesickness. Yet Nehemiah did not give up. Then when you see him going among these desolated streets, and by these dismantled towers, and by the torn up grave of his father, you would suppose that he would have been disheartened, and that he would have dismounted from his horse and gone to his room and said: ·"Woe is me. .My father's grave is torn up. The temple is dishonored. The walls are broken down. I have no money with which to rebuild. I wish I had never been born. I wish I were dead." No so says Nehemiah. Although he had a grief so intense that it excited commentary of his king, yet that penniless, expatriated Nehemiah rouses himself up to rebuild the city. He gets his permission of absence. He gets his passports. He hastens away to Jerusalem. By night on horseback he rides through the ruins. He overcomes the most ferocious opposition. He arouses the piety and patriotism of the people, and in less than two months, namely, in fifty-two days, Jerusalem was rebuilt. That's what I call busy and triumphant sadness.

THE TEMPTATION TO "GIVE UP."

My friends, the whole temptation is with you when you have trouble, to do just the opposite to the behavior of Nehemiah, and that is to give up.

You say, "I have lost my child and can never smile again."

You say, "I have lost my property, and I never can repair my fortunes."

You say, "I have fallen into sin, and I never can start again for a new life."

If Satan can make yon form that resolution, and make you keep it, he has ruined you. Trouble is not sent to crush you, but to arouse you, to animate you, to propel you. The blacksmith does not thrust the iron into the forge, and then blow away with the bellows, and then bring the hot iron out on the anvil and beat with stroke after stroke to ruin the iron, but to prepare it for a better use. Oh that the Lord God of Nehemiah would arouse up all broken hearted people to rebuild.

Whipped, betrayed, shipwrecked, imprisoned, Paul went right on.

The Italian martyr Algerius sits in his dungeon writing a letter and he dates it "From the delectable orchard of the Leonine prison." That is what I call triumphant sadness.

TOUCHING STORY OF A MOTHER.

I knew a mother who buried her baby on Friday and on Sabbath appeared in the house of God and said, "Give me a class; give me a Sabbath school class. I have no child now left me, and I would like to have a class of little children. Give me real poor children. Give me a class off the back street" That, I say, is beautiful. That is triumphant sadness.

At three o'clock this afternoon in a beautiful parlor in Philadelphia—a parlor pictured and statuetted—there will be from ten to twenty destitute children of the street. It has been so every Sabbath afternoon at three o'clock for many years. These destitute children receive religious instruction, concluding with cakes and sandwitches. How do I know that that has been going on for many years? I know in this way:

That was the first home in Philadelphia where I was called to comfort a great sorrow. They had a splendid boy, and he had been drowned at Long Branch. The father and mother almost idolized the boy, and the sob and shriek of that father and mother as they hung over the coffin resound in my ears to-day. There seemed to be no use of praying, for when I knelt down to pray, the outcry in the room drowned out all the prayer. But the Lord comforted that sorrow. They did not forget their trouble. If you should go on the snowiest winter afternoon into Laurel Hill you would find a monument with the word "Walter" inscribed upon it, and a wreath of fresh flowers around the name. I think there has not been an hour all these years, winter or summer, when there was not a wreath of fresh flowers around Walter's name. But the Christian mother who sends those flowers there, having no child left, Sabbath afternoons, mothers ten or twenty of the lost ones of the street. That is beautiful. That is what I call busy and triumphant sadness.

Here is a man who has lost his property. He does not go to hard drinking. He does not destroy his own life. He comes and says, "Harness me for Christian work. My money's gone. I have no treasures on earth. I want treasures in heaven. I have a voice and a heart to serve God." You say that that man has failed. He has not failed—he has triumphed. Oh, I wish I could persuade all the people who have any kind of trouble never to give up. I wish they would look at the midnight rider of the text, and that the four hoofs of that beast on which Nehemiah rode might cut to pieces all your discouragements and hardships and trials. Give up! Who is going to give up, when on the bosom of God he can have all his troubles hushed? Give up! Never think of giving up.

Are you borne down with poverty? A little child was found holding her dead mother's hand in the darkness of a tenement house, and, some one coming in, the little girl looked up, while holding her dead mother's hand, and said, "Oh, I do wish that God had made more light for poor folks." My dear, God will be your light, God will be your shelter, God will be your home. Are you borne down with the bereavements of life? Is the house lonely now that the child is gone? Do not give up.

Think of what the old sexton said when the minister asked him why he put so much care on the little graves in the cemetery—so much more care than on the larger graves, and the old sexton said: "Sir, you know that of such is the kingdom of heaven,' and I think the Saviour is pleased when he sees so much white clover growing around these little graves." But when the minister pressed the sexton for a more satisfactory answer, the old sexton said, "Sir, about those larger graves, I don't know who are the Lord's saints and who are not; but you know, sir, it is clean different with the bairns." Oh, if you have had that keen, tender, indescribable sorrow that comes from the loss of a child, do not give up. The old sexton was right. It is all well with the bairns. Or, if you have sinned, if you have sinned grievously—sinned, until you have been cast out by the church, sinned until you have been cast out by society, do not give up. Perhaps there may be in this house one that could truthfully utter the lamentation of another:

> Once I was as pure as the snow, but I fell—
> Fell like a snowflake, from heaven to hell—
> Fell, to be trampled as filth on the street—
> Fell, to be scoffed at, spit on and beat;
> Praytng, cursing, wishing to die,
> Selling my soul to whoever would buy,

Dealing in shame for a morsel of bread,
Hating the living and fearing the dead.

WHERE COMFORT IS FOUND.

Do not give up. One like unto the Son of God comes to you to-day, saying, "Go and sin no more," while He cries out to your assailants, "Let him that is without sin cast the first stone at her."

Oh! there is no reason why anyone in this house, by reason of any trouble or sin, should give up.

Are you a foreigner and in a strange land? Nehemiah was an exile.

Are you penniless? Nehemiah was poor.

Are you homesick? Nehemiah was homesick.

Are you broken hearted? Nehemiah was broken hearted. But just see him in the text, riding along the sacrileged grave of his father, and by the dragon well, and through the fish gate, and by the king's pool, in and out in and out, the moonlight falling on the broken masonry, which throws a long shadow at which the horse shies, and at the same time that moonlight kindling up the features of this man until you see not only the mark of sad reminiscence, but the courage, the hope, the enthusiasm of a man who knows that Jerusalem will be rebuilded. I pick you up to-day out of your sins and out of your sorrow, and I put you against the warm heart of Christ.

"The eternal God is thy refuge, and underneath are the everlasting arms."

THE END.

TEACHING THE DEAF TO SPEAK.

The Teeth the Best Medium and the Audiphone the Best Instrument for Conveying Sounds to the Deaf, and in teaching the partly Deaf and Dumb to Speak.

Address Delivered by R. S. Rhodes of Chicago, Before the Fourteenth Convention of American Teachers of the Deaf, at Flint, Michigan.

Mr. President and Ladies and Gentlemen:

I would like to recite some of the causes which led to my presence with you to-day.

About sixteen years ago I devised this instrument, the audiphone, which greatly assisted me in hearing, and discovered that many who had not learned to speak were not so deaf as myself. I reasoned that an instrument in the hands of one who had not learned to speak would act the same as when in the hands of one who had learned to speak, and that the mere fact of one not being able to speak would in no wise affect the action of the instrument. To ascertain if or not my simple reasoning was correct, I borrowed a deaf-mute, a boy about twelve years old, and took him to my farm. We arrived there in the evening, and during the evening I experimented to see if he could distinguish some of the vowel sounds. My experiments in this direction were quite satisfactory. Early in the morning I provided him with an audiphone and took him by the hand for a walk about the farm. We soon came across a flock of turkeys. We approached closely, the boy with his audiphone adjusted to his teeth, and when the gobbler spoke in his peculiar voice, the boy was convulsed with laughter, and jumping for joy continued to follow the fowl with his audiphone properly adjusted, and at every remark of the gobbler the boy was delighted. I was myself delighted, and began to think my reasoning was correct.

We next visited the barn. I led him into a stall beside a horse munching his oats, and to my delight he could hear the grinding of the horse's teeth when the audiphone was adjusted, and neither of us could without. In the stable yard was a cow lowing for its calf, which he plainly showed he could hear, and when I led him to the cowbarn where the calf was confined, he could hear it reply to the cow, and by signs showed that he understood their language, and that he knew the one was calling for the other. We then visited the pig-sty where the porkers poked their noses near to us. He could hear them with the audiphone adjusted, and enjoyed their talk, and understood that they wanted more to eat. I gave him some corn to throw over to them, and he signed that that was what they wanted, and that now they were satisfied. He soon, however, broke away from me and pursued the gobbler and manifested more satisfaction in listening to its voice than to mine, and the vowel sounds as compared to it were of slight importance to him, and for the three days he was at my farm that poor turkey gobbler had but little rest.

With·these and other experiments I was satisfied that he could hear, and that there were many like him; so I took my grip and audiphones and visited most of the institutions for the deaf in this country. In all institutions I found many who could hear well, and presented the instrument with which this hearing could be improved and brought within the scope of the human voice. But at one institution I was astonished; I found a bright girl with perfect hearing being educated to the sign language. She could repeat words after me parrot-like, but had no knowledge of their value in sentences. I inquired why she was in the institution for the deaf, and by examining the records we learned she was the child of deaf-mute parents, and had been brought up by them in the country, and although her hearing was perfect, she had not heard spoken language enough to acquire it, and I was informed by the superintendent of the institution that she preferred signs to speech. I was astonished that a child with no knowledge of the value of speech should be permitted to elect to be educated by signs instead of speech, and to be so educated in a state institution. This circumstance convinced me more than ever that there was a great work to be done in redeeming the partly deaf children from the slavery of silence, and I was more firmly resolved than ever that I would devote the remainder of my life to this cause.

I have had learned scientists tell me that I could not hear through my teeth. It would take more scientists than ever were born to convince me that I did not hear my sainted mother's and beloved father's dying voice with this instrument, when I could not have heard it without.

It wou lake more scientists than ever were born to convince me that I did not hear the voice of the Rev James B. McClure, one who has been dear to me for the last twenty years, and accompanied me on most of my visits to institutions spoken of above, and who has encouraged me in my labors for the deaf all these years, say, as I held his hand on his dying bed only Monday last, and took my final leave from him (and let me say, I know of no cause but this that would have induced me to leave him then), "Go to Flint; do all the good you can. God bless your labors for the deaf! We shall never meet again on earth. Meet me above. Good-by!"

And, Mr. President, when I am laid at rest, it will be with gratitude to you and with greater resignation for the active part you have taken in the interest of these partly deaf children in having a section for aural work admitted to this national convention, for in this act you have contributed to placing this work on a firm foundation, which is sure to result in the greatest good to this class.

You have heard our friend, the inventor of the telephone, say that in his experiments for a device to improve the hearing of the deaf, (as he was not qualified by deafness,) he did not succeed, but invented the telephone instead, which has lined his pocket with gold. From what I know of the gentleman, I believe he would willingly part with all the gold he has received for the use of this wonderful invention, had he succeeded in his efforts in devising an instrument which would have emancipated even twenty per cent. of the deaf in the institutions from the slavery of silence. I have often wished that he might have invented the audiphone and received as much benefit by its use as I, for then he would have used the gold he derives from the telephone in carrying the boon to the deaf; but when I consider that in wishing this I must wish him deaf, and as it would not be right for me to wish him this great affliction, therefore since I am deaf, and I invented the audiphone, I would rather wish that I might have invented the telephone also; in which case I assure the deaf that I would have used my gold as freely in their behalf as would he. [The speaker then explained the use of the audiometer in measuring the degree of hearing one may possess. Then, at his request, a gentleman from the audience, a superintendent of one of our large institutions, took a position about five feet from the speaker, and was asked to speak loud enough for Mr. Rhodes to hear when he did not have the audiphone in use, and by shouting at the top of his voice, Mr. Rhodes was able to hear only two or three "o" sounds, but could not distinguish a word. With the audiphone adjusted to his teeth, still looking away from the speaker, he was able to understand ordinary tones; and repeated sentences after him; and, when looking at him and using his eyes and audiphone, the speaker lowering his voice nearly as much as possible and yet articulating, Mr. Rhodes distinctly heard every word and repeated sentences after him, thus showing the value of the audiphone and eye combined, although Mr. Rhodes had never received instructions in lip reading. The gentleman stated that he had tested Mr. Rhodes' hearing with the audiometer when he was at his institution in 1894, and found he possessed seven per cent. in his left ear and nothing in his right,

A NEW BOOK.

1910 PUBLICATION.

CLOTH BOUND, - - - $1.00

Captain W. F. Drannan, Chief of Scouts, as Pilot to Emigrant and Government Trains Across the Plains of the Wild West of Fifty Years Ago.

This book, being a sequel to the famous "Thirty-one Years on the Plains and in the Mountains," of which over 100 editions have been printed in less than ten years, does not need any recommendation; the author being an abundant warrant as to its value.

So we launch this little volume into "The Public Sea" with perfect confidence that it will float with flying colors, and soon share the honor of wide-spread popularity with its elder brother.

The book contains over 400 pages of reading matter, and is illustrated with ten full page engravings from original drawings by E. Bert Smith.

TEN YEARS A COW BOY. A full and vivid description of frontier life, including romance adventure and all the varied experiences incident to a life on the plains as cow boy, stock owner, rancher, etc., together with articles on cattle and sheep raising how to make money, description of the plains, etc, etc Illustrated with 1oo full-page engravings, and contains reading matter 471 pages.

WILD LIFE INTHE FAR WEST By C. H. Simpson, a resident detective, living in this country. Giving a full and graphic account of his thrilling adventures among the Indians and outlaws of Monana—including hunting, hair-breadth escapes, captivity, punishment and difficulties of all kinds met with in this wild and lawless country. Illustrated by 3o full-page engravings by G. S. Littlejohn and contains reading matter 264 pages.

A YANKEE'S ADVENTURES IN SOUTH AFRICA (In the diamond country) By C. H. Simpson. Giving the varied experiences adventures. dangers and narrow escapes of a Yankee seeking his fortune in this wild country, which by undaunted courage, perseverance, suffering, fighting and adventures of various sorts is requited at last by the ownership of the largest diamond taken out of the Kimberly mines up to that time, and with the heart and hand of the fairest daughter of a diamond king. Containing 3o full-page illustrations by H. DeLay and reading matter 22o pages.

WIT Contains sketches from Mark Twain, witticisms from F. H. Carruth Douglas Jerrold, M. Quad, Opie Reid, Mrs. Partington, Eli Perkins, O'Malley, Bill Nye, Artemus Ward, Abe Lincoln Burdette Lance, Webster Victor Hugo Bret Harte Gardner, Clinton Scollard, Tom Hood, L. R. Catlin, Josh Billings Chauncey Depew and all humorous writers of modern times. Illustrated with 75 full-page engravings by H. DeLay, and contains reading matter 407 pages.

BENONI AND SERAPTA A Story of the Time of the Great Constantine, Founder of the Christian Faith By Douglas Vernon. A religious novel showing a Parsee's constancy and faith through many persecutions, trials and difficulties, placed in his way by priests nobles and queens of his time and his final triumph over all obstacles. Being an interesting novel intended to show the state of the religious feelings and unscrupulous intrigues of those professing religion at the time of the foundation of the Christian faith. Illustrated with 88 full-page engravings by H. DeLay, and contains reading matter 22o pages

They are idols of home and of house-
holds;
They are Angels of God in disguise.
His sunlight sleeps in their tresses;
His glory still gleams in their eyes.

STORIES FOR THE LITTLE ONES AT HOME. 320 pages. "This handsomely illustrated book has been compiled and arranged by one who is best able to tell what is good for the instruction and amusement of the children."—A MOTHER. Many of the rhymes are original, but a large number are old favorites that will interest the old folk as reminiscences of their childhood days. The illustrations are numerous and designed to amuse and interest the little ones at home.

GEMS OF POETRY. 407 pages. Finely illustrated. Contains a very choice and varied selection of our most popular, beautiful and time-honored poems, written by the poets of all ages and climes. A magnificent gift book for a friend; a splendid book for the holidays; appropriate for a birthday or wedding present; a fine center table book, interesting to all.

KIDNAPPED: OR, SECRETS OF A GREAT MYSTERY. By A. Stewart Manly. Illustrated by H. S. De Lay. 428 pages.

SOCIAL KNOTS UNTIED. A Series of Practical and Popular Sermons delivered by T. De Witt Talmage, D. D. Handsomely illustrated. 475 pages

LUCKY TEN BAR OF PARADISE VALLEY. His humerous pathetic and tragic adventures. Copiously illustrated by H. S. De Lay. His travels by reproductions from photographs, constituting almost a Pictorial America. By C. M. Stevens. 600 pages.

PEARLS FROM MANY SEAS. A collection of the best thoughts of four hundred writers of wide repute. Selected and classified by Rev. J. B. McClure. Illustrated with 51 full page engravings selected especially for this work from the great art galleries of the world. A volume of rare value and interest to all lovers of good literature. Reading matter 528 pages